P9-CCR-062

Out by a Step

Out by a Step

The 100 Best Players Not in the Baseball Hall of Fame

Mike Shalin and Neil Shalin

DIAMOND COMMUNICATIONS

An Imprint of the Rowman & Littlefield Publishing Group

Lanham • South Bend • New York • Oxford

3 3210 0366191

Copyright © 2002 by Mike Shalin and Neil Shalin.

All rights reserved.
No part of this book may be reproduced in any form or by any electronic or
mechanical means, including information storage and retrieval systems,
without written permission of the publisher.

Published by Diamond Communications
An Imprint of the Rowman & Littlefield Publishing Group
4720 Boston Way
Lanham, Maryland 20706

Distributed by National Book Network

Library of Congress Cataloging-in-Publication Data

Shalin, Mike, 1954–
    Out by a step : the 100 best players not in the Baseball Hall of Fame /
    Mike Shalin and Neil Shalin.
        p. cm.
    ISBN 1-888698-44-6 (cloth : alk. paper)
    1. Baseball players—Rating of—United States. I. Shalin, Neil, 1944– II. Title.

    GV865.A25S45 2002
    796.357'092'2—dc21   2002003514

♾ᵀᴹ The paper used in this publication meets the minimum requirements of
American National Standard for Information Sciences—Permanence of
Paper for Printed Library Materials, ANSI/NISO Z39.48–1992.
Manufactured in the United States of America.

"When I was a kid, I saw Waite Hoyt on the subway. He was like a God. Handsome as a movie star, dressed in the most stylish suit, and his shoulders were so broad he took up two seats." —Sid Shalin

"Leo Durocher's not in the Hall of Fame? Baseball should be ashamed of itself. When he opened up that mouth, that WAS baseball." —Ronnie Shalin (1986)

This book is dedicated in loving memory of our parents:

To our father, Sid Shalin, who took his six-year-old son to the movies to see *The Jackie Robinson Story* and explained right from wrong, and that maybe this was a start. He would never have dreamed of the influence he had on his children and grandchildren.

And

To our mother Ronnie Shalin, who was charismatic, funny, loved baseball, and knew exactly what her influence was on her children and grandchildren.

Contents

Acknowledgments

The authors gratefully acknowledge the following people whose generous assistance made this book possible:

Dan Shalin, for his ideas, objective criticism, and editorial expertise.

Bonnie and Joanna Shalin, for their editorial input, patience, and support.

Steve Shalin for his historical input.

Rob Rains for his help and support in the publishing process.

We thank the following people for their assistance in providing research material, interview contacts and for generally making this a pleasant experience:

Steve Gietschier and Jim Meier of The Sporting News Research Center for their help and generosity in providing access to materials in The Sporting News files.

Scott Mondore and Jeff Idelson, National Baseball Hall of Fame and Museum for providing information and archive files.

Keri Naeger, Media Relations, Major League Baseball Players Alumni Association, who put the authors in contact with numerous former major leaguers.

Holly Yeates and the research staff at the Nichols Library, Naperville, Illinois.

The public relations staffs of the Boston Red Sox, Chicago Cubs, Chicago White Sox, Houston Astros, Los Angeles Dodgers, New York Yankees, San Francisco Giants, and all other Major League Baseball organizations.

Boston Red Sox, Chicago White Sox, Houston Astros, Milwaukee Brewers, Negro Leagues Baseball Museum, New York Yankees, Topps Company, Inc., George Brace, Ron Vesely, and Mary Ann and John Sain for photos used in the book. Also Bob Soelke for his cover photo of Neil Shalin.

And the following major league players, managers, executives, broadcasters, and writers:

Buzzie Bavasi, Yogi Berra, Wade Boggs, Lou Boudreau, Larry Bowa, Bobby Bragan, Bob Broeg, Dr. Bobby Brown, Rod Carew, Roger Clemens, Tony Cloninger, Darren Daulton, Tommy Davis, Bucky Dent, Dom DiMaggio, Carl Erskine, Ed Farmer, Bill Fischer, Whitey Ford, and Charlie Fox.

Rich Gale, Cito Gaston, Tom Grieve, Dick Groat, Tommy Harper, Ken Harrelson, Ernie Harwell, Roland Hemond, Art Howe, Randy Hundley, Monte Irvin, Jim Kaat, Bruce Kison, Jim Landis, Buck Martinez, Lee Mazzilli, Tim McCarver, Hal McRae, Minnie Minoso, Paul Molitor, Joe Nossek, Joe Nuxhall, Tom Paciorek, Johnny Pesky, Billy Pierce, Jim Piersall, and Lou Piniella.

Dick Radatz, Willie Randolph, Jerry Remy, Arthur Richman, Eddie Robinson, Cookie Rojas, Johnny Sain, Ron Santo, Bill Skowron, Hal Smith, Rusty Staub, Syd Thrift, Joe Torre, Alan Trammell, Frank White, Maury Wills, Bobby Wine, and Don Zimmer.

Introduction

The player who inspired this book is not on our list. He's now in the National Baseball Hall of Fame in Cooperstown, N.Y.

Several years ago, just for fun, we selected an All-Star team for the second half of the twentieth century. We were being generous, picking three or four players at each position, but ranking them in order. We discovered that if we listed Stan Musial as an outfielder, Orlando Cepeda became our All-Star first baseman. We put aside career statistics and were left with the conclusion that we would take Cepeda at the height of his career slightly ahead of Willie McCovey, Johnny Mize, and Willie Stargell—all of whom were already in the National Baseball Hall of Fame. (Eddie Murray was still active at the time, and therefore not eligible for our team.)

This exercise led to consideration of other players who were rejected by the Hall of Fame selectors and, subsequently, to the first list of those we thought were "Out by a Step."

The list included Bill Mazeroski, perhaps the best fielding second baseman of all time. It included Norman "Turkey" Stearnes and Raleigh "Biz" Mackey, a pair of Negro League greats who are mentioned on every "greatest ever" list. Also included were Dick Allen and Tony Oliva, arguably the best right-handed and left-handed hitters of the 1960s and 1970s. And no list would be complete without Maury Wills, the man who brought speed back into fashion when he starred for the great Dodgers teams of the early 1960s.

We came to the conclusion that these and other great and near-great players should be recognized for their achievements as major leaguers.

Since we began, Cepeda, Stearnes, and Mazeroski have all been rewarded with a rightful place in Cooperstown. But there's still plenty of talent for a Top 100. We're honoring those players who remain on the outside—those players who will eventually be in the Hall of Fame, those who should be in the

Hall of Fame, or, at least, those who shouldn't be forgotten by the average base-ball fan. The players who are "Out by a Step" may not be regarded as highly as Babe Ruth, Willie Mays, and Ted Williams, but they are important figures in baseball history.

The National Baseball Hall of Fame has become the official conferrer of baseball immortality. Until the recent media revolution, nobody outside of hardcore baseball fans talked much about Cooperstown. Oh, there was a flurry of publicity surrounding the annual election and ceremony, but most average or even passionate baseball fans didn't know or care much about who was in and who wasn't.

That's all changed in the past two decades. The Hall of Fame is now an integral part of most baseball talk. There's even talk about twenty-four- and twenty-five-year-old infielders as future Hall of Fame candidates after two or three years in the majors. Personal conversations, newspaper columns, and sports talk radio are all preoccupied with questions about who belongs in Cooperstown and which players will be first-ballot selections.

The Hall of Fame has become the official memory of Major League Baseball—and of the Negro Leagues, for that matter. The players whose accomplishments will live as the years pass are those who are elected into the Hall of Fame. The average fan will be able to talk about highlights from the careers of Babe Ruth, Joe Dimaggio, Sandy Koufax, and Ted Williams. Visitors will encounter the plaques of Josh Gibson, Lefty Grove, and Lou Gehrig. And highlight films on classic sports programs and documen-taries will recount the history of Jackie Robinson's breaking the color line, Willie Mays's catch, Hank Aaron's 715th home run, and Reggie Jackson's magnificent October home runs. Everyone else, including most of our "Out by a Step" Top 100, will be the subject of trivia questions for the truly addicted.

The exceptions, of course, will be those players who are remembered for specific achievements, some of whom are on our list: Roger Maris for break-ing Babe Ruth's home run record; Johnny Sain as the greatest pitching coach of all time and the mantra "Spahn and Sain, then Pray for Rain"; and Kirk Gibson for his dramatic World Series home run limp—none of these will ever be forgotten.

The stars of today and the coming years will replace our old-time heroes in the minds of future fans, and some day the achievements of all but the truly great players of the twentieth century will be dismissed as ancient history—the way we talk about nineteenth-century players today. This will be especially true if the hitting numbers continue to increase the way they have in recent years. Soon the home runs, runs batted in, and total hits numbers of the twentieth century will be as obsolete as early statistics on nineteenth-century pitchers' victories, innings pitched, and complete games look to us today.

In making our cases either for Hall of Fame inclusion or just plain "please-don't-ever-forget-this-guy" status, we're not saying that these players are the equals of Ruth, Mays, and Aaron—although some former players we interviewed did make that claim for several of our top players, notably Dick Allen and Tony Oliva.

We are spotlighting the diamond heroes who were the greats of their time, but have been denied their places in baseball history. While a good case can be made for enshrining many of the players we recognize, others clearly have no chance based on accepted career statistical standards. In many cases, careers that were headed to Cooperstown were short-circuited by injury or illness. Some of those profiled came to the majors late or slipped from their prime a bit prematurely. As time passes, statistics play an increasing role in evaluating a career, and many of these players just don't have the numbers to be given serious consideration for the Hall of Fame.

Our "Out by a Step" players were among the best of their time. Some will eventually make it to Cooperstown. Others were the equals of or better than many of those already elected.

Some of our honorees were among the most popular players ever to play in a particular city. Try telling someone who lived in Cleveland in the late 1950s that Rocky Colavito doesn't belong in the Hall of Fame and you are risking a violent confrontation. The memories of Rocky's home runs and powerful throwing arm are ingrained in the collective memory of the city. Don't suggest to a Chicagoan that Ron Santo wasn't one of the best third baseman ever. St. Louis fans will tell you that Ken Boyer was even better.

When this project was getting off the ground I mentioned it to a friend, an Ohio native, and the first thing he said was "Ted Kluszewski is on the list, isn't he?" He is. There are senior citizens in Cleveland and New York who insist that Joe Gordon was a better all-around second baseman than his Boston contemporary Bobby Doerr. This isn't taking anything away from the brilliant Hall of Famer Doerr, but a case can be made for Gordon. The message is "don't forget Joe Gordon. He was a gem."

America's love affair with baseball is not *just* about the greatest players of all time, it's about your own personal favorites. In these pages we will profile 100 players who were among the very best at their profession or at their position for a significant number of years. There are even a few exceptions to that statement: Pete Reiser, Tommy Davis, and Joe Wood are three whose brilliance was diminished by injury at a very young age.

There have been volumes written about the past century of baseball, much of it by great writers, historians, and statistical analysts. We drew upon this wonderful material in preparing this book. Those who evaluate the careers of ballplayers past give credit to a player for his achievements but they usually let the record tell the story. We've read that you can't say what would have happened if a certain pitcher hadn't thrown out his arm, or if a certain slugger hadn't suffered a back or hand injury.

For the purposes of this book, we say we can say what would've happened. We're considering the facts and then adding in memories, emotions, and testimony. We are giving "Big Klu," Al Rosen, J. R. Richard, and Don Mattingly five or six more healthy years. We're imagining what Minnie Minoso's career would have been had he reached the majors at an earlier age. We're giving Bert Blyleven the benefit of all those one-run decisions. And we're curing Hal Trosky's migraines. We're also recognizing that, despite what the numbers say, Jim Rice, Dick Allen, and Tony Oliva are three of the top players of the second half of the twentieth century. We're also claiming that the best you saw of winners such as Don Newcombe and Elston Howard was probably more an indication of the kind of players they were than their statistics reveal. Even though Jackie Robinson broke the color barrier in 1947, baseball was not fully integrated until the early 1960s, and those players whose careers peaked in the first two decades of that integration faced extraordinary struggles, both personally and professionally.

In compiling our Top 100, we followed the Baseball Writers Association of America's (BWAA) rules of eligibility. For consideration, a player must have ten years in the majors, be retired five years, and not be on the suspended list. So you won't find Pete Rose, Shoeless Joe Jackson, or Ed Cicotte among our honorees. You also won't read about Herb Score, Tony Conigliaro, Lyman Bostock, or Dick Radatz, four worthy candidates whose careers were sadly ended before they reached the required ten years. And we haven't included future Hall of Famers Eddie Murray, Cal Ripken Jr., or Ryne Sandberg, because they are not yet eligible. To make the task manageable, we have also not considered players from the nineteenth century.

You would think that producing this list would be relatively easy—that we're really scrambling to find a worthy 100. The opposite is true. We found *at least* 100 players who would not devalue our Top 100. At the end of the book, we list those Honorable Mention candidates who were given consideration. Many of these were even in the Top 100 at some point in the process.

How did we arrive at our Top 100? A great many of our choices were made from personal observation, following the game we love for five decades. Mike Shalin was a baseball beat reporter for almost twenty years and is a voting member (for the Hall of Fame) of the Baseball Writers Association of America. Neil Shalin is a sports writer and sports historian. We were influenced by the testimony of former players, managers, broadcasters, and writers, both in personal interviews and through the research of books, newspaper, and magazine stories.

Obviously the choices of the pre-1950 players were made as a result of extensive research of records and the commentary of those who saw some of them play. Negro League players were chosen because of the almost unanimous opinion of former players and observers that these players are worthy of selection to the Hall of Fame.

In making our evaluation, like any writers, we come to the table with our own biases. Our list is in no way definitive and, in truth, changed many times right up until its publication. But we're not copping out and we'll stick by our choices and defend them at any time with a good-natured argument. There are at least forty players who were on the list at one time who did not make the final cut. I wish we had the room to include them all. The Top 100 represents the entire century but is weighted somewhat on the side of post–World War II players. There are two reasons for this. One, the obvious—these are players we actually saw play and therefore we can testify to their abilities and achievements with some accuracy. Also, in looking at the roster of the Hall of Fame, it seems as though the Veterans' Committee has taken care of most of the great players from pre–World War II baseball. Our representatives from this era are the remaining players we believe were overlooked.

We hope you enjoy reading about the great players of your youth, of your father's youth, or of somebody's youth, and that you get some satisfaction in knowing that someone agrees with you about their greatness. Maybe you'll discover a new hero or two as we did in working on this project. One thing is certain: You will form your own opinions about who does or doesn't belong on this list. And if we could all meet around a hot stove, we could argue right through next winter. These arguments are the lifeblood of the game and they account for a great deal of the hold that baseball has on the public and why, despite the claim of football loyalists, it is still our national pastime.

Baseball is only partially about athletic achievement. It is also about fathers and sons going to games together, or fans sitting around watching television, or kids who should be asleep listening to night games from the

West Coast. It's about following your favorite player in the newspaper box scores or sneaking a minute at the office to follow the play-by-play on the Internet. It's about heated arguments over controversial plays, the relative abilities of certain players, and the direction in which the game is headed.

And it's just as much about Orlando Cepeda and Tommy Henrich—the 100th player on our list—as it is about Babe Ruth.

Enjoy.

Neil Shalin
June 2002

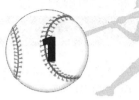

Richie (Dick) Allen

1B, 3B, OF, 1963–1977, Phillies, Cardinals, Dodgers, White Sox, A's

C all him Richie. Call him Dick. Call him a pain-in-the-you-know-what to management. Call him anything you want—he's number one in our book.

Dick/Richie Allen, the slugger with the big, heavy bat and the penchant for getting himself into hot water was, simply put, as feared a hitter as there has been in the modern era.

"I have played on some great teams and played with some of the best play-ers in baseball history," said former pitcher Rich Gossage (also a member of our distinguished list) in a passage of the book, *Pen Men*. "But I'll tell you this—the best player I ever played with was in a league of his own, and that's Dick Allen. Nobody else is even close. I played with him in 1972 in Chicago when he was MVP. I saw him do the most incredible things with the bat, the glove. He hit more balls hard. I could take you to any ballpark we played and show you balls that he hit so hard, balls that looked like rockets.

"You kinda listen to stories about the old guys but it doesn't sink in because you don't have any recollection of them at all. You can't imagine how good they were: Mays, Mantle, and Maris . . . but I saw Dick Allen—he was the best. Just unbelievable."

Allen was one of those baseball figures that was larger than life—and the legend he created off the field tends to take away from the man who put up some marvelous numbers and won that 1972 Most Valuable Player (MVP) award with a tremendous year—a .308 batting average, 37 home runs, 113 runs batted in, only 10 points off the Triple Crown in a pitchers' year that was also shortened by eight games by a players' strike.

Dick Allen *at a glance*

- 1964 NL Rookie of the Year
- 1972 AL MVP
- .292 career BA, with 351 HRs, 1,119 RBIs, and .534 slugging pct.
- AL home run champion in 1972 and 1974
- 1974 AL RBI champion
- Seven-time All-Star

People tend to forget all the numbers and focus on the negative (the horses; the partying, which some contend was exaggerated; etc.), but you should know this about the man who hit .292 with 351 homers and 1,119 RBIs in his career—Allen was, most of the time, anyway, a good teammate. His problems were mainly with management (although there were battles with teammates, too), and all of that started early, when Allen thought white players with less talent than he had were being signed to bigger contracts. It was exacerbated when the Phillies played hardball with his contract after he was National League (NL) Rookie of the Year in 1964.

"I think had he had some of the things available today in terms of counseling and psychological help to help him deal with the media, the responsibility, and things like that, I think maybe he would have been a more popular figure," says former teammate Jim Kaat. "But he had his own rules."

In Chicago, Chuck Tanner let it be known that Allen had his own rules. He told the team this. Once, when Allen was late for a bus, other players said, "Let him take a cab, he can afford it." Tanner said, "You can take a cab. I'm waiting for Dick Allen."

And so the stories went. Former Phillies shortstop Bobby Wine says, "Me and (Bob) Uecker love to sit down and start telling Richie Allen stories. There's so many of them."

There were suspensions, scuffles—but the man could play. In 1972, Tanner says, "He was on a rampage, a man on a mission."

He didn't always do things on time. "We're playing in Shea Stadium and at that time they were still playing doubleheaders at 1:05," Wine says. "It's about quarter to one, ten to one, we took infield, we took our batting practice, and we're back in the clubhouse and we're changing and getting ready. [Manager Gene] Mauch has been back and forth between the dugout and the clubhouse looking for him. No Richie. So Richie walks in and we said, 'Rich, where ya been? We're getting ready to play and you're the third hitter.' He says, 'I'll be ready, don't worry about it.'

"He's standing there, getting dressed, putting his socks on, and he's talking. We say, 'Rich, we got eight minutes and you're the third hitter.' He says, 'I'll be there, I'll be there.' He gets his stuff on, walks out, and they're playing the National Anthem. First guy out, second guy, I don't know what happened to them and—BAM!—home run [by Allen]. He hadn't hit a ball. I don't even know if he's awake yet. That's the kind of talent he had."

"(Don) Drysdale thought Stan Musial was the best hitter he ever faced but he said Richie Allen was in the top five," says Ken Harrelson. "Coming from Drysdale . . . that shows that Richie was just a wonderful player.

"Richie was a great hitter and a great guy. He's a Hall of Fame player."

The home runs were special, often leaving the playing field on the way up. And it was clear from his first season that he was a special talent. "But the Phillies wouldn't give him a raise. They told him to put back-to-back years together and they'd pay him then," says Wine. "He went south after that with management. He just wrote everybody off."

"They'd say, 'be here at five,' and he's here at six. They say, 'be here at three' and he'd be here at five. They say, 'we're gonna do this' and he'd do that. We'd be working out in spring training and he'd be on a plane somewhere else. He just came and went as he pleased. From that day on, management was dog meat for him."

Allen's problems with management started before that—when he felt white players got the aforementioned better treatment. He was rebellious against the powers that be even before he got to the major leagues. And, until he got to Chicago, the fourth stop on a six-team trail (counting the Phillies twice), there were problems—until Tanner laid the rules out for the other players.

Harrelson says the "off-field stuff" wasn't that bad. Kaat remembers a great teammate who would do anything to win—and anything for one of his teammates. "He was beyond just a power hitter," Kaat says.

And beyond just a legend.

Tony Oliva

OF, DH, 1962–1976, Twins

Count former Twins teammate—and fellow Out by a Stepper—Jim Kaat among the many who believe Tony Oliva should be in the Hall of Fame.

"The comparison I always make is [Rod] Carew is in the Hall of Fame—and he should be," Kaat says. "[Harmon] Killebrew's in the Hall of Fame and he should be. But if you ask Andy Etchebarren, Duane Josephson, Bill Freehan, Bob Montgomery—guys that caught in that era—who they feared [in the Twins lineup] and it wouldn't be Carew or Killebrew first or second. It would be Oliva. He was still our most feared hitter.

"Tony, without bad knees, would have played a long time—but he was, I think, the best at his position [right field] during his era, which should qualify him for the Hall of Fame.

"He was like, if you took Tony Gwynn and Rod Carew . . . he was those guys with extra base power."

Adds Lou Piniella: "This guy was a batting champion who could hit 35 home runs. Jesus Christ!"

But Oliva hasn't come close to the Hall of Fame—and now awaits good news from the revamped Veterans Committee. Crippling knee injuries kept this product of Cuba from the all-important longevity criteria for the Hall. Basically, this is a man who had a million-dollar swing and ten-cent knees.

"Tony was a complete player," says Carew. "Tony could run, he could hit, he could throw—he could hit anybody! It didn't matter who it was. He was just a good all-around player. You look at a kid now and say, 'five-tools'—that was Tony.

"Tony could hit for power, he could steal bases. He had a great arm but it's just that injuries cut short his career.

"He should be in the Hall of Fame."

Tony Oliva *at a glance*

- Three-time AL batting champion, including his first two seasons
- 1964 AL Rookie of the Year
- .304 lifetime hitter
- Hit first home run by a DH
- Eight straight All-Star appearances between 1964 and 1971
- 1966 Gold Glove
- Led AL in hits five times

Seven operations on Oliva's right knee mangled the leg, but never stopped him from hitting. Even at the end—when Oliva's crooked knee made it almost impossible for him to get up to the plate—the Twins would lead him off for road games, let him take his one shot in the first inning, and then take him out of the game. Or they would let him pinch hit later in the game.

After sneaking into the United States with his brother's papers (his brother's name was Tony) and almost getting sent back by the Griffith family after a less-than-spectacular tryout as a seventeen-year-old, Pedro Oliva, using a wide batting stance born of trying to hit pieces of corn cob with a stick in Cuba, won the American League batting title his first two years, the only player ever to do that. That was in 1964 and 1965—just after *Baseball Digest* described him as a "fair hitter" who "can make somebody a good utility outfielder."

Oliva had 217 hits in his rookie season starting his career by batting .410 his first year as a pro. He wound up hitting .304 lifetime, adding a third batting title in 1971 (a season that started with Oliva hitting .375 before another injury forced him to limp through the rest of the year). He led the league in hits five times, in doubles four times, and in runs scored once. On April 6, 1973, he hit the first homer ever hit by a designated hitter.

Oliva wound up playing only eleven years of 126 games or more, getting 1,917 hits—220 of them home runs. He batted .440 in six playoff games, but only .192 in the 1965 World Series.

Style? A plan? This guy learned to hit diving for pieces of corn cob with a stick! Basically, Oliva went up, saw the ball, and hit it—and he hit bad balls, walking more than 50 times in a season just once in his career. "You wouldn't want to teach anybody to hit like that," says longtime Twins manager Tom Kelly, "but that son of a bitch could swing the bat."

"There was no right way to pitch him," says former catcher Buck Martinez. "One time, he came up against us [in Kansas City] and we threw him a nasty pitch down and in and he pulled it for a double. Next time, same pitch, same place, and he went the other way for a double." Martinez recalled a double-header at the old ballpark in Kansas City, where Oliva went 6-for-8 and hit two balls out of the park and out onto Brooklyn Avenue—"something that had been done like twelve times and he did it twice on the same day."

Says Kaat: "One of the things that stands out about Oliva, how I rank a ballplayer, is he could hit good pitching. You have a lot of guys who can compile pretty good career stats, but he was always a guy you could count on to hit Dean Chance and Mickey Lolich, Mike Cuellar, and Jim Palmer and guys like that. He hit good pitching."

Adds Piniella: "He hit the ball harder to left field than any left-handed hitter I've ever seen."

And, Kaat says, "I came up with him in Instructional League. We used to hit him fly balls, and he would literally miss the ball. I mean, it would land three or four feet from him. Yet, four years later, he was Gold Glove winner in the American League. He was a good outfielder, had an accurate throwing arm, and was a good base runner."

But, because of those knees, "Here's a guy that couldn't do anything but hit." says Joe Torre. "That's why the DHs really get passed over at this point in time because nobody knows if they could play a position, but Tony Oliva—he had physical ailments and would still go out there and limp through a .330 season. He was pretty incredible."

Bruce Sutter

P, 1976–1986, 1988, Cubs, Cardinals, Braves

The latest Hall of Fame balloting tells the story. Bruce Sutter just isn't getting much support for Cooperstown and we can only wonder why.

"He was awesome," says Art Howe, who played with and against Sutter in the National League. "I guess [his lack of support] is because he was like the first of his ilk—probably the first real closer."

"In his era, in his time, I don't think there was anybody better in the National League," adds Alan Trammell. "I guess people are enamored by power. Here's a guy who did it with a trick pitch. That shouldn't matter [for Hall consideration]. The bottom line is results."

While Roger Craig gets much of the credit for the split-finger fastball, it was Sutter, taught the pitch by then-Cubs pitching coach Freddie Martin, who perfected the pitch—a drop-off-the-table forkball-type pitch that drove hitters crazy—and Craig actually came to *them* for tips on how to teach it. Sutter, who pitched for the Cubs, Cardinals, and Braves, was the master.

And many feel he should be in the Hall of Fame.

"First of all, he broke ground," says Joe Torre, one of the believers. "He was *the* reliever. Bruce Sutter was the reason that you had to be ahead of the Cubs by the sixth inning—because at that time closers pitched the seventh, eighth, and ninth innings. When you think of it now it's like, wow, I feel like I'm tempting fate pitching my guy [Mariano Rivera] two innings. In those days, it was every day and it was three innings."

A pitch that was born from the adversity of a blown-out right elbow led Sutter to 300 saves—most of them recorded primarily with that that one pitch. "The amazing thing is that it worked right off the bat," Sutter said. "Fred started me out throwing it with a slightly different grip and then he made a slight adjustment and, baby, that was it."

Bruce Sutter *at a glance*

- 1979 NL Cy Young winner
- 300 career saves
- First pitcher with 40 saves in a season
- Had five years with over 100 innings pitched
- Set a record (since broken) with 45 saves in 1984
- Four straight All-Star Games 1978–1981

"I've never seen anybody, for a guy who didn't throw in the 90s . . . I've never seen anybody embarrass the big hitters like he did," says Larry Bowa. "He'd make them swing and miss at pitches that just disappeared out of the zone. You'd see that with Nolan Ryan and his fastball and curveball, you'd see that with Steve Carlton's slider that's down and in. But for somebody that didn't have 90-plus velocity, he could embarrass you."

Even though you knew it was coming. "He basically threw it 90 percent of the time, if not more," says Howe. "Everybody knew that it was coming, you just couldn't hit it—that's how good it was." Randy Hundley, one of his early catchers, said, "The interesting thing about Bruce was that he threw the split-finger about 95 percent of the time and you would think guys would eventually learn how to hit it. But they never did."

Adds Howe: "He was one of the best I ever played with. He was just an ultimate professional. No situation ever rattled him. I never saw the man sweat. It was like he was playing catch in his back yard."

And you can go back and check those saves—this was the era before the one-inning freebie. For instance, Sutter, the National League Cy Young award winner for the Cubs in 1979, had 37 saves that year, the first of a six-year span that saw him lead the league in saves five times and saw him become the first ever to get past 40 in a season. He appeared in 62 games and worked 101 innings in 1979, the second of five years over 100 innings. By comparison, Rivera saved 45 games in 1999, with 69 innings of work over 66 outings.

In 1984, Bruce Sutter saved a then-record 45 games and pitched 122⅔ innings in 71 appearances.

"When he got saves, they weren't from a 1–2–3 ninth inning and that was it," says Bowa. "They were three-inning saves, two-inning saves. Durability—I remember a four-game series against us [the Phillies], he pitched every single game and it wasn't just the ninth inning."

"Johnny Franco was one of my proteges when I coached in Cincinnati," says Jim Kaat. "Now, everybody gets excited about 400 saves. It's not the same. It's not the same as when Sutter and [Rich] Gossage and [Rollie] Fingers and maybe Eck [Dennis Eckersley], but even Eck started getting the one-inning saves.

"These guys are getting 400 saves today and it's not the same as Sutter because Sutter and Fingers and Gossage used to pitch two innings, two-and-a-fraction innings. Then they'd come back the next day and do it again. They didn't just come in with a three-run lead and pitch one inning."

Sutter, called "a great, great teammate" by Howe, got a World Series ring with the Cardinals in 1982—closing out the Milwaukee Brewers with his second save of the seven-game series. He would eventually sign a big six-year deal with the Braves in 1984 but would be hampered by shoulder problems and struggled through the 1988 season long enough to reach the 300-save mark.

Gary Carter

C, 1974–1992, Expos, Mets, Giants, Dodgers

Gary Carter's wife had a surprise party planned for January 8, 2002—the day her husband would get the news he had been elected to the Baseball Hall of Fame. Gary Carter even had plane reservations to fly to New York for the happy press conference.

But the celebration was put on hold, at least for another year. Gary Carter fell eleven votes shy of the total needed for induction. Ozzie Smith was the only one voted into the class of 2002. "If 129 of those 472 [voters] don't feel Gary Carter is deserving, that's their decision," the former catcher said that day. "It's frustrating. I'd like to know who they might be. I'd like to know their reasoning."

Said Smith: "I'm very surprised, when you look at Gary's numbers. I thought for sure he would probably get in this year. I think eventually he will."

Some speculated Carter was *too* nice to the media, too accessible. Some even thought he was a phony. Some think all the years he played in Montreal were holding him back. None of that should have mattered—Carter will get his shot.

When people think of Gary Carter, the first thing that comes to mind is that big smile, that all-American, apple-pie look. But baseball people will tell you the look wasn't what this borderline Hall of Fame catcher was about at all.

"Sometimes, you couldn't believe it was the same guy," one opponent said of Carter. "Meet him off the field or around the batting cage, and he was always this smiling, friendly guy. But then during the game, try scoring on a close play, and it's like running into the side of a wall. I tell you, he can be *mean* at the plate."

He was also accused of being *too* nice—teammates often jealous of his ability to grab the attention with that personality. Even his nickname—"The Kid"—annoyed some people. In some ways, it all took away from what Carter really meant to the game while he was in it.

Gary Carter *at a glance*

- Two-time All-Star MVP
- Eight straight All-Star starts
- Three straight Gold Gloves
- *Sporting News* NL Rookie of the Year 1975
- Had only one passed ball in 152 games in 1978, a record
- 324 homers, 298 as a catcher

In short, he can be overlooked when you're talking about the great catchers of his—or *all*—time. The one-time pride of the Expos, who would win a World Series with the New York Mets in 1986 (his was one of those three straight singles that keyed the bottom of the tenth inning of that Game Six against the Red Sox), Carter was as solid as they came. He also may have been the best catcher of his time had it not been for a fella named Johnny Bench.

"It wasn't fair to Gary," one writer wrote, "but that's the way it goes. Bench was already a legend when Gary came up, and the truth was Johnny was beginning to slip just a bit, but there was no way you were going to say that *anybody* was better than Johnny Bench."

The Hall of Fame voters certainly weren't saying the pair belong together in Cooperstown. Not yet, anyway.

"In the late '70s and early '80s, there were a lot of good catchers," says Buck Martinez, a decent catcher in his own right who turned to broadcasting and then became the manager of the Toronto Blue Jays prior to the 2001 season. "You had [Thurman] Munson and [Carlton] Fisk and [Jim] Sundberg and all those guys—those guys that were in the league at the same time, so [Carter] had a tendency to be lumped in with all those guys. Then [Bob] Boone came in.

"Gary was a prototypical catcher. He certainly had all the qualities to be a Hall of Fame–type player. He was a strong-armed catcher."

Said former teammate Rusty Staub: "He was a great catcher . . . The Kid will have his day. That's my opinion. I would be hard-pressed to put anybody (in his era) ahead of him—except Bench."

Carter, who came up as an outfielder, played eighteen years in the major leagues, becoming a regular catcher at just twenty-three—when he hit .284 and banged 31 home runs for the 1977 Expos. Before that, he was *The*

Sporting News Rookie of the Year in 1975, but lost the Baseball Writers' award to John Montefusco.

In 1978, in his second year as a catcher, he had *one* passed ball, a record for 150 or more games.

The only drawback Martinez could recall to Carter's game was that Carter "may have worried too much about offense, [whereas] the number one concern of a catcher is to get the best out of your pitchers—and he may have taken some of his at-bats back behind the plate with him and that may have caused him some problems.

"He had a reputation of being a good leader," Martinez said. "Later on [in] his career, he became quite an impact offensive player."

Carter's reputation as a leader may not have been entirely accurate. More than one teammate resented that perpetual smile, Larry Parrish once said, "He smiled an awful lot, especially with cameras around. I didn't like him for years."

But Parrish admitted that changed when he, and others around him, realized how tough Carter was *on* the field, how much he wanted to win. He almost got there in Montreal (he hit .360 and drove in 22 runs down the stretch in 1981 but it wasn't enough as the run of the talented Expos was coming to an end with nothing to show for all the players they had) and then was able to do it in New York, two years after the Mets traded four young players to get him. He helped the Mets to their second title.

Carter and Keith Hernandez—also prominent in this book—weren't true buddies in New York. They played together and won together, surviving one of the strangest endings to a World Series ever that gave the Mets their first title since 1969 (their only two through the end of the century).

Career numbers? Carter batted .262 lifetime, with 324 homers, 1,225 runs batted in. He hit ten career grand slams. He was a two-time All-Star Game MVP and won three straight Gold Gloves from 1980 to 1982.

Staub is probably right—The Kid probably will have his day, and that day will probably be in 2003. He deserves it.

Don Mattingly (Donnie Baseball)

1B, 1982–1995, Yankees

It was Don Mattingly's first year on the ballot. Yankee fans everywhere, knowing his career numbers weren't what they should have been, were hoping against hope that the man they call "Donnie Baseball" would get a real look from the Hall of Fame voters.

It didn't happen.

In a year in which one of his former teammates, Dave Winfield, and another guy, Kirby Puckett, whose career numbers were strangely similar to his, found their way into the Hall, Mattingly had to settle for ninth place on his first try—with 145 votes.

Ian Browne of Sportsline.com came up with the matchup between the former Yankee captain and first baseman and Puckett, who, like Winfield, went in on the first try, the class of 2001. Mattingly then got only 96 votes his second year.

Browne wrote: "They played in an almost identical number of games—1,785 for Mattingly, 1,783 for Puckett. Puckett hit .318 and had 2,304 hits, compared to .307 and 2,153 for Mattingly. Mattingly had 222 homers, Puckett had 207. Mattingly drove in 1,099 runs, Puckett 1,085. Mattingly won nine Gold Gloves while Puckett had six."

Continuing Browne's piece, "Both retired following the 1995 season and this was their first time on the ballot. So it's fair to ask why Puckett got 423 votes and Mattingly finished with a paltry 145, 242 votes shy of the 387 necessary for enshrinement."

Browne then pointed to Puckett being "on top of his game" when glaucoma forced him to retire, while Mattingly had gone downhill in the 1990s because of his back—after spending 1984–1989 as a dominating player in the American League. Then there's the World Series—it took Mattingly, the 1985

Don Mattingly *at a glance*

- 1985 AL MVP
- 1984 AL batting title
- Once hit homers in eight straight games
- Six-time All-Star
- Nine Gold Gloves
- Hit 6 grand slams in 1987
- Had Yankee record 238 hits in 1986
- .307 lifetime hitter

MVP, until his final year to even play in a playoff game (he batted .417 with a homer and 6 RBIs in five playoff games) and he never got to a World Series. Puckett led the Twins to two titles.

"Without the back thing, certainly a Hall of Famer," says Lou Piniella, Mattingly's former hitting coach and manager. "First of all, when you look at his defensive prowess, excellent around first base—great hands, excellent range, could turn a double play. He threw from the left side as well as anybody. I would say in the period Mattingly played, he played first base as well as anybody (and he played in New York at the same time as fellow Gold Glover and "Out by a Stepper" Keith Hernandez)."

And offensively, Piniella says, "I was the hitting coach when he came to the Yankees. He had a wonderful stroke, had a line-drive stroke, and hit the ball to left-center field. And because of the short dimensions at Yankee Stadium, Yogi said, 'Lou, see if you can work with him and get him to the pull the ball.' And we worked on it and it started to come for him—he started to hit home runs. He became a legitimate 30–35 home run guy and tied the record for 8 home runs in eight consecutive games."

"Great hand-eye coordination, wonderful weight shift. In the thirty-two years or so that I've been involved with major league baseball as a player, coach, and manager, one of the shortest takeaway [cocking the bat, which reduces the time it takes to get the swing to the ball] I've ever seen. I would think that Paul Molitor was the only other guy I've seen like that.

"Legitimate .300 hitter, legitimate RBI guy, legitimate home-run hitter, Gold Glove-type first baseman. You take away the back injury from Donnie and you have a guy that, say, plays another five or six years (in top shape)—Hall of Fame numbers."

"His run was as good as any I've ever seen for that period of time," says former teammate Willie Randolph. "He was into one of those zones—he had [a] great supporting cast around him. Donnie had a great situation. He was in a beautiful spot. It always amazed me, as much as he was raking back then, as much as he was doing, they still would pitch to him rather than pitch to Dave Winfield. I always thought that was kinda weird—you have to respect Winfield, too, he's a Hall of Famer, but it just seems that sometimes Donnie was a tougher out than Winfield at certain times. But they would just continue to go after him and he would continue to rake.

"People don't remember, when Donnie first came up, he wasn't a power hitter. He's flipping the ball, he's hitting line drives, and also he got into this little run where he was hitting a lot of home runs but I think that he would say, if he was honest with you, he would say that he was surprised, too.

"He was a student of the game—he worked hard, all the time, always trying to refine his swing. I think he surprised himself with the home run power."

Adds Puckett: "I idolized Donnie. Like me, he was the first person there, the last to leave [the park]. The only difference between Don and myself, I went to ten All-Star Games in a row. Donnie went to several. But the Yankees didn't win the World Series [until just after Mattingly left, when they re-established their dynasty]. I won two in [five] years. That may be the thing that put me over the top. Other than that, we were pretty much the same type of ballplayers. I know that we both played hard every day."

6. Ron Santo

3B, 1960–1974, Cubs, White Sox

Randy Hundley has an interesting theory on why former teammate Ron Santo is not in the Hall of Fame—even though, Hundley says, he should be.

"When you look at his record, he should be in the Hall of Fame," the ex-catcher says. "One of the big things holding him back is that three guys from our team—Ernie Banks, Billy Williams, and Fergie Jenkins—are in and we never won a pennant."

"Our team," of course, was the Chicago Cubs, who turned from losers into near- and should-have-been winners during the 1960s—with Santo playing a marvelous third base. A decade that would start with the coaches taking turns managing the team for two weeks at a time—Phil Wrigley's infamous College of Coaches—ended with Leo Durocher's team falling apart and losing the 1969 National League East race to the "Miracle" Mets, despite having a big lead heading down the stretch.

Through it all, as the Cubs turned into one of the great teams that never won, like fellow hitters Banks and Williams, Santo was a star—both offensively and defensively. From 1963 to 1970, Santo batted .300 twice, but hit 30–33 home runs four straight years at one stretch (1964–1967) and had 98 or more RBIs seven of eight years from 1963 to 1970. He also won five Gold Gloves—his defense always overshadowed by Brooks Robinson over in the American League.

"Was Brooks Robinson a better fielder than Ron Santo?" Williams asks. "I played left field behind Santo in Chicago all those years and I'm telling you that sucker was quick. I saw him make plays that nobody else could have made. He was out there every day, hurt or not, he had marvelous instincts and he could hit."

Ron Santo *at a glance*

- Nine-time All-Star
- Five straight Gold Gloves
- Led NL in chances nine times
- 342 career homers
- 1,331 career RBI
- 98 or more RBI in one stretch of seven of eight years

But he's on the outside looking in, not a Hall of Famer but ranked number six in a book created just for people like him. There are eleven players in the Hall listed as third basemen—Santo matches up with at least a few.

Take George Kell, for example. Playing in the 1940s and 1950s, with his big years coming for the Detroit Tigers, Kell was a nice player. He hit .306 lifetime, with one batting title, one 200-hit season, 78 career homers, 870 RBIs, and 51 steals. He led the American League in doubles twice, had 100 RBIs in a season once. No postseason play. He's in.

Santo, who played his entire career while keeping his battle with diabetes a secret, hit .277 lifetime, with 342 homers, 1,331 RBIs, 35 steals. He's out.

His five Gold Gloves don't match Robinson's 16—but Robinson batted 10 points lower and hit 74 fewer homers. Robinson did drive in 26 more runs and had postseason success—which is where that Cubbie factor comes in again.

"The Cubs haven't done anything and haven't won anything—but as an everyday player this guy was tough," says former National League shortstop Bobby Wine. "He played every day, he hit, he hit with power, hit for average.

"He played a great third base—but he's one of those guys that's in that mix and you're gonna say, 'ahhhh, he's got an outstanding chance,' but how many guys are gonna vote for him?"

Says Hundley: "If you saw how quick his hands were, it would explain a lot about why he was such a good hitter."

Defensively, Santo went from a young guy who once led the Texas League with 53 errors in a season to a Gold Glover in the majors. He led the National League in total chances nine times and shares the National League mark for most years leading the league in assists (seven) and double plays (six).

Santo had to have an incredible work ethic. While a player in this new millennium would probably wear the badge of playing with a disease with honor and become an active spokesman in the fight against it, Santo played in a different time. He begged those who knew about his diabetes not to say anything and his problem didn't become known until after he finished his career with a season with the cross-town White Sox in 1974 (he had a verbal battle with Dick Allen, who was angered when he thought Santo was trying to take over his team).

"I was always careful not to give myself a shot of insulin in the locker room in front of anybody. I always did it in private," he said, adding the disease actually drove him on the field. "[It was] one reason I played so hard," he said. "I keep thinking my career could end any day. I never really wanted out of the lineup. The diabetes thing was hanging over my head."

Wanting to play is one thing, missing 23 of a possible 1,595 starts from 1961 to 1970 is another. The guy was always in there.

But he's not in the Hall of Fame.

"He was a great competitor, a tough, get-dirty, get-down guy, an outstanding third baseman," says former reliever Dick Radatz, a Santo teammate in 1967. "You talk about a borderline Hall of Famer . . . I think it bothers him he's not in the Hall of Fame. He's got a big ego—a lot of ballplayers do."

And he also has a resume many feel is worthy of entrance into the great Hall.

Dave Parker (Cobra)

OF, DH, 1973–1991, Pirates, Reds, A's,
Braves, Angels, Blue Jays

T hose who saw Dave Parker only in the American League—as a hulking, hobbling designated hitter—have no way of knowing what this very large man could do on a baseball field.

"He did everything," fellow "Out by a Stepper" Larry Bowa says. "He had a cannon [for an arm], he could run, steal bases, hit home runs, hit doubles, get walks."

Adds Paul Molitor, who would become a teammate of Parker's in Milwaukee: "When you talk about a guy who was a five-tool player with major league high marks across the board, I think Dave, particularly in his younger years, filled that bill."

"He had a presence because of his size alone [6'5", 225 early and weighing more later, sometimes much more] but he hit line drives as hard as anybody I've ever played with—and that was in the latter stages of his career. He could beat you in a lot of ways."

The flamboyant Parker, one of the first players to wear an earring (he once said he wouldn't switch from a diamond to a pearl because "a pearl would be ostentatious"), got in trouble off the field with cocaine. He also got hurt and never actually became what he probably should have. But there are many in baseball who believe he was as good as it gets from a pure-talent standpoint. There was also a general feeling he was the best player in the National League in the late 1970s, when he still had a "bad boy" label that would eventually transform to the image of team-leader, a type people wanted to have around.

"I think a lot of the times when there's a problem and you've had a drug problem, it always inhibits [your chances] of being in [the Hall of Fame]—but

---

Dave Parker *at a glance*

- 1978 NL MVP
- NL batting champion 1978 and 1979
- Three straight Gold Gloves
- Hit .300 five straight years
- Six-time All-Star
- Finished with a .290 career batting average, 339 homers, and 1,493 RBIs

---

Dave Parker was definitely an impact player," says Joe Torre. "Defensively, offensively, he could run, he could do everything. He was an all-tool guy. He could steal bases. He had a rocket for an arm.

"I remember, when I was managing the Mets. We were talking about helping our club and free agency was new, this was in the late '70s. I had made mention to our general manager, I said, 'the one guy you gotta take a shot at is Dave Parker—give him a million dollars.' At that time, my general manager, Joe McDonald, looked at me cross-eyed. I said, '. . . he's the one guy if you're going to pick out to make your club legitimate, he'd be the one guy.'"

For his career, which carried into the early 1990s, Parker hit .290 with 339 home runs and 1,493 RBIs. He won three Gold Gloves, two World Series titles (one with Pittsburgh, with the 1979 "Fam-A-Lee," and one with Oakland), hit .300 five straight years, winning the batting title in 1978, when he was also National League MVP, and in 1979. He added a sixth .300 season with the Reds in 1985, and hit .289 with 21 homers and 92 RBIs for the Brewers in 1990—when he turned thirty-nine and was a designated hitter. Parker also stole 76 bases in a four-year stretch with the Pirates, 154 in his career.

"Eventually, his size worked against him because it broke him down," said Torre.

When Parker went from Pittsburgh to Cincinnati, he said, "Pittsburgh took a lot out of me. I always sacrificed my body in Pittsburgh. I tried to come back too soon from injuries. That was my stupidity. It made my game decline. I should have done what every player does when he's hurt—sit on the bench."

Parker became one of baseball's first big-money guys after 1978 and, often playing hurt at the start of the 1980s, was the focal point of Pirate fans' frustrations over the decline of the team. There were death threats, batteries, and even bullets throw at him. He got heavy. He got miserable. "I wasn't treated right in Pittsburgh," he said after signing with his hometown Reds, where his career again took off. "I let it affect my performance in those later years, and I never should have."

Hall of Famer Rod Carew remembers an All-Star appearance with Parker, Ellis Valentine, Andre Dawson, and Reggie Smith. "I saw those guys put on an exhibition of throwing at the All-Star Game in Yankees Stadium—I was just in awe," Carew recalls. "I mean, they showed it off. They were throwing balls from right field that were clotheslines, all four of them. They knew it and they wanted guys to see it."

Parker made one legendary All-Star throw and never hesitated to show off his gun. "To me, his arm stood out," says Buck Martinez. "We used to go watch him throw during infield and marvel at his arm. The next thing that was so impressive about him was his size. He was big, he could run and he played very aggressively. He had a very good swing and he became a very good hitter. He hit for a good average all the time and he had that mentality that said, 'you're not going to beat my ass—I'm gonna hit your ass and there's nothing you have that can get me out.'"

"He was intimidating, it had to be intimidating for a pitcher to face him," recalls Lou Piniella. "A guy that probably, basically, most closely resembled Willie Stargell than any other player in a Pittsburgh uniform. He had tremendous power, could hit for average, hit the ball to left field as well as right field— and a great throwing arm and a guy basically when he first came up, at his size, could steal bases and rather easily. You're talking about a heck of an athlete."

Jim Rice

OF, DH, 1974–1989, Red Sox

I f you ask baseball people, there doesn't seem to be much doubt—Jim Rice deserves to be in the Hall of Fame.

"Jimmy is a Hall of Famer, there's no question about Jim Rice being a Hall of Famer in my opinion," says Hawk Harrelson. "You look at some of the guys in the Hall of Fame, who deserve to be there, and Rice was a better player."

Adds Jim Kaat: "Here's a guy who was a perennial All-Star. He was a[n] MVP. If you ask, 'was he the dominant player at his position in his era?' he certainly was that. To me, for a decade, if a guy does that he qualifies as a Hall of Fame player."

Says old friend and former coach Johnny Pesky: "I don't know why he's not in."

Mention Rice to Joe Torre and he says: "There's a certain amount of politics [that] go into this thing where you have a chance to be voted in by somebody but if they remember that Rice didn't talk to them or was hard to get along with, it's going to be a problem."

Rice was 89 votes short of election in the 2000 voting, 94 in 2001. There appeared to be hope. Yet, he still wasn't in. Some say he'll get there, but many wonder if his relationship with the media is what's keeping him out. Looking at his numbers, you have to think.

Funny thing about Rice: If you spent the time trying to talk to him, his answers were better than the average player—and always honest. If he got mad at you, though, it wasn't pleasant. Don Zimmer, his old manager, who lauds Rice in his recent autobiography, says Rice was misquoted in an article during his rookie season and that changed Rice's attitude toward the press.

"This guy was a big hitter," says Zimmer. "I don't think people realize Jimmy Rice's numbers. I asked some people one day about [Dale] Murphy. I

Jim Rice *at a glance*

- AL MVP 1978
- .298 lifetime batting average
- *Sporting News* Minor League Player of the Year 1974
- Eight-time All-Star
- 382 career homers, 1,451 RBIs
- Hit into 315 double plays, third-most ever

said, 'you think Murphy will go to the Hall of Fame?' and people hesitate a little bit and they say, 'possibility.' Then I would say, the very next question, 'you think Rice will go?' and they'd say, 'oh, no.'"

"Well, go look at their records. I mean, my goodness, Jim Rice put up some numbers. Unfortunately, Jim Rice did not have a great rapport with the press. It wasn't that Jim Rice was a bad guy. He was [misunderstood]—that's probably what hurt his chances for being voted into the Hall of Fame."

Breaking in with the Red Sox in 1975, along with fellow "Out by a Stepper" Fred Lynn (the MVP and Rookie of the Year that year, with Rice hitting .309 with 22 homers and 102 RBIs before breaking his hand in September). Rice put together numbers over the next twelve years (before a three-year downturn and then an abrupt end to his career) that should warrant more attention. But his special year was 1978.

If you're a Boston fan, you'll never forget 1978—Bucky Dent and all that—but it seems you, and others, do forget what Rice did that year in winning the MVP award. Think about it—he hit .315, with 46 homers, 139 RBIs, 121 runs, 213 hits, and 406 total bases—the highest American League total since Joe DiMaggio's 418 in 1937. Rice beat out an incredible Ron Guidry for the MVP that year, but Guidry had the best laugh by beating the Red Sox in a playoff for the American League East title.

Rice wound up with 382 career home runs. He did go downhill fast, costing him the wind-down years that would have carried him over 400 homers (he was thirty-six when he retired). He drove in 1,451 runs, batting .298.

Comparison? Teammate and first-ballot Hall of Famer Carl Yastrzemski hit .285 with 452 homers and 1,844 RBIs—the power edge run up in over 1,200 more games. Rice had eight 100-plus RBI seasons; Yaz had five.

Yes, Rice hit into double plays—he hit balls very hard right at people. Yes, there was a rap he collected useless RBIs and didn't hit all that well in the clutch at times—and people say he wasn't a good fielder, even though he became more than adequate, especially at Fenway Park. Most of the raps are shaky. Another thing: that close Green Monster probably hurt Rice more than it helped him—his hard liners often became singles instead of extra base hits.

"If you had to pick a cleanup hitter who epitomized the role of a guy who hit in the middle of the lineup and got big hits when you needed them, it would have been Jim Rice," says ex-player and executive Tom Grieve. "He had power to all fields, he was a good hitter, he hit for average."

Adds Buck Martinez: "You think of an impact player . . . the problem with Jim Rice was you couldn't pitch around him because everyone else in that lineup could hit, too. He's going to get overshadowed and I don't think it's fair." Adds Lou Piniella: "My God, I remember the short stroke he had. It looked like he could hit a ball 450 feet in a phone booth."

Harrelson says Rice was underrated as a fielder and adds, "That's the best outfield I've ever seen, when they had Rice, Lynn, and [Dwight] Evans." All three are in this book.

Perhaps Alan Trammell summed it up best by saying of Rice, "He was a man! He got the head of the bat on it, he used a big bat with a huge head and he didn't get cheated. I don't know why he's somehow been put to the side. That son of a gun, in my era, the era of Jim Rice, was one of the best all-around outfielders in baseball.

"He hit the ball so hard, as a shortstop, you almost felt like a third baseman because you never felt like you were back far enough."

Adds Frank White: "He put fear in pitchers."

Well said.

Maury Wills

SS, 3B, 1959–1972, Dodgers, Pirates, Expos

The [new] Veterans Committee might as well put Maury Wills in the Baseball Hall of Fame because most fans assume he's already been selected.

Of all the players on this list, Maury Wills' name draws the biggest look of disbelief and exclamation of surprise when we tell people that he is included among the overlooked Top 100.

Most who follow baseball don't know about the statistics that are considered for selection, and they don't keep up with the annual baseball writers election or veterans committee meetings. They just remember the name Maury Wills and the effect he had on the game during his days as the offensive catalyst for the great Dodgers teams of the 1960s.

"That's crazy. He should be in!" said an old-time Dodgers fan. That's the typical reaction heard when you inform someone that Wills is being recognized in this book. "I don't care what his career stats were. He was one of the greatest and most exciting players I've ever seen."

Maury Wills was a latecomer to the major leagues and he had a tough act to follow. When he became the Los Angeles Dodgers shortstop midway through the 1959 season, he was almost twenty-seven and he stepped into the formidable footsteps of Pee Wee Reese, who had held the position, with time out for World War II military service, since 1941. Not only had Reese been an outstanding all-around player, but he was the captain of the "Boys of Summer," one of the most storied teams in history, and he led the Dodgers to seven National League pennants.

Before Wills took over, he had been an obscure minor leaguer who was in danger of having his name added to the long list of infielders whose careers were either thwarted or sidetracked by the presence of the great Pee Wee.

Wills proved, however, that he wasn't just any old sequel because with him batting leadoff and anchoring the infield, the Dodgers kept on winning after Reese's retirement.

Maury Wills *at a glance*

- 1962 NL Most Valuable Player
- 104 SBs in 1962 broke Ty Cobb's single-season record (96)
- Five-time All-Star
- Two Gold Gloves
- Lifetime .281 BA, with 1,067 Rs, and 586 SBs
- Six NL stolen base titles (1960–1965)

He, more than anyone, revolutionized the game of baseball into a running and base-stealing game—one that it hadn't been since the great sharpened spikes of Ty Cobb. While not in the defensive class of his contemporary Luis Aparicio, it was Wills who eventually broke Cobb's "unbreakable" single-season record of 96 stolen bases.

He also had a .281 lifetime batting average compared to Hall of Famer Aparicio's .262. While we're not comparing the two (Aparicio was one of the great shortstops of all time and certainly deserves his niche in history), Wills's effect on the game was probably greater, because he was the every day centerpiece for one of the great teams of the 1960s.

The Los Angeles Dodgers were led by the superior pitching duo of Sandy Koufax and Don Drysdale, but it was "Wills singles, steals second, (and maybe third), and scores on a single or sacrifice fly" that was key to the team's National League pennants in 1963, 1965, and 1966. The hit could have been supplied by Tommy Davis, Willie Davis, Wes Parker, or Jim Gilliam, but Wills was the guy who put fear into the hearts of the opposition. His base-stealing heroics changed baseball from a straight power game to a more balanced power-speed offense.

"That used to be our attack," Sandy Koufax said. "Maury would get on, get around somehow, come to the dugout, and say, 'There's your run Sandy.' I had to make it stand up."

In his first season, Wills, who was taught to switch-hit by Bobby Bragan the preceding year, hit an unspectacular .260, but his competitive drive was apparent and he was the team's starting shortstop in the 1959 World Series six-game victory over the White Sox. There was both good news and bad news the following year, as Wills proved he could hit major league pitching, batting .295, but he led the league in errors by a shortstop with 40. He also stole 50 bases—the highest in the National League since Max Carey stole 51 in 1923.

In 1961, he improved in the field, winning one of his two Gold Glove awards, hit .282, scored 105 runs, and won the second of his six consecutive base-stealing titles (then a National League record) with 35.

In 1962, Wills did something so special, according to writer David Smith, that he "changed how the game was played."

"His base running was a major weapon for the Dodgers and others learned that greater daring on the base paths could pay off," said Smith in *The Top 100—The Best Individual Seasons of All Time.*

In that year, Wills stole 104 bases and broke a record that had stood since 1915—Ty Cobb's record of 96 stolen bases. In 1962 no other *team* in the major leagues stole more than 99. And, remarkably, Wills was caught stealing only 13 times. In comparison, Cobb was caught 38 times in 1915. Wills also hit .299 that year, led the league in triples with 10, and scored a career high 130 runs. He was named the National League MVP over Willie Mays.

Smith pointed out that most leading base stealers attempt to steal 25 percent of the time. In 1962, Wills attempted 49 percent of the time. He said the percentage went up to 58 percent when the score was tied or the Dodgers were ahead by one run, when the base was most needed. Further, with Wills on base opposing teams committed 4 balks, 1 passed ball, 7 errors on pickoff attempts, and 6 errors while he was stealing. With Wills on base the Dodgers' number two hitter batted .322, compared to .267 with the bases empty.

Wills would go on to win the base-stealing title three more times, with a high of 94 in 1965 (a Dodger championship year) and set the stage for future base thieves like Lou Brock, Willie Wilson, and Rickey Henderson.

Wills was so effective that Giants' manager Herman Franks was forced to come up with a creative way to stop him from stealing. According to Charlie Fox, who coached under Franks, "Twice with two out, we walked the pitcher to keep Wills from leading off the next inning, and then we walked Wills so he couldn't steal second because the base was occupied. It worked."

Wills later played for the Pirates, hitting .302 in 1967 and the Expos before returning to the Dodgers to close out his fourteen-year career in 1972.

Doug Krikorian of the *Long Beach Press–Telegram* is one of many, including the authors of this book, who believe that Wills should be given his rightful place in the Hall of Fame.

"I look at Maury Wills, and I get the feeling the old shortstop smiles through a wounded heart because he has become the Forgotten Man of his sport, shunted into the shadows in recent years despite his heroic achievements across fourteen blazing seasons he spent in the major leagues . . . no one has vocally stood up and railed about the injustice of Wills not having a plaque in the Cooperstown. All Wills did . . . was bat .281, collect 2,134 hits, steal 586 bases, play on four NL pennant-winning Dodger teams, and alter forever the contours of his sport."

Amen!

Jack Morris

P, 1977–1994, Tigers, Twins, Blue Jays, Indians

He probably didn't get the credit or recognition for it—and some of that may have been his own fault—but there's no denying Jack Morris was the winningest pitcher of the 1980s.

He argued with his manager, didn't get along very well with the press, had a nasty look on his face—but he won, and he won when it counted. He won 162 times in the 1980s, 22 more than any other pitcher. He helped the Detroit Tigers to the world championship in 1984 by winning 19 games and pitching a no-hitter (he had a midseason slump that may have been created by his team—after a 35-5 start—being so far in front of the pack).

Leaving the decade, Morris capped his career by leading his hometown Minnesota Twins to the 1991 title—pitching ten shutout innings in an incredible Game Seven win over the Atlanta Braves (adamantly telling Twins manager Tom Kelly to leave him in during a mound chat late in the game). Morris then went to Toronto as a free agent, won 21 games and another World Series (despite going 0–3 in the postseason) in 1992.

Yes, his career ERA was 3.90, a little high by Hall of Fame standards. But he was a righty pitching in a lefty-friendly Tiger Stadium, where the right field upper deck was actually a little closer to home plate than the lower stands. High fly balls would drop into that upper tier that would have fallen short of the right field fence. And Morris pitched entirely in the era of the designated hitter, never facing a pitcher at the plate.

ERA or no ERA, this guy won.

Guts and determination. Enough nasty to make it all work. This is Jack Morris.

"He had the stubbornness of a mule and the grace of a thoroughbred," Tiger manager Sparky Anderson said in his autobiography. "When we absolutely had to win a game, I wanted Morris on the mound over any pitcher

Jack Morris *at a glance*

- Winningest pitcher of the 1980s
- 7–4 postseason, despite 0–3 finale in 1992
- Four-time All-Star
- Pitched 10-inning shutout in Game Seven of 1991 World Series
- 254–186 lifetime
- Won 21 games and 3 World Series games with Toronto in 1992
- Pitched a no-hitter in 1984

you'd give me. Nine out of ten times, he'd win. The other time he'd keep you close enough for a shot at the end.

"Jack is the perfect lesson in determination. It's so easy in life to give up when the going gets rocky. That's when Morris got going."

And these two guys—Anderson and Morris—it should be pointed out, didn't always get along very well. When Sparky arrived in Detroit in 1979, he angered Morris with comments like, "I'll weed out the rats." He was talking about Morris' friends—people Anderson wanted to dump to turn the Tigers around (which he did). There were shouting matches, and disagreements over Morris coming out of games.

"Once he started a game, it took an act of Congress to get him out," Sparky said in *They Call Me Sparky*. "Jack was a great believer in always finishing what he started. Quitters want to bail when the arrows start flying. Jack stared at those arrows and dared them to come his way."

Fellow Out by a Stepper Willie Randolph remembers not liking Morris much—but respecting him a lot. "I have mixed feelings about Morris because I couldn't stand the guy," the ex–second baseman said. "He was a hell of a competitor, he had great stuff, but we faced each other for so many years and battled each other for so many years, we just had a little thing going where he'd try to brush me back and stuff.

"He's one of those guys who when they're out there on the mound looking down at you, you can see the fire burning in their eyes. You can see these guys are not going to play—they ain't bs-ing around and to boot they have great stuff to go with it . . . when you played Detroit and when you faced Jack Morris, you knew you were in for a battle that day because he would try to sometimes intimidate you but he was also going to come after you and try to embarrass you, too.

"He was one of those real nasty kind of competitors that you really had to come to play if you wanted to beat them. He had a certain arrogance about him, a certain cockiness . . . we used to love to beat him because of that, but he was, to me, the way old-school pitchers were supposed to be. They didn't pussyfoot around, fraternize, act like it was another game—these guys went to war with you. Those are the guys I remember as real gamers. [Dave] Stewart, Jack Morris—those are the guys I call bulldog guys."

Which is why Morris hated to leave games. Paul Molitor recalls there was "no way" Morris was leaving that Game Seven. Anderson said Morris actually "broke blood vessels in my fingers slamming the ball in my hand" when he took him out of a game once. Former teammate Darrell Evans said, "He's a great closer. If he has the lead in the seventh, eighth, and ninth innings, he's going to hold it."

Or want the chance to—Morris also led the 1980s with 133 complete games.

Through it all, he was quiet. He didn't like to talk in public and even shunned the mayor of Detroit during the Tigers' 1984 victory celebration—saying, "I'm not running for mayor. I'm not much of a speaker. I'm trying to go hunting sometime this afternoon." You have to wonder if his attitude led to a pitcher with a 254–186 lifetime record and three rings getting only a smattering of Hall of Fame votes early in his election eligibility.

"I respect anyone who ain't afraid to stand in the middle of the ring when all the punches are coming from the other direction," says Sparky. "He's the best pitcher I ever had. And one of the toughest competitors."

Steve Garvey

1B, 3B, 1969–1987, Dodgers, Padres

Steve Garvey was a genuine hero in the age of the anti-hero. If he had come along at any other time but the late 1960s or early 1970s, Garvey would have been hailed as "Jack Armstrong, All-American Boy." Parents would have pointed to him as an example of good, clean-cut American values and they'd have instructed their kids to be like Steve. That would have been the case if Garvey's superb major league career had happened a decade or two earlier, or even a decade or two later, when conservative values came back into fashion.

But, Steve Garvey, the pride of the Los Angeles Dodgers, the National League iron man, the great clutch hitter of his time, was considered by many to be arrogant, self-promoting or "too good to be true." Although a leader on the field, he was sometimes shunned socially by his teammates.

Steve Garvey was born to be a Dodger. He grew up in Tampa, Florida. His dad was a bus driver who often drove chartered buses for the baseball teams during spring training. For a time he drove the Dodgers bus and Steve served as the Dodgers batboy. He idolized Gil Hodges.

"He was a gentleman on and off the field. I always admired him," Garvey said. "I can still remember his handshake."

Garvey went to Michigan State on a football scholarship, playing in the defensive backfield for the Spartans. When he was drafted by the Dodgers, his favorite team, he left East Lansing and his football career for Dodgertown.

Garvey, who was a solid 5'10" and 195 lbs., was first tried at third base, but was never comfortable there. Finally in 1973 he was moved to first base and, according to Manager Walter Alston, he took to it right away. "He began making all the plays, especially digging out low throws," Alston said.

Alston also noticed that Garvey's football experience came in handy in his approach to the game, especially as a first baseman.

Steve Garvey *at a glance*

- 1974 NL Most Valuable Player
- Lifetime .356 BA in NLCS (five years) and .319 BA in World Series (five years)
- Ten-time All-Star
- Four Gold Gloves
- Lifetime .294 BA, with 2,599 hits (twice led league), 272 HRs, 1,143 Rs, and 1,308 RBIs
- Seven-time .300 BA, six times with 200 hits, five times with 100 RBIs

"He was good at making the sweeping tag play, which sometimes brought him into the path of the runner," Alston said. "He had some pretty rough collisions, but he always bounced right up. I guess that was his football experience. He was used to getting banged around and wasn't afraid of it. He wasn't afraid of anything."

Garvey was tough. He still holds the National League record for durability, having played in 1,207 straight games. He was also consistent, hitting between .280 and .319 thirteen times. He hit over .300 seven times and registered 200 or more hits six times. He batted in 100 runs five times.

When he retired in 1987, Garvey also held a boatload of career fielding records for first basemen, including highest fielding average for a season, 1.000, in 1984 when he was a member of the San Diego Padres. He held the record for most consecutive errorless games by a first baseman, 193, achieved from June 26, 1983, to April 14, 1985 (in that period he accepted 1,319 chances, also a major league record). He won four Gold Glove awards and led the league in fielding average for a first baseman five times. His career fielding average was .996. The Dodgers infield—with Garvey at first, Davey Lopes at second, Bill Russell at short, and Ron Cey at third—stayed together from 1973 to 1981, an all-time major league record for longevity.

Garvey's career record was impressive, but as a man who thrived in the spotlight, he really came forward in important games during the pennant stretch, often getting the key base hit that led to a Dodgers victory. He played in the postseason five times, hitting .356 in five National League Championship Series, each year leading his team to the World Series. In the 1978 NLCS, Garvey hit four home runs to help eliminate the Phillies.

Garvey held the NLCS records for home runs with eight and RBIs with 24. He was named NLCS Most Valuable Player in 1974 and 1978. He hit .319 in 28 World Series Games.

A participant in ten All-Star Games, Garvey hit .393 and fielded flawlessly. He was MVP of the All-Star Game in both 1974 and 1978.

Tommy LaSorda, who succeeded Alston as manager of the Dodgers, marveled at Garvey's businesslike approach to the game.

"He comes to the ball park every day ready to play," LaSorda said. "He's ready to give you his best, every day. He doesn't make trouble, he doesn't, give anyone a headache, he just does his job."

Despite friction with teammates (in 1978 he had a well-publicized fight with pitcher Don Sutton), he was very popular with Los Angeles fans. There was even a junior high school named for him while he was an active player.

Garvey always defended his rapport with the press and the fans.

"It's not so much my publicity as it's baseball's," Garvey said. "If somebody wants to write something about baseball, I make myself available. Anything I say is going to be positive."

He saw his relationship with the fans as the most positive part of the game and was known for patiently signing autographs and chatting with fans after the game. He made numerous public appearances for the community and for charity.

"I enjoy the people," Garvey said. "They are so much a part of this game. I get a lot of my energy from the people."

Garvey shocked the Dodger blue faithful before the 1983 season by signing with the Padres as a free agent. He quickly established himself as a leader on his new team. His new manager Dick Williams became a believer in Garvey's charisma and work ethic.

"Steve Garvey is infectious," Williams said. "Young players who see someone like Steve working as hard as he does cannot help but be inspired."

In 1984, Garvey hit the home run in game four of the playoffs that broke the hearts of Chicago Cubs fans everywhere and set the stage for the Padres to go to their first World Series.

When his playing days were over, Garvey's clean-cut image lost some luster when he admitted to having fathered children with several women. He was also embarrassed by a tell-all book written by his ex-wife, Cyndy.

The memory of Steve Garvey as a baseball player could never be tarnished and he should some day be selected for the Hall of Fame. He definitely has the credentials.

Ken Boyer

3B, OF, 1955–1969, Cardinals, Mets,
White Sox, Dodgers

K en Boyer was that rare individual who was regarded as a hero by
those who knew him. Years after his playing career ended, Boyer's
former teammates still called him "Captain." He was a complete
ballplayer and a team leader respected by opponents, managers, and fans alike.

In a career that spanned fifteen seasons, eleven with the St. Louis Cardinals,
Boyer won five Gold Gloves, was an All-Star for six straight years and won the
1964 Most Valuable Player award in his team's championship season. He led
third baseman in double plays five times, batted .287, scored and drove in more
than 1,000 runs, and smashed 282 homers. Fans who followed baseball at the
time but don't keep up with the statistics and the Hall of Fame annual voting
are incredulous that he has not been enshrined in Cooperstown.

The sturdy 6'2", 200-lb., right-handed hitter was the third baseman for the
Cardinals in the 1950s and 1960s. Because his career spanned the two decades,
he often gets lost in the shuffle—Eddie Mathews is justifiably chosen as the
best National League third baseman of the 1950s, while Ron Santo gets the
nod for the 1960s. Many think Boyer was the equal of these two greats.

Fred Hutchinson, manager of the Cardinals when Boyer matured as a
major leaguer in the late 1950s said, "Ken is the kind of player you wish you
had twelve of, so you could play nine and have three on the bench just to stir
things up. He's the kind of guy you dream about: terrific speed, great arm, and
brute strength. There's nothing he can't do."

Veteran St. Louis columnist Bob Broeg, who watched Boyer throughout his
career, thought the third baseman was one of the greats of the game and one
of the most versatile.

David Halberstam, in his book *October 1964*, recounts Broeg's "Eight Boyer
Theory of Baseball," which is that if the pitching was equal and eight Boyers

Ken Boyer *at a glance*

- 1964 NL MVP
- Five Gold Gloves
- Seven-time All-Star
- Twice hit for the cycle
- Led third basemen in double plays five times
- Five-time .300 hitter

were playing other positions, they would stand a good chance of beating a team made up of any other ballplayer in baseball.

Also from *October 1964*: "Boyer, as far as the younger players on the Cardinals were concerned, was a great role model, a consummate professional who played hard every day and never lost sight of his essential purpose. It was as if he had a God-given instinct about what was real and what was not real in baseball."

Once Boyer made a great play at third base, and umpire Dusty Boggess told Cards' catcher Tim McCarver "Take a good look, son, because you're not going to see anyone like him again." Later, after the game, McCarver told Boyer what Boggess had said.

"Never get caught up in stuff like that," Boyer said.

Boyer wasn't influenced by the emotional swings that affected other players' ability to perform. He was consistent and focused on winning and on what was good for his team.

In his attitude toward younger players he saw himself as carrying on a Cardinals tradition set by Stan Musial, who helped Boyer a great deal throughout his career. In 1964, the year after Musial retired, Boyer felt an extra sense of responsibility to the younger players on the team.

"They come to the older players for advice and an older player can help by giving the younger player compliments, pats on the back, to help him gain confidence," Boyer said. "Another player can reach a ball player better than coach or a manager by helping him with some points on hitting and base running."

His first Cardinals manager, Eddie Stanky, recognized Boyer's abilities and professionalism early. "He's not colorful, but he's deadly efficient with no apparent weakness."

Boyer's record is a model of consistency, efficiency, and durability. Playing mostly in what is remembered as a pitchers' era, Boyer hit over .285, 20-plus home runs, and 90-plus RBIs eight times. He was considered an outstanding clutch hitter. He twice hit for the cycle and he usually played in 150-plus games during his years with the Cardinals. The only flaw in his game was that he could have been a more patient hitter and taken more walks.

As a third baseman he made all the plays, and made them look easy. He was also a great baserunner. Boyer even had the speed and skills to take over center field for the Cards in 1957 and he played it well, although his offensive production suffered.

In the Cards' 1964 championship year, Boyer was voted the NL Most Valuable Player, hitting .295, with 24 homers and a league-leading 119 RBIs. In the World Series against the Yankees (his younger brother Clete was the Yankees' third baseman), he hit a grand slam off Al Downing to win Game Four 4–3 and tie the Series at two games apiece. In Game Seven, his home run off Steve Hamilton was instrumental in the Series-clinching victory.

In June of that year, Boyer, bothered by a bad back but refusing to come out of the lineup, slumped badly and heard about it from the fans. But, in his typical, stoical manner he said, "You hear the booing, but I don't think you can permit yourself to think about it. If you do, you could start to lose your confidence and that's the worst thing possible."

Teammate Dick Groat said unequivocally in 1964: "Ken Boyer is the best third baseman in the major leagues. He's carried our club all year. Without him, we would be a second division team. You can't be chosen the number one third baseman by your fellow players unless you're great like Ken. He's a ballplayer's ballplayer."

According to several of his black teammates, in October 1964 Boyer's leadership was one of the keys to the racial harmony on the Cards that made them what is often considered the first truly integrated team in Major League Baseball.

To Boyer, his baseball career was a dream come true. He grew up in the Ozarks, one of thirteen children, seven of them boys who played professional baseball (older brother Cloyd pitched for the Cards in the early 1950s). And Boyer grew up a Cardinals fan.

"I hope I never have to leave St. Louis," Boyer told *The Sporting News*. "Ever since I was six-years-old, all I wanted to do was play ball for the Cardinals."

After his playing career ended, Boyer managed in the Cardinals minor league system for seven years and was brought up as manager of the big club in 1978. He spent two years as the Cardinals' manager, leading them to a third place finish in the National League East in 1979.

Boyer was voted the third baseman on the Cardinals' All-Time Team and his number, 14, has been retired.

In 1982, Boyer succumbed to cancer at the age of fifty-one.

Rich (Goose) Gossage

P, 1972–1994, White Sox, Pirates, Yankees, Padres, Cubs, Rangers, Mariners

The way Lou Piniella sees it, it's all pretty simple: "Rollie Fingers is in the Hall of Fame," Piniella says. "Taking away nothing from Rollie, although Rollie pitched on those dominating Oakland teams of the '70s . . . Goose should be in the Hall of Fame. He was as good as you wanted for a period of eight or ten years. You didn't want any better out there."

Yet Rich Gossage is *not* in the Hall, which lands him in our select circle. He finished sixth in the 2000 voting, placing the big right-hander with an even-more-pronounced mustache than Fingers (he of the fabled facial hair) well short of where he needed to be—and he was sixth again in 2001.

Piniella thinks that's crazy.

"When you look at Goose's era, he had to be in the top three or four relief pitchers," he says of his teammate through those crazy Bronx Zoo years. "He had that intimidating posture about him on the mound and he could back it up with a 97- or 98-mile-an-hour fastball and a heck of a breaking ball.

"He loved to compete, loved big-game situations, was as reliable as reliable could be closing out ballgames, had some leadership qualities on the pitching staff."

And he was all business—on the mound, anyway.

"Gossage was an easy-going guy until the eighth inning," recalled ex-Goose catcher Barry Foote. "Then you'd see a metamorphosis occur. All of a sudden he looked like a wild man. I remember the first time I caught him he'd gotten behind on the hitter and there was a runner on first, so I step out in front of the plate and say something and he yells, 'Get your ass back there and catch.' Finally, I go back, Goose throws three straight strikes and we're out of the inning."

Rich Gossage *at a glance*

- Pitched twenty-two years in the big leagues
- 310 career saves
- 151 saves as a Yankee was a club record broken by Dave Righetti
- Pitched in 1,002 career games
- Had 1,502 career strikeouts in 1,809 innings

Unlike today's closers, Gossage wasn't always called on for only one inning. While the Yankees did develop Gossage into a true closer, with Ron Davis ahead of him, Goose threw as many as 134 innings in relief for the Yankees and threw over 100 for the 1984 San Diego Padres.

Says former foe Frank White, "He took the ball in the seventh, where today the guy wants the ball in the ninth inning. Those guys were pitching 130, 135 innings a year and today's closers are pitching 50 innings a year. When they put him in the pen [Gossage only had one full year as a starter, going 9–17 with the 1976 Pittsburgh Pirates before Chuck Tanner put him back in the pen the following year], he began to shine. He was good; he was very good.

"Very intimidating. His awkward delivery, the speed of his fastball, good slider, would throw the ball up and in on you—he wouldn't give in to hitters. Commanding his respect on the mound."

Gossage pitched twenty-two years in the major leagues. He finished with 310 saves, pitched in more than 1,000 games. He won 115 games as a reliever, which left him third behind Hoyt Wilhelm and Lindy McDaniel in that department.

He always seemed to be involved in dramatic situations. He got Carl Yastrzemski to pop out to end the 1978 "Bucky Dent" playoff game; he yielded George Brett's monster playoff home run; he was involved in a clubhouse scuffle with teammate Cliff Johnson and missed much of the 1979 season with a hand injury and surgery as the Yankees started the year looking for their fourth straight pennant and ended it mourning the death of leader Thurman Munson; and he let loose with the infamous "Take it to the fat man upstairs" tirade aimed at owner George Steinbrenner.

The outburst came following Gossage blowing both ends of a double-header in Chicago and a *New York Post* headline reading "Goose Is Cooked." Frustrated over his own failure—which he never took well—he exploded. He was that intense as a competitor.

"The great players are hard on themselves," says Piniella. "They don't take to mediocrity kindly. They push themselves and they strive for almost absolute perfection. Nothing wrong with it at all.

"He was just a great competitor, a great guy and, more important, great stuff on the mound."

Gossage came to the Yankees in 1978, taking over the closer role from Sparky Lyle, who just happened to have won the American League Cy Young Award the previous year. Lyle could have resented Goose's arrival and probably did—but did nothing but support Gossage. It didn't help—Gossage suffered through a tough season his first year in New York, later saying the only reason there was a playoff game with the Red Sox was because he had struggled so badly during the season.

Then came 1979. First Goose got hurt and then Munson died. "The season was just eleven games old when we lost Goose," Reggie Jackson says in his autobiography. "Lyle had been traded to Texas [in a deal that brought future Yankee closer Dave Righetti to New York] during the offseason, so we all knew Goose had to be it in '79. That was no problem—we were positive because it was clear that Goose just could have been Gossage when he was closing for the Yankees in the late '70s . . . he could strike fear in you—definitely wild enough to keep you from digging in."

Raleigh (Biz) Mackey

C, 1920–1947, Negro Leagues: Hilldale Daisies,
Baltimore Elite Giants, Newark Eagles,
Philadelphia Stars

Biz Mackey will some day be named to the Hall of Fame by the Veterans' Committee. It's surprising it hasn't happened already because as a catcher and later as a pennant-winning manager, Negro League historians believe that Mackey had few peers. There are some who would even rate him ahead of Josh Gibson.

With Turkey Stearnes selected to the Hall of Fame in the year 2000, Mackey is probably the greatest of the Negro League greats still on the outside looking in.

Raleigh "Biz" Mackey, the big, affable Texan who starred as a catcher (although he played other positions when needed) from 1920 to 1947 is usually considered second only to the great Josh Gibson as the best Negro Leagues catcher of all time.

Buck O'Neil said that while he was no equal to Gibson as a hitter, "Biz was the best pure defensive catcher we ever produced."

There are those who will tell you that, as a total package, Mackey would be their choice. In a 1952 poll conducted by the *Pittsburgh Courier*, Mackey was named the greatest catcher in the history of black baseball, ahead of Gibson, Louis Santop, and Bruce Petway.

Cumberland Posey, who managed Gibson in his days with the Homestead Grays, also rated Mackey as his number one catcher of all-time.

"For combined hitting, thinking, and physical endowment, there has never been another Biz Mackey," Posey said. "He was a tremendous hitter, a fierce competitor."

Raleigh Mackey *at a glance*

- Regarded as the best defensive catcher in Negro Leagues history
- .322 lifetime BA
- Hit .300 for season fourteen times
- Led Hilldale to three straight championships
- Hit .375 in 1925 Negro World Series over Kansas City Monarchs
- Chosen for four East–West Negro Leagues All-Star games

Mackey was admired by his peers for his positive, upbeat personality, his coolness under pressure, and his leadership skills. He didn't smoke or drink and was considered a great role model for young players and fans. Although he was barely literate, Mackey was one of the most intelligent baseball players of all time.

A keen student of the game, Mackey used his fine memory to learn the strengths and weaknesses of opposing batters and pitchers, as well as the talents and emotional makeup of his battery mates. Thus, he was at his best when it came to calling a game. He was also known for his fine sense of humor and talkative style behind the plate. He had the knack, which Campanella and Yogi Berra later displayed, for distracting enemy batters by engaging them in "harmless small-talk."

Mackey was the best when it came to calling a game, and his teammates said that he had a special knack for framing pitches to convince umpires that they were strikes.

His strongest attribute, however, was his howitzer arm.
According to James A. Riley in the *Biographical Encyclopedia of the Negro Leagues*, "Mackey could snap a throw to second from a squatting position and get it there harder, quicker, and with more accuracy than most catchers can standing up.

"Mackey delighted in throwing out the best base stealers and his pegs to the keystone sack were frozen ropes passing the mound belt high and arriving on the bag feather soft."

While not in Gibson's class with the bat, Mackey was one of the game's great hitters, batting for both power and average from both sides of the plate. He had a .335 lifetime average in league play and .326 against major leaguers in exhibition games. Mackey achieved the latter mark while touring against some of the best major leaguers, including Lefty Grove and Bob Meusel.

Though he was a big man and not fast on the base paths, Mackey was a good runner. His natural agility, combined with an excellent pair of soft hands, made him a pretty good defensive infielder or outfielder when he was needed at those positions.

Mackey was held in such high esteem during his playing days that, as a member of the Philadelphia Stars, he was chosen over the young Gibson as the starting catcher in the first Negro League All-Star Classic held in Comiskey Park in Chicago in 1933. He played in four of the first six All-Star Classics, in a career that saw him lead the Hilldale club to three successive Eastern Colored League pennants and the Philadelphia Stars to three Negro National League titles.

He also earned a reputation as an astute teacher and one of the most successful managers in the Negro Leagues, and is remembered as the man who "taught Roy Campanella everything he knows" when the teenage Campy came up with the Baltimore Elite Giants.

In his last public appearance in 1959, Mackey attended a special ceremony to honor Campanella before a Los Angeles Dodger home game. In his remarks, Campy glanced at Mackey and told the crowd "I couldn't carry his glove."

Mackey went on to manage the Newark Eagles to two Negro League championships during the 1940s. At Newark he mentored future big league stars Larry Doby, Monte Irvin, and Don Newcombe. With Mackey at the helm, the Eagles won the Negro League Championship in 1948.

In his thirty-eight-year career, Mackey did it all both as a player and manager.

Hall of Famer James "Cool Papa" Bell offered this assessment of the beloved catcher: "As much as I admired Campanella as a catcher and Gibson as a hitter, I believe Biz Mackey was the best all around catcher I ever saw."

Joe (Flash) Gordon

2B, 1938–1950, Yankees, Indians

Joe Gordon is still regarded by many of those who saw him play as one of the all-time great second basemen, drawing comparisons with Eddie Collins, Frankie Frisch, Charley Gehringer, and most of all with his contemporary, Bobby Doerr. And yet Gordon is not in the Hall of Fame. He was a superb, acrobatic fielder; a solid home run hitter; a leader on six championship clubs; and was voted American League MVP in 1942. The explanation for why he doesn't have a plaque in Cooperstown is in the numbers.

Although he hit .322 in his MVP season, his lifetime .268 average is undoubtedly a drawback in the eyes of the voters. His two years in the service during World War II and an off-year in 1946 when he returned left Gordon just short of 1,000 career RBIs and runs scored—and it may have also cost him the 2,000 hit plateau. These are important numbers in the eyes of the electors. Otherwise, we're talking about someone who in all-around ability can be compared with Joe Morgan, who came along much later, and gets a great deal of support as the greatest of all time.

Phil Rizzuto, who played alongside Gordon in the Yankees infield said "Gordon is the most acrobatic fielder I have ever played with. The plays he could make off balance, throwing in midair, or off one foot or lying down. Unbelievable!"

Gordon had no weakness in the field. He could go to his left, to his right, come in on slow grounders, or cover a great deal of outfield territory on pop flies. He was a thrill to watch making the pivot at second base and he had a strong throwing arm.

Tommy Henrich, who played right field for those Yankees championship teams and has been an outspoken advocate of Gordon for the Hall of Fame, said it was a pleasure just playing behind Gordon every day and having the opportunity to watch him play.

Joe Gordon *at a glance*

- AL MVP in 1942
- Nine-time All-Star
- Held AL career record (246) and season record (32) for HRs by a second baseman
- Starting second baseman in six World Series
- Hit .400 in 1938 World Series and .500 in 1941 World Series
- Hit for the cycle in 1940

After Gordon starred in the 1941 World Series victory over the Dodgers, Yankees manager Joe McCarthy, recognizing his second baseman's contribution to the team's success, said, 'I'll say right now that the greatest all-around ballplayer I ever saw—and I don't bar any of them—is Joe Gordon.

"I don't care what he hits and, what's more, neither does Gordon. You say he hit .500 in the Series and led both teams? Well, I'll bet you a cigar that if you went up to him . . . and asked him what he hit, he wouldn't have the slightest idea. He don't give a hoot, so long as we win. But when you need a hit from him, or a great play or a great piece of base running, that guy will come through. Ask Brooklyn."

Gordon, a 5'10", 170-lb. California native, was brought up to the Yankees in 1938 to replace an aging and injured second baseman Tony Lazzeri, who was dealt to the Chicago Cubs.

From the beginning, "Flash" Gordon displayed the agility in the field that he owed to his time as a varsity gymnast at the University of Oregon. He could also hit for power, which was rare for a second baseman. He hit 25 home runs and drove in 97 runs in his rookie year. In his career, he hit 20 or more homers seven times (his best was 32 in 1939 and 1940) and he batted in 80 or more runs eight times (four times over 100).

Though he was often compared to Doerr, Gordon usually finished higher in the MVP award voting. That does not take anything away from Doerr, who was a great second baseman and a fine hitter. In fact, the two stars were amused by the comparisons and often joked about it. Sportswriter Dan Daniel of the *New York World–Telegram*, called Gordon the "absolute successor to Charley Gehringer. Doerr? Yes, a grand ball player, a fine hitter, a nimble guy, Gordon? Just the best in the business today."

Connie Mack, who had seen just about everybody play, was also a Gordon admirer. "Gordon is a whole infield himself. He is the greatest second baseman. Yes the greatest of all infielders today," Mack said.

In 1942, Gordon's MVP year, he hit 18 home runs and drove in 103 runs and was the linchpin of the best infield in the league. He had a 29-game hitting streak in May and June that helped to all but decide the pennant race. After the season, he was named MVP in a close vote over Ted Williams.

After his bad year in 1946, the Yankees thought Gordon was washed up and traded him to the Indians for Allie Reynolds, who went on to help them to six World Championships. Gordon, however, regained the old magic for a few years. In Cleveland, he teamed with player-manager Lou Boudreau to form one of the best double-play combinations in history.

Gordon had his best year with the Indians in 1948, hitting .280 with 32 home runs and 124 RBIs and combined with Boudreau to lead the Indians to the World Championship. It was Gordon's sixth World Series, and his stellar play and leadership were key factors to Cleveland's success.

Boudreau, looking back on the years Gordon played for him in Cleveland, said that Gordon contributed so much to the team besides his powerful bat and his defensive acrobatics. "Joe was a great man to have on the ball club. He talked baseball day in and day out. He knew how to play the hitters. You never had to move him. He knew the pitchers very well.

"He helped me tremendously in my managing," Boudreau said. "He was a good guy who took a lot of problems on his shoulders that would have been mine. He would talk to the other players and give them guidance, tell them what they were doing wrong. He later made a very good manager. There is no doubt in my mind that Joe Gordon belongs in the Hall of Fame."

Note: In 1958 Joe Gordon was named Cleveland's manager, and, after finishing second in 1959, was involved in one of the most bizarre transactions in baseball history. He was traded by Cleveland General Manager Frank "Trader" Lane, to the Kansas City A's for their manager, Jimmy Dykes.

Ron Guidry
(Gator, Lou'siana Lightning)

P, 1975–1988, Yankees

J im Kaat doesn't pull any punches when he's asked about fellow left-
hander Ron Guidry. "At that time, if you were to pick one guy to win
an important game for you, he probably would be the guy you'd
pick," says Kaat, himself a pretty fair pitcher who is also one of the Top 100 in
this book.

Picking Guidry, all 5'11", 162 lbs. (soaking wet) of him, for one game is
exactly what Bob Lemon did, when Guidry, 24–3 over the first 162 games of the
1978 season, went out and beat the Red Sox in a one-game playoff. It wasn't a
gem, a real Guidry outing, by any means, but he won and he did it with toughness on short rest.

"This thin, little guy the writers call 'Lou'siana Lightning' had been the
leader all season," Reggie Jackson says in his autobiography. "When everything
else had fallen apart, he just kept quiet and kept winning. Again, he was the
truest Yankee of all.

"The next season, when [Rich] Gossage got hurt in the shower fight with
[teammate] Cliff Johnson, Guidry went to the bullpen by choice because he
thought he could do the team the most good there. He never got the credit he
deserved for that one. He's a winner, and he always managed to get the job
done with a great mixture of humility and pride.

"Gimme the ball. Let me spit a little tobacco. Here comes the fastball and
sliders. Hell of a man . . . Ron Guidry."

And the man they called "Gator" and "Lou'siana Lightning" had a sense of
knowing what was important. Guidry seemed to relish serving up a homer to
Reggie ("It was the only fun I had all night") when the slugger returned for his
first Yankee Stadium game after George Steinbrenner decided not to bring him

Ron Guidry *at a glance*

- 1978 AL Cy Young winner
- Won 24 games and then beat the Red Sox in a one-game playoff
- 111–45 from 1977 to 1983
- 5–2 in postseason, 3–1 in the World Series
- Three-time All-Star
- Winningest pitcher in majors from 1977 to 1987

back for the 1982 season. Anyone at that game who watched what happened in a steady rain knows Guidry wasn't trying his best to get Jackson out on that final at-bat of an emotional night.

Guidry doesn't have the career numbers of many of the pitchers in the Hall of Fame. But he has a six-year run that's strangely similar to the one Sandy Koufax had in the 1960s. In fact, if you toss out strikeouts, the numbers of the two lefties during their great years are very similar. The career numbers are similar, too.

From 1961 to 1966, Koufax, regarded as the best pitcher ever by many, was 129–47, with 35 shutouts. For a career that ended too soon because of elbow arthritis, the Dodger ace was 165–87 (a .655 winning percentage) with a 2.76 ERA. He was also 4–3 with an amazing 0.95 ERA in the World Series.

From 1977 to 1983 (excluding the strike year, 1981), Guidry was 111–45, with 23 shutouts. He was also 11–5 in the strike year and 22–6 in 1985. For his career, Lightning was 170–91 (a .651 percentage), with a 3.29 ERA (remember, he faced the designated hitter, Koufax did not). He was also 5–2 in the postseason and 3–1 with a 1.69 ERA in the World Series, and the majors's winningest pitcher from 1977 to 1987.

This is not to say Ron Guidry was Sandy Koufax. But what about Koufax's mound mate, Don Drysdale (and others)? Drysdale, a huge right-hander who would knock his mom off the plate if she were too close and one of the great workhorses of all time, was 209–166 (.557) with a 2.95 ERA and 3–3 with the same ERA in the World Series. His best year was 25–9 (2.83 ERA). But he had three losing seasons (Guidry had one as a full-timer) and he lost in double figures ten times (admittedly, pitching in a ton of games), while Guidry did it three times.

And Guidry won that playoff game—the Bucky Dent game. "Gid started and didn't really have his good stuff 'cause he was going with only three days' rest again," Sparky Lyle said. "But he was still good enough to hold them to two runs in six and a third [innings], quite an accomplishment for a left-hander in Fenway."

It was just Guidry being Guidry. Doesn't he deserve *some* Hall of Fame consideration? He got 27 votes in the 2000 balloting, barely staying on the ballot for 2001, when he garnered 23 and was gone.

"What comes to mind when I think of Ron Guidry is 1978: 25–3," says fellow Out by a Stepper Alan Trammell. "I think of that slider down and in and I think of the crowd noise in New York every time he'd get two strikes, which became kind of a thing in New York.

"The people would get up and, as a hitter, you'd hear that crowd goin' crazy in the background and, ultimately, you'd check-swing and miss at a ball in the dirt. Everybody from the dugout or from the stands would say, 'how could you swing at that pitch?' You'd say, 'well, when you're 60 feet, 6 inches away, and somebody throws that Steve Carlton-type of slider, it's very hard to lay off of it.'

"He's almost like Pedro Martinez is now—you're not supposed to have that good an arm in that type of frame, but Lord knows he did."

And that two-strike eruption, by the way, has become Guidry's legacy in New York. It's even referred to by name, honoring the little lefty from Louisiana— a hell of a man in pinstripes.

17. Gil Hodges

1B, 1943, 1947–1960, Dodgers, Mets

No player in baseball history has come as close to being elected to the Hall of Fame as many times without making it as Gil Hodges. The slugging first baseman of the Brooklyn Dodgers "Boys of Summer" team of the 1950s finished in the top five in voting in twelve of the fifteen years his name appeared on the Hall of Fame ballot. Twenty-four players—meaning everyone—who received more votes than Hodges in fourteen of his fifteen years—is now enshrined in Cooperstown. Twenty-two players who finished in the top ten but behind Hodges in the balloting are now in the Hall of Fame. (This includes many of those who were elected while he was still on the ballot). Four of his teammates have been elected—and rightly so—but the popular Hodges, who is considered one of the greatest fielding first basemen of all time, is still outside.

Above and beyond his greatness as a ballplayer, Hodges was loved and admired by teammates, fans, opponents, and the community. Many who knew him say that Hodges was as close as we come to a genuine American hero. As Pee Wee Reese told Marino Amoruso in *Gil Hodges: The Quiet Man*, "If you had a son, it would be a great thing to have him grow up to be just like Gil Hodges. He was just one helluva man."

After his playing days, Hodges managed the "Miracle" Mets to a World Championship in 1969, and the legend of Hodges grew into folk legend proportions. His players remember him as being quiet, yet stern. He commanded respect.

Hodges's hold on the loyal and vocal Brooklyn fandom was attributed to his image of quiet strength and that he seemed to be a genuinely nice guy. He was also given extra points because he married a Brooklyn girl and settled in as a visible, active member of the community.

Gil Hodges *at a glance*

- Eight-time All-Star
- Three-time Gold Glove
- Starting first baseman in six World Series
- Eleven straight seasons hit 20 HRs (40 HRs twice), seven straight seasons with more than 100 RBIs
- Set record of 14 career grand slams
- Hit 4 home runs in one game (1950)

In the 1952 World Series against the Yankees, Hodges went 0–21 and each time he came to the plate, the cheer from the crowd would get louder. The slump continued for two months into the 1953 season and rather than get down on him, the borough of Brooklyn united behind him. Sermons were said for him in churches, children included him in their prayers. He received thousands of encouraging letters, many containing good luck charms. In mid-May he was batting .187, finally causing Manager Charlie Dressen to bench him for five games to help take the pressure off. He finally came in to pinch-hit and broke the slump against the Giants, and even the Polo Grounds faithful let out a big cheer for Gil.

He and Ted Kluszewski were considered the most powerful men in baseball and they were both gentle men who "wouldn't hurt a soul."

According to pitcher Rex Barney in *Bums* by Peter Golenbeck: "Anytime we'd have a fight on the field, Gil was the peacemaker. Big and strong as he was, he wouldn't touch a flea. He might pick up one fighting player in one arm and the other one in the other. When he got into it, there was no more fight."

The ex-marine from Princeton, Indiana, came up with the Dodgers after World War II as a catcher. They said he would have been a great one, but the presence of rookie receiver Roy Campanella necessitated moving Hodges to first base in order to keep both bats in the lineup. The move sent second-year Dodger great Jackie Robinson, who had been named Rookie of the Year in 1947, to second base. Hodges, whose hands were so large that teammates joked that he didn't need a glove, went on to become the best first baseman in the league, one of the best of all time, winning three Gold Glove awards.

Longtime teammate Carl Erskine called him the best he ever saw. "He had great footwork and great range," Erskine said. "And, boy, did he have good hands. Just tremendous in size, but soft. He never dropped anything that was near him. He was so smooth he made difficult plays look easy. Like throwing to the pitcher covering the bag. He was a master at it. The throw was always perfect, even if his momentum in catching the ball was carrying him toward second."

As he matured, Hodges also became one of the most feared power hitters in the league. Both Hodges and outfielder Carl Furillo are probably under-rated, having performed most of their careers in a lineup that included Hall of Famers Robinson, Campanella, Reese, and Duke Snider.

Hodges topped the 20 home run mark eleven times, with a high of 42 in 1954. He batted in 1,274 runs in his career, including seven 100-plus RBI seasons. Eight times he had a slugging average above the .500 mark. His career batting average was .272, and he was good for about eighty walks a year.

In a game against the Braves in 1950, Hodges became the first National League player in the twentieth century to hit four home runs in a nine-inning game.

When his famous slump ended in 1953, Hodges went on a tear and finished the year with 31 home runs and 122 RBIs. He also hit .302 and starred in the World Series against the Yankees, hitting .364 in a losing cause. Hodges played in seven World Series with the Dodgers, six in Brooklyn. The last of his 5 World Series home runs came as a member of the Los Angeles Dodgers against the White Sox in 1959.

When he retired, Hodges held the National League record for most grand-slam home runs in a career with 14. Hank Aaron (16) and Willie McCovey (18) passed this mark in later years.

After retiring as a player, Hodges returned to New York in 1968 to manage the Mets and, after a ninth-place finish, led the "Miracle" Mets to the World Championship the following year, in one of the biggest upsets in sports history.

In *The Greatest First Basemen of All Time* by Donald Honig, Tom Seaver gave Hodges most of the credit. "All season people kept waiting for the bubble to burst," Seaver said. "But Gil wouldn't let it happen. He'd been through too many grueling pennant races. He never let us get too high, he wouldn't let us get too low. He instilled confidence, he made you feel like a winner, he kept you motivated."

Gil Hodges died just before the 1972 season began, in Florida, two days before his forty-eighth birthday.

"Gil Hodges is a Hall of Famer," said Duke Snider. "I'm sure Gil's going to get in. He deserves it. It's just a shame that his family and friends have to wait so long for that day."

Thurman Munson

C, 1966–1979, Yankees

"M r. Yankee."

It's a title that's been passed on through the years—shared by names like Ruth, DiMaggio, Mantle—special names in baseball history. But if you were looking for a Mr. Yankee of the real turbulent years of the George Steinbrenner era, you need look no further than Thurman Munson. Yes, you'd take him even over Reggie Jackson.

"Had he lived, I bet we would have won two more World Series in New York, both in 1980 and in 1981," Jackson wrote in his autobiography.

"He could hit second, third, fourth, or fifth. In all those spots you have to be able to do different things with the bat . . . he was one of the few guys I ever played with who could have done all that, hit anywhere from second to fifth, and I've played with some hitters."

Munson didn't live. He died landing his own plane during the 1979 season. The effect on the Yankees was devastating. Jackson claimed the Yankees still hadn't replaced their captain. It would take a long while after that before it happened—and as good as Jorge Posada would become for the later Yankee champions, he was no Munson.

Jackson saying kind things about Munson wasn't easy. They didn't always get along (Jackson angered Munson with his famed "I'm the straw that stirs the drink" comment). They were friends at the end, when Munson asked Reggie to go with him on that fateful day. Jackson had other commitments. He lived.

It was impossible to play alongside—or against—this guy without having a world of respect for him. "I love Munson—he's one of my all-time greats," says Ken Harrelson. "I didn't like him personally but I liked him as a player. I loved his competitive spirit."

Thurman Munson *at a glance*

- 1976 AL MVP
- 1970 AL Rookie of the Year
- Hit .339 with 2 homers, 10 RBIs in 14 ALCS games
- Hit .373 with 1 homer, 12 RBIs in 16 World Series games
- Six-time All-Star
- Won three straight Gold Gloves

You had to. But he's not in the Hall of Fame. Rival Carlton Fisk of the Red Sox (and later the White Sox) got in because of longevity. Munson, battered and bruised and apparently slipping when he died, was denied his declining years—years he might not even have taken because he was talking retirement anyway.

"They were the premier catchers of their era [in the American League]," says Jim Kaat, a Yankee teammate when Munson was killed. "It's just unfortunate he didn't get to play longer."

When Munson died, a group of New York writers tried to get the five-year waiting period waived so Munson could go right into the Hall of Fame. A few years later, support for Munson had disappeared. Should it have gone away?

Munson, the 1970 Rookie of the Year and 1976 MVP, played eleven years in the major leagues. He batted .292 with 113 home runs and 701 RBIs. But he hit .339 with 2 homers and 10 RBIs in fourteen playoff games and .373 with a homer and 12 RBIs in sixteen World Series contests. His mammoth two-run homer off Doug Bird that won the third game of the 1978 playoffs will never be forgotten.

"He loved to talk," Buck Martinez says. "If he was getting hits, he would talk all day long. If he didn't get any hits, he wouldn't talk. He'd step into the batters box and he'd say, 'where should I stand?' I'd say, 'why don't you stand right there?' He'd stand there and he'd get a hit. Next time up he didn't get a hit and he'd say, 'I ain't listening to you anymore.'

"He had so much energy behind the plate. He was very quick behind the plate, very agile. You wouldn't say you'd want anyone to catch like Thurman Munson—he was kind of awkward and crude in what he did, but he was good, and he had the personality to lead his pitching staff and, like (Ted) Simmons, the pitchers would do whatever he wanted."

Talk? Rod Carew said he did more than talk, that Munson would throw dirt on his shoes, grab at his shoelaces in the batters box, or "hit my bat when the ball was on his way in." Frank White says Munson was so quick he'd step on your foot as you were trying to bunt for a hit and he was already scrambling for the ball. Said Carew: "Thurman was as tough as nails, as tough as they came." But you know he liked him.

"He was a catcher who couldn't throw well but he could throw guys out because he was a quick as a cat," says Don Zimmer, who managed against Munson in the great Red Sox-Yankees rivalry. "He was like a second baseman that doesn't have a strong arm but gets rid of the ball very quick. That's the way Munson caught.

"[Roy] Campanella didn't have a strong arm but the ball got down there quick, he was like a cat. That's the way Munson was. He was an outstanding catcher, knew the game—he was a great hitter, a situational hitter. You'd never have to ask him: hit the ball to the other side. Munson was a home run hitter but he was a situational hitter. You could play hit and run with him. Munson was a great player."

Teammate Willie Randolph agrees, saying, "I thought he was as clutch as anyone. He wasn't a prototypical power guy but he hit third or fourth. He was one of the first power guys who knew how to hit, get the job done when he had to.

"He would do anything to win. He played hurt. I saw him, like, crawling around at home plate, knees were bad, shoulders were hurting—he would get that ball to second base with a little tail on it. His arm was hurting. A real blood and guts kind of guy. He went through some real bad years with the Yankees and I was glad he was there when we came back in '76, '77, and '78 and people got to see what kind of leader he was."

Luis Tiant (el Tiante)

P, 1964–1982, Indians, Twins, Red Sox,
Yankees, Pirates, Angels

Denny McLain won 31 games in 1968, the year of the pitcher. But there was at least one hitter who insists McLain wasn't even the best pitcher in the American League that season. "Denny McLain was the second-best pitcher in the league that year—behind Luis," Hawk Harrelson says. "You ask the hitters who hit against them and they'll tell you."

Luis, of course, is Luis Tiant. El Tiante, the flamboyant righty whose herky-jerky motion spun him to a career many—most of them apparently in Boston—feel should have landed him in the Hall of Fame. "He was 20–9 with nine shutouts playing for a horseshit ballclub," said Harrelson, referring to the 1968 Cleveland Indians. "He threw harder than [Sam] McDowell that year."

In fact, Tiant, who had gone 45–35 in his first four years in the big leagues, was 21–9 with a 1.60 ERA that season. McLain finished 31–6 with a 1.96 ERA. Over in the National League, Bob Gibson was 22–9 with a ridiculously low 1.12 ERA. Three incredible years that came in the season before they changed things to make them better for the hitter. Three incredible years—but most people talk about McLain and Gibson, forgetting Tiant.

Tiant had nine shutouts. McLain had six. The rest of the numbers were all similar—except McLain got a lot more support playing for a Tiger team that would win the World Series. The Indians finished 17½ games behind Detroit. But Cleveland wasn't a bad team, winning 86 that year, with Tiant leading the way.

That was the first of four, 20-win seasons for Tiant, who would have to reinvent himself in Boston and go on to record a 229–172 lifetime record. After that big year, he lost 20 games for the 1969 Tribe and was 8–10 over the next two seasons before turning it around with the Red Sox.

Luis Tiant *at a glance*

- Won 20 games four times
- Went 2–0 in 1975 World Series
- Went 21–9 with a 1.60 ERA and 9 shutouts in 1968
- 229–172 career record
- Lost 20 games in 1969
- Three-time All-Star

In Boston, el Tiante became legend. After he would warm up, the sound of the latch opening the bullpen door would trigger the fans waiting for his arrival. The chants of "Lou-ie, Lou-ie" would resound through Fenway Park. Tiant won 81 games for the Sox from 1973 to 1976 and was a World Series star in 1975 (2–0 in three starts).

"He was a hell of a competitor—just a tremendous, tremendous competitor," says Lou Piniella. "Very intelligent on the mound—used a lot of different arm angles to throw the ball, knew how to pitch hitters, didn't back down. Toward the end of his career, he was in the Top 10 of all the pitchers, starting-wise, that were pitching in his era."

And there was so much more to the mustachioed Tiant, called "the Fred Astaire of Baseball," by Reggie Jackson, who would become a teammate in New York in 1979 and 1980.

"You gotta look at his character," says Piniella, who would also become Tiant's teammate with the Yankees. "He was a fun-loving guy who brought looseness to a clubhouse, to a team and, you know what—when you needed a big game won, you could give the ball to Loo-ie and he was going to give you an excellent chance to win it."

Adds Joe Torre: "He was colorful. Adding to what he accomplished and how many good years he put together, I'd like to see him celebrated. Again, when you think about how they didn't allow blacks or Latin players in [the majors] for the longest time, he certainly made a great impression and made you look forward to seeing the more talented Latinos. I don't know what our game would be without Latin players."

Harrelson calls Tiant "a wonderful, wonderful teammate" and remembered a confrontation with the guy who would actually turn his back on hitters in his wind-up. "I hit two homers off him in a game in Cleveland one night," Hawk says. "The next time they come to play us [in Boston], I'm standing by the cage and he comes walking out—and he said, 'Hawk, I'm gonna blow your ass away four times today.' I said, 'Luis, get outta here man.' He said, 'I'm gonna get you four times today.'

"Well, the fourth time I come to the plate, he looks at me and says, 'where you want it?' I said, 'right here.' He gave it to me and I hit a ground ball to short but he blew my ass away the first three times.

"With Luis, it was none of this and none of that. It was just whoosh and I was one of the better fastball hitters in the league and he just blew me away. I had no chance. I think he's special. To this day, people don't understand what a power pitcher he was."

And what a finisher! In that four-year stretch that included three, 20-win seasons with the Sox, Tiant completed 85 games. "One thing about Tiant—he had a knack if it got to be into the ninth inning, set your bullpen down," says Don Zimmer. "He knew how to finish the game. I don't care whether it was 2–1, 8–7, 9–8, if he got into the ninth and he was still pitching, he knew how to get those last three outs.

"He was a character. He was a showman. When I say showman, I don't mean over-cocky or a smart aleck. He was a showman. I could hear it today, him coming out of the bullpen, 'Lou-ie, Lou-ie,' just coming from the bullpen to warm up. He was a showman and a heck of a pitcher.

Roger Maris

OF, 1957–1968, Indians, A's, Yankees, Cardinals

I
t took the home run battle between Mark McGwire and Sammy Sosa in 1998 to get Roger Maris the credit he deserved for being an outstanding multi-talented ballplayer. It was thirteen years after Maris's death and thirty-seven years after he surpassed Babe Ruth's single-season home run record of 60 in one season, but the modern baseball fans finally found out that the crewcut outfielder was a pretty damn good baseball player.

During the McGwire-Sosa march to the home run record, Maris's family was on hand for many of the milestones, and received a great deal of attention and the opportunity to set the record straight about Maris, who was a fine player and a man respected by all those who really knew him.

Maris was certainly not popular in his time, because beginning in 1961 he was, at least in the eyes of the media and the public, in direct competition with two baseball icons—teammate Mickey Mantle and the ghost of Babe Ruth. In 1961, the New York press still included a group of veteran reporters and columnists who were Babe Ruth idolaters. To them, The Babe was simply the greatest, and it was pure sacrilege for his most memorable record to be challenged by any modern ballplayer, let alone a modest young man from Fargo, South Dakota, who, before joining the Yankees in 1960, never hit more than 28 home runs.

During the 1961 season, the eyes of the nation were on Maris and Mantle as they chased the original Ruthian feat—the 60–home run mark. Mantle, who had been a Yankee since 1951, had never been fully appreciated, but next to Maris, he became the public's fair-haired boy. Maris, a private person who could be blunt and standoffish, was cast as a surly brat, who was not a worthy successor to the Bambino.

When the media attention became really intense, Maris received no support from the Yankees—no press conferences, no publicity department state-

Roger Maris *at a glance*

- 61 HRs in 1961 broke Babe Ruth's thirty-four–year-old record of 60
- 1960 AL MVP, with .283 BA, .581 SA (led league), 39 HRs, and 112 RBIs (led league)
- 1961 AL MVP, with .269 BA, .620 SA, 61 HRs (led league), 132 Rs (led league), and 142 RBIs (led league)
- 1960 Gold Glove
- Played in more World Series (seven) than anyone in 1960s with Yankees (five) and Cardinals (two)

ments, no spin doctors—just Maris answering the same silly questions, day after day. In reaction, the beleaguered slugger got impatient and gradually became less communicative. The negative publicity increased and continued through 1962 and Maris's reputation never recovered.

Teammate and friend Clete Boyer observed the 1961 media circus: "The guy was a great player. They like to say that 1961 was a fluke, but Roger hit 39 homers and was the American League MVP in 1960. Not too many stiffs become back-to-back MVPs." Boyer said.

"In 1961 he got on this unbelievable roll, and the press made him out to be nothing but a home run hitter. Roger knew he couldn't hit 40 or 50 home runs year after year, but he found himself in the position of being something that he's not. And there was the press asking him about being another Babe Ruth. Then they made Mickey out to be the good guy and Roger the bad guy because it gave them good stories. What a bunch of crap! He was 26, just a kid. Some guys say he didn't handle everything the best. Well, how could anyone handle it? Roger was like the rest of us. What he wanted to do most was win. He wanted to get into the World Series for two reasons—the prestige and the check. Believe me, that $8,000 check came in handy every Christmas."

In 1959, the Yankees finished third, 15 games behind Chicago's "Go-Go Sox." When they acquired Maris in a seven-player trade with the Athletics in December 1959, they knew he was good, but probably didn't expect the greatness he achieved in a Yankee uniform.

He was a smart, fearless outfielder with a great arm (he easily moved to center fielder when Mantle was injured), a strong base runner and a good clutch hitter. And, of course there were those home runs. Without Maris, the famed Yankee dynasty probably would have been over in 1958. With Maris, they went on to a second string of five-straight pennants.

In 1960, Maris won the American League MVP Award with 39 homers, 112 RBIs, and a .283 batting average.

Casey Stengel, who managed Maris in 1960, appreciated his MVP's abilities. "I give the man a point for speed," Casey said. "I do this because Maris can run fast. Then I can give him a point because he can slide fast. I give him another point because he can bunt. I also give him a point because he can field. He is very good around the fences—sometimes on top of the fences. Next, I give him a point because he can throw. A right fielder has to be a thrower or he's not a right fielder."

"So I add up my points and I've got five for him before I even come to his hitting. I would say this is a good man."

In 1961, Maris proved to be a very good man, exceeding Mantle, who was injured toward the end of the year, and hitting the 61 homers that would break Ruth's record. Maris led a Yankee team that is mentioned with the greats of all time to the World Series where they defeated the Cincinnati Reds in five games. But 1961 proved to be the high point of his career. While he did smack 33 round trippers and knock in 100 runs in 1962, a series of injuries took their toll and, in 1965, a broken hand caused him to miss most of the year. Never completely healthy in 1966, Maris was traded to the Cardinals the following year. He contributed to two-straight St. Louis pennant winners and retired after the 1968 season.

Roger Maris was a key contributor to seven pennant-winning teams in his twelve-year career, and he held the record for most home runs in a season for thirty-seven years. Ruth held the record for thirty-four years. Maris was a complete ballplayer and a good man.

Call it delayed justice, but the McGwire-vs.-Sosa duel finally set the record straight. Maybe some day the Veteran's Committee will overlook the career statistics and admit a great all-around player for a unique achievement.

Jim Kaat (Kitty)

P, 1959–1983, Senators, Twins, White Sox,
Phillies, Yankees, Cardinals

Ask the modern baseball fan—especially the young one—about Jim Kaat and you might get a blank stare. Who? Some might know him as a New York Yankee announcer—and a good one, a nice guy with the ability to analyze the game. Some might recall a pretty good pitcher who was a great fielder for a long time—a very long time.

What most fans, especially those young ones, probably don't remember about this classy left-hander was that he won 283 games in a career that touched four decades. They also might not remember that he was one of the best all-around players of anyone who ever pitched in the major leagues.

"I think Jim Kaat should go into the Hall of Fame," says Ken Harrelson. "He was maybe as good a fielding pitcher as there ever has been. He was a good hitting pitcher as maybe there ever has been and he was a great pitcher for a long time.

"Kitty, to me, is a Hall of Famer."

But, so far at least, he's not. Perhaps he said it best himself when he said, after retiring, "I'll never be considered one of the all-time greats, maybe not even one of the all-time goods. But I'm one of the all-time survivors."

But—and this question has been asked oh so many times—is the Hall of Fame filled with only the all-time greats? There are, in fact, many, many all-time goods in Cooperstown.

Always one of the nicest guys in the game, Kaat, who also lost 237 times in the big leagues, was a strapping 6'4", non-athletic looking type who won 20 games three times—once with the Minnesota Twins and twice, at ages thirty-six and thirty-seven, after being reunited with old pitching coach Johnny Sain with the Chicago White Sox. Kaat was 41–27 over those two years.

Jim Kaat *at a glance*

- 283 career wins
- Pitched in four decades
- Won his only World Series in 1982 at age forty-four
- Sixteen straight Gold Gloves
- Batted 16 homers in career
- 25–13 in 1966
- Won 20 games three times, including two at ages thirty-six and thirty-seven

Neither of those 20-win seasons was as good as Kaat's 25–13 record in 1966. He had 19 complete games in 41 starts that year and probably would have won the Cy Young award—but that was the last year there was only one Cy awarded and Sandy Koufax (27–9, 317 strikeouts in his final season) won it.

Kaat won 18 games for the 1965 pennant-winning Twins, beat Koufax in Game Two of the World Series, but lost Games Five and Seven, both to Koufax.

Kaat won sixteen straight Gold Gloves from 1962 to 1977 and hit .185 with 16 homers during the pre–designated hitter era and, later, his National League days.

"I might go along with him for the Hall of Fame," says fellow broadcaster Ernie Harwell. "He was a great candidate because of his longevity and he had a good record. I liked the way he worked fast and he was on some winning teams."

Some winning teams? Yes. Heck, Kaat was almost forty-four when he pitched for the St. Louis Cardinals in the 1982 World Series. But Kaat pitched in only nine postseason games in a career that started in 1959 (with the Washington Senators, before they moved to Minneapolis) and ended in St. Louis in 1983. In addition to the 1–2 mark he posted in the 1965 World Series, he pitched four times in earning his only Series ring with the 1982 Cardinals. He also pitched in the playoffs for the Twins and Phillies.

"I played my second major-league game against the Twins and got my first major-league hit against Jim Kaat," says former catcher Buck Martinez.

Kaat jokes there are "guys all over the place who got their first big-league hits off me."

But, Martinez adds, "He was always a competitor. He never gave in. He was always trying something. You'd never get a pitch in the middle of the plate from him. You could see it and then you went to hit it and it was gone—and then he'd see you leaning and he'd bust you inside. He had enough on the pitch to move you off the plate."

"He was a tremendous fielder with all those Gold Gloves," Martinez says. "But he was a baseball guy. He was aware, and he could hit, too. He was a complete player."

Yet Kaat finds himself in a victory group with fellow non–Hall of Famers Tommy John and Bert Blyleven—a trio that can't get serious consideration for the Hall. Rod Carew, a former Kaat teammate, thinks his buddy's in trouble because, "I guess winning 300 games puts you in the Hall of Fame."

Kaat says in the Tommy John chapter of this book that he'd be upset if Tommy John made it and he didn't. He also says TJ would have the right to be upset if that was reversed. Ask him how he would be remembered and Kaat says, "I don't know so much about what people remember but if you ask the guys you played with, that's probably where you'd get the true picture."

One of them, Carew, recalled, "Jimmy worked as hard as any player, any pitcher, I've ever played with in the major leagues."

Says Kaat: "I guess I took pride in the fact I never missed a start. I never went on the disabled list with an arm injury [he did break his wrist sliding in 1972, when he was off to a 10–2 start]. I guess the durability factor was my greatest asset. I was never really a dominant pitcher. I was usually a No. 2 guy but I was durable.

"Like Johnny Sain used to say, you learn how to pitch when you hurt your arm and I really hurt my arm for the first time when I was nineteen. I took a lot of pride in learning how to adjust year after year. You don't pitch that long without making some kind of adjustments."

Andre Dawson (Hawk)

OF, DH, 1976–1996, Expos, Cubs, Red Sox, Marlins

There were three new names on the 2001 Hall of Fame ballot that jumped right out at you: One, Ozzie Smith, was a sure-fire first-ballot Hall of Famer; the other two, Andre Dawson and Alan Trammell, were not.

And when the votes came back, that's exactly the way it read: Smith was a slam dunk. Dawson got 214 of the 354 votes needed for selection, Trammell just 74. "I'm kind of shocked at only 45 percent and being fifth," Dawson said when he got the news. "The first ballot, you know there are problems getting in. Ozzie getting 91 percent was amazing. But what can I say? I'm fine."

Andre Dawson was always fine. Even when his knees were so bad he could barely walk, let alone do the things you have to do to play baseball—at a high level—Dawson was fine. He accepted his problems and worked through them, until it finally became time to give in.

People love to talk about what Mickey Mantle might have been without his knee injuries. Here's a news flash—Dawson may well have been Mantle without the off-field troubles. In fact, Dawson might be the anti-Mick. Trying to find someone to say anything negative about the man they called "The Hawk" isn't easy.

"There is no one else like Andre Dawson," Ernie Banks wrote in the fore-word of Dawson's autobiography. "He is a living example of what a human being should be and can be. Amazingly, the influence he had while he was a Cub is still strongly felt years after he has moved on. In fact, I feel that what he left behind will never leave us. He touched us all—the players, the fans, everyone.

"All who touch his life, just by his example, better who they are."

Like Banks, Andre Dawson never played in a World Series. He did play in fifteen postseason games with the Expos and Cubs and didn't do well. Both of

Andre Dawson *at a glance*

- 1977 NL Rookie of the Year
- 1987 NL MVP
- Eight-time All-Star
- Eight-time Gold Glove, at two positions
- 2,774 career hits
- 438 career home runs

those things work against him in terms of Hall of Fame consideration. But neither had as much of an effect as injury, which tends to cloud the memories of a great player.

When his name came up for that first ballot, writer Scott Miller wrote: "Dawson is an extremely difficult case. I didn't go with him because, aside from his outstanding MVP season in 1987 (.287, 49 homers, 137 RBI), he hit more than 25 homers in a season just three times, and, more important, he only broke the 100-RBI mark three other times. A very, very good player, yes. But most dominant? Not quite, even as an eight-time All-Star. Besides, in '87, Dawson's best season by far, the ball was heavily juiced. Matt Nokes—remember him?—smashed 32 homers that summer."

Valid point. But let's not take away from what Dawson did the rest of the time. He had four seasons overall with 100 RBIs. Hall of Famer Carl Yastrzemski had five. He had four, 25–home run seasons; so did Yaz. He had 438 career homers; Yaz had 452. He had 2,774 career hits and batted a career .279; Yaz had 3,419 career hits and a lifetime .285 average—the hit total a tribute to Yaz's longevity (he played 3,308 games to Dawson's 2,627).

In 1967, Yaz won the Triple Crown, hitting .326, with 44 homers and 121 RBIs. In 1987, Dawson hit more homers and drove in more runs than Yaz did in 1967. But Yaz carried a team to Game Seven of the World Series. Dawson's Cubs finished last in their division.

"Dawson was a front-line, major star, impact player," says former outfielder and general manager Tom Grieve. "He was a five-tool player, he had excellent speed, one of the greatest arms in the game, he was a Gold Glove–caliber defensive player. He had great power."

And he had that very special 1987—one of Dawson's eight All-Star seasons. After destroying his knees on the artificial turf in Montreal, Dawson was looking for a home with natural grass. But this was the era of collusion, and

Dawson, represented by Dick Moss, wound up signing a blank contract with the Cubs, allowing the team to fill in the amount, which turned out to be a paltry $500,000.

He then went out and delivered. But, please, let's not use the juiced-up ball to diminish what Dawson did in his career. He was Rookie of the Year with the Expos in 1977, an MVP in 1987. He finished second in the MVP voting on two other occasions, led the National League in hits in 1983, in extra base hits in 1982 and 1983, and in total bases in 1983 and 1987. He stole 314 bases (and was successful 75 percent of the time). Oh—and he won eight Gold Gloves, both as a center fielder and after he had to move to right because of his knees.

And Dawson was a leader. Everywhere Dawson went, he left a positive impression. More from Banks: "While with the Expos, Andre's presence saved Tim Rainses's career and even his life from becoming a disaster. In recognition of Andre's influence, Raines named his first son after the future Hall of Famer. Andre was there for Shawon Dunston of the Cubs during the young shortstop's time of need, as well. Andre's words also lifted newly acquired Hubie Brooks to a new level of play in Montreal."

Even in Boston at the painful end of his career, Dawson was a presence. And this was long after his thoroughbred days.

"Just the force that he was," Bucky Dent said when asked what stood out about Dawson. "When I was coaching third base for the Cardinals, and he was in the outfield, he could really throw. I saw him at the tail end [of his career] when his knees were bothering him a little bit. I didn't get a chance to see him much when he was young but just the time I saw him when he was with the Cubs, he was just a tremendous, intense guy. He was a force. He could run, he could throw, power . . . he played the game."

The Yankees Big Three—
Allie Reynolds

P, 1942–1954, Indians, Yankees

Vic Raschi (P, 1946–1955, Yankees, Cardinals, A's)

Ed Lopat (P, 1944–1955, White Sox, Yankees, Orioles)

I n the late 1940s and early 1950s it was one word: ReynoldsRaschiLopat. It meant reliability, savvy, competitiveness, excellence, and dominance. It also meant five-straight World Championships for the New York Yankees, the only time that's ever been done in the history of baseball. Broken down to its components, the word stands for Allie Reynolds, Vic Raschi, and Ed Lopat—the "big three" of the Yankees pitching staff.

Though their career numbers may not warrant admittance to the Hall of Fame, the big three shared pitching duties during baseball's most glorious run. Between 1948 and 1953, their combined record was an amazing 307 victories and only 143 losses, and they won 15 of the 20 World Series victories between 1949 and 1953.

Reynolds, the "Superchief," who was part Creek Indian, was acquired from Cleveland after the 1946 season in a "good-for-both-teams" trade for Joe "Flash" Gordon, also a member of the Top 100. He was a winner right from the beginning, but his early Yankees years were marked by wildness and giving up key hits in the clutch.

When Casey Stengel and pitching coach Jim Turner came in 1949, turning Reynolds from a thrower into a pitcher was a top priority. Reynolds also credited Lopat with helping him mix up his speeds and teaching him how to slow down his pitches to fool batters.

Allie Reynolds *at a glance*

- Starting pitcher on six World Champions, compiling a 7–2 record with 2.79 ERA, 2–0 relief record, and four saves in World Series games
- First American League pitcher to throw two no-hitters (1951)
- Won Hickock Belt in 1951 as the top professional athlete, with a 17–8 record, 3.05 ERA, 7 shutouts (led league), and 7 saves
- Twenty-game winner (20–8) and led league with 2.06 ERA, 6 shutouts, and 160 SOs in 1952, second in MVP voting
- Six-time All-Star

Reynolds became the workhorse of the staff. He would take his regular turn as a starter and then come in as an effective reliever in critical situations. He was a tough, mean competitor who had no problem buzzing a fastball past a batter's ear to keep him from digging in.

Stengel said in 1951: "They told me, don't count on this guy when the chips are down. All I can see is this fellow keeps getting tougher and tougher and better and better. There's no use kidding about it. That big guy comes close to being the most valuable pitcher in baseball right now."

In 1951, Reynolds won the Hickock Belt as the Professional Athlete of the Year. He pitched two no-hitters, the first American League pitcher to accomplish this, and had a 17–8 record with 7 shutouts and 7 saves. He finished third in the MVP balloting.

The following season was even better. At the age of thirty-seven Reynolds was 20–8, led the league with a 2.07 ERA and 160 strikeouts and 6 shutouts. His 2–1 record against the Dodgers in the World Series included a four-hit shutout in Game Four.

Johnny Sain, who was brought in during the 1951 season as a spot starter and to share the relieving assignments with Reynolds, was an admirer of the "Superchief."

"There's no reason why he shouldn't be in the Hall of Fame." Sain said. "In a big game Allie Reynolds was a Koufax-type pitcher. In the five consecutive World Championships he was a dominating pitcher. He had a great curveball and he could overpower you with his fastball."

Sain told Whitey Ford one day that he would love to have just ten Allie Reynolds fastballs to throw in a game. "When would you throw them?" Ford asked. "I'd throw them with my first ten pitches and then they'd be looking for them for the rest of the game," Sain said.

During his career as a Yankee, Reynolds won 131 games and lost only 60. He had a 7–2 career record in the World Series.

Vic Raschi, "The Springfield Rifle," was the Yankees' most consistent pitcher on the staff, winning many big games. The scowling, unshaven Raschi could be a frightening sight for batters. He had a sharp-breaking slider and a blazing fastball and he never missed a start, despite chronic pain in his knees. His career record with the Yankees was 120–50. He was a three-time 20-game winner and had victories in four World Series, including a two-hit shutout in Game One of the 1950 Series against the Phillies.

Stengel considered Raschi his best pitcher for nine innings. "That guy in the eighth and ninth innings he'd give me, he'd give me, I mean he was almost a sure bet . . . Boy, he was the best on the club in the eighth or ninth inning."

In the 1949 World Series, Raschi was in a jam and Stengel instructed his young catcher, Yogi Berra, to go out and tell the fiercely independent pitcher to work more deliberately. Reluctantly, Berra called time and headed for the mound. Before he got there, Berra was met by a wad of tobacco juice and an angry Raschi shouting, "Gimme the goddamn ball and get the hell out of here!"

Raschi was traded to the Cardinals after the 1953 season after a contract dispute. Some Yankees believed that he would have been the difference in the 1954 pennant drive that was won by Cleveland, the only year that kept the Yankees from winning ten consecutive pennants.

Steady Eddie Lopat, a native, street-smart New Yorker, whom the Yankees acquired from the White Sox in 1948, contributed a 113–59 record to the five championship teams. An intelligent pitcher, Lopat, "The Junkman," had a repertoire of off-speed pitches, including a dancing screwball, and a keen knowledge of when and how to throw them.

Casey Stengel once said that Lopat looked like he's throwing wads of tissue paper. "Every time he wins a game, fans come down out of the stands asking for contracts," Stengel said.

Ed Lopat, who could occasionally cross up the batter with a sneaky fastball, was a great clutch performer and a control artist. He was a student of pitching, who knew the strengths and weaknesses of every batter and a fine teacher and steadying influence on his teammates, especially younger pitchers such as Whitey Ford.

Stengel would often use Lopat between Raschi and Reynolds in a series in order to keep the opposition off-balance. Lopat won 21 games in 1951 and averaged 16 victories a year between 1949 and 1953. He led the league in ERA and winning percentage in 1953.

Whitey Ford picked up the torch from ReynoldsRaschiLopat and led the Yankees next generation of dominance from 1955 to 1964, but no trio of starters in the history of baseball ever won championships with the consistency of the Big Three between 1949 and 1953.

Dom DiMaggio
(The Little Professor)

OF, 1940–1942, 1946–1953, Red Sox

I t isn't quite Cooperstown, but the Ted Williams Museum in Hernando, Florida, is quickly turning into a happening baseball site. And if you ever get down there, you'll find a booklet entitled "Why Dom DiMaggio Belongs in the Hall of Fame" there for your reading enjoyment.

We called the museum for the information and received a rather large press kit. The case made for DiMaggio is an impressive one. The man, who will forever be known as one of Joe D's two brothers, has impressive numbers—and friends—behind him.

"I can't understand why he's not in the Hall of Fame," says old pal Johnny Pesky, who calls DiMaggio "the perfect player." "He was one of the premier outfielders of his time. Why he's not in I'll never know. He deserves to be there. I thought he was as good as any player who ever played the game."

Strong words—and perhaps even a bit skewed when you consider the source, but let's understand how good this guy really was. "He was as good a center fielder as I ever saw," said Williams, who lobbied for years to have the Veteran's Committee, of which he was a member, install his buddy. "Dom saved more runs as a center fielder than anybody else. He should be in the Hall of Fame."

In 1959, the great Grantland Rice wrote: "Dom can do everything that Joe can do—and don't forget that Dom is faster than Joe. Joe will tell you that."

In a recent "Where Are They Now?" piece in *Sports Illustrated*, Dom DiMaggio displayed his usual class and dignity when it came to talking about himself. This guy didn't look like a player when he played—he was small and wore glasses—and hasn't really acted like one since.

Dom DiMaggio *at a glance*

- .298 lifetime BA
- Averaged almost 31 doubles per season
- Averaged almost 105 runs per season
- Seven-time All-Star
- Owns hitting streaks of 34 and 27 games

Asked if his brother thought he belonged in the Hall, Dom said, "Joe never expressed an opinion, not to me. I would have loved him to, but we're not that kind of people. I know that when people used to ask him who was the best defensive center fielder he ever saw, he would say, 'My brother, Dom.' But he would never say, 'Dom belongs in the Hall' because if he had said that and I had gotten in, he knew people would have said, 'Dom's only in because Joe pushed for him.'"

The tributes have gone on for years. But what about the numbers?

Dom DiMaggio's career was shortened because of the war—and, at the end, by a manager's decision to sit him on the bench. But the information obtained from the museum, notably an editorial by famed broadcaster Curt Gowdy that called DiMaggio the most underrated player of all-time, shows that in his ten full years in Boston, no one had more hits and only Williams scored more runs.

And that was just offense, where DiMaggio's .298 lifetime batting average would have been an estimated .304 if sacrifice flies didn't count as at-bats—as they did throughout his career before the rule was changed. He averaged almost 31 doubles and almost 105 runs a year, and also swiped 100 bases.

Defensively, you won't find anyone to tell you DiMaggio, a seven-time All-Star, wasn't a great center fielder. Casey Stengel, "The 'Ol' Professor," once had this to say about Dom DiMaggio: "With the possible exception of his brother, Dom, Joe is the best outfielder in the league."

"There are a lot of guys in the Hall of Fame who are not as good as Dominic," says Pesky. "Here's a guy who just did his job quietly, but he was a good player. In those years—'48, '49, '50 and '51—we had as good a team as anyone and he was one of the big reasons for it. But the Yankees were always just that much better."

Wrote Gowdy: "Dom was the most underrated ballplayer I ever saw—from the day Dom arrived in the big leagues, people underestimated him."

On the .300 thing, Gowdy writes: "DiMaggio was cheated out of a .300 lifetime batting average because of a quirk in the rules. In the years he played, the Sacrifice Fly Rule was not in effect. If a player drove in a runner from third with a fly ball to the outfield, he was charged with a time at bat. The Sacrifice Fly Rule was reinstated in 1954, shortly after his retirement, and has remained in effect ever since. Had it applied during his career, Dom DiMaggio's lifetime average would be over .300 rather than the .298, which appears in the record books. His on-base percentage, .383, is higher than that of almost sixty percent of the position players now in the Hall of Fame."

And then there's hitting streaks. While brother Joe has the record 56-gamer, Dom had streaks of 34 (still the Red Sox record) and 27 games.

His career ended abruptly during the 1953 season. At age thirty-six, after hitting .296 and .294 the previous two seasons, DiMaggio was benched by Sox manager Lou Boudreau in favor of a guy named Tommy Umphlett. It was May and DiMaggio had batted three times and not appeared in the field. He went to general manager Joe Cronin and asked for a trade. Cronin, holding on to a final link to the Sox' recent past, said no, and, as Gowdy put it, "on May 13, 1953, Dom DiMaggio, the best outfielder in the American League, retired from baseball."

The voters never considered DiMaggio a viable Hall of Fame candidate during his brief stay on the ballot and then time turned the cause over to Williams. But as Ted grew older, his efforts failed. The Veteran's Committee is no more and it will be interesting to see if Dom DiMaggio gets another look when the new Veterans system goes into effect in 2003.

Keith Hernandez

1B, 1976–1990, Cardinals, Mets, Indians

t's easy to forget Larry Bowa—one of the members of the club that is this book—finished his fine major-league playing career with the New York Mets, heading to New York in a late-season 1987 trade. In the short time he was with the Mets, though, Bowa was there long enough to notice something: Keith Hernandez was a very strange man.

Not strange in any particular character trait—although Hernandez got himself in trouble with some of those—or strange in that he was a bad guy or did voodoo in the clubhouse. No, strange in something he did on the field.

"You watch the things that this guy did in the field, it was amazing," says Bowa. "This guy could go to the mound . . . he was like a pitching coach out there. Talk about leadership qualities—he was probably as good a leader as anybody I've ever seen. He would settle a pitcher down, tell him the situation, what to do."

Sounds like something a quality defensive catcher might do. But Hernandez was a Gold Glove–winning first baseman—perhaps the best there ever was at the position.

"He would come to the mound all the time and I asked him one day, 'what are you telling [the pitcher]?'" recalls Bowa, a pretty good field general in his own right. "I said, 'you're always in there and you do that every time?' He says, 'yeah, some of these guys don't know what they're doing out there.' He literally took it as a challenge."

Hernandez took command. He got into some trouble later in his career (admitting cocaine use in that Pirates drug scandal) and became known as much for being Seinfeld's buddy on the TV sitcom as anything else. But this guy could play—and he could take over in the infield.

When the Mets were trying to finish off the Houston Astros in the sixteenth inning of game six of the 1986 National League Championship Series, Houston had rallied for two runs in the bottom of the inning after the Mets had

Keith Hernandez *at a glance*

- Eleven-straight Gold Gloves
- Shared NL MVP with Willie Stargell in 1979
- 1979 NL batting champion
- Twenty-four game-winning hits in 1985
- .400 on-base percentage seven times
- Five-time All-Star
- Hit .333 in NLCS
- Eight RBIs in 1982 World Series

scored three times in the top half as the teams finished off one of the great playoff games ever played. Kevin Bass, a tough hitter, was up and the tying run was on second base. Hernandez came to the mound and reportedly told pitcher Jesse Orosco (even though one version of the story had him saying the words to catcher Gary Carter), "if you throw this guy a fastball, I'm going to fucking kill you." Orosco listened (or Carter called a slider), and the Mets won and went on to win the World Series in seven games over the Red Sox. It was the second World Series title in five years for Hernandez, who hit .333 in the playoffs and drove in eight runs in the World Series in 1982, before a so-so 1986 postseason that ended with a huge two-run single in Game Seven of the World Series.

"He's as good a first baseman as I've ever seen for doing everything," says Bowa. "Bunt plays . . . his bunt plays were unbelievable! First and second, he'd charge and throw to third. Man on first, he'd charge and throw to second—he could do it with anybody."

There were even times Hernandez would charge a bunt down the third base line and make the play at third. His quickness and ability to know what was going to happen were incredible.

"The only thing he didn't do was hit a lot of home runs," says Bowa. "But both parks he played in (Busch Stadium and Shea Stadium) were big ballparks."

This is not to say Hernandez didn't hit—or that all he did was win eleven-straight Gold Gloves. No, this was a career that included him sharing the 1979 National League Most Valuable Player award with Willie Stargell of the Pirates— Hernandez winning the batting title by hitting .344 (his first .300 season) for the Cardinals, with 210 hits, 48 doubles, 105 RBIs, and 116 runs scored.

His trade to the Mets came with Whitey Herzog looking to dump the off-field headache (Herzog insisted the trade for Neil Allen was baseball-motivated, but it clearly wasn't) and Hernandez, who would provide a perfect balance in a lineup that would include Carter and Darryl Strawberry, set a major-league record in 1985 when he had 24 game-winning RBIs. In fact, he had 129 of those things when it was an official stat and also became the Mets' captain in 1987—both the season and career totals setting records.

Hernandez, a tough out who had an on-base percentage over .400 seven times in a career that would end with a brief stop in Cleveland in 1990 (he signed a two-year contract but injuries ruined him), led the National League in that category in 1979 and 1980. He drove in 21 runs in thirty postseason games and had more than 90 RBIs in a season six times, his high the 105 in the MVP year. The 48 doubles he had that year was also a career-best and he wound up hitting .296 lifetime (he was a .300 hitter until the injury-hampered last two seasons), with 162 homers, 1,071 RBIs, 1,124 runs scored, and 108 errors in 1,931 career games in the field. A master at the 3–6–3 double play, he led the National League in double plays a record six times.

There was no stat kept on how many times he went to the mound—or how many pitchers he was able to help avoid disaster by telling them the right thing to do. But anyone who played with him knows how important Keith Hernandez was to his teams.

Carl Mays

P, 1915–1929, Red Sox, Yankees, Reds, Giants

I f the Hall of Fame could correct one oversight and elect one pre–World War II, twentieth-century major league player, it should be five-time 20-game winner Carl Mays. Baseball immortality has eluded him in large part because he threw the only pitch in baseball history that killed an opposing batter.

On August 16, 1920, while pitching for the Yankees, Mays, a tough submarine ball pitcher, struck the popular twenty-nine-year-old Cleveland shortstop Ray Chapman with a fastball that caught him in the left temple. Chapman died in the hospital later that night.

After the pitch hit Chapman, it bounced onto the playing field and Yankee's catcher Muddy Ruel fielded the ball and threw it to first baseman Wally Pipp for what he thought was a put out. He was shocked to turn around and see Chapman on the ground.

"I heard a dull sound and I was sure Ray had bunted," Ruel said.

The contrasting personalities of Mays and Chapman provided the case with an ironic twist. Even before the incident, Mays was considered a mean, sullen loner who was disliked by teammates, a man with a nasty streak who was certainly capable of throwing at a batter's head.

He had become a submarine pitcher early in his career because of a sore arm. His demeanor, his unorthodox motion and tendency to throw inside were calculated to inspire fear in batters.

Chapman, who was in his prime as one of the league's top shortstops, had an all-American-boy image. He was a team leader beloved by his teammates and fans. Immediately after Chapman's death, there was widespread belief that Mays had purposely thrown the fatal pitch at the batter's head. Rumors circulated that members of the Red Sox and Tigers would refuse to play against the Yankees if Mays was not banished. But eyewitnesses absolved Mays of any malice in the

Carl Mays *at a glance*

- Lifetime record of 208–126, with a .623 winning percentage and 2.92 ERA
- Five-time 20-game winner (twice with Red Sox, twice with Yankees, once with Reds)
- Led AL in relief wins (5) and saves (7) as a rookie in 1915
- Led AL in complete games (30) and shutouts (8) and won 21 games in 1918 (Red Sox)
- Led AL in shutouts (6) in 1920, with 26–11 record
- Led AL in victories and winning percentage (27–9, .750), games pitched (49), innings pitched (336.2), and saves (7) in 1921

tragic death. They said that Chapman, who was known for crowding the plate, seemed to be about to run up as if to bunt the ball. He just didn't see the under-handed fastball as it sailed up and toward him; he was still over the plate.

Tris Speaker, Cleveland's manager, made his feelings known soon after the incident. "I do not hold Mays responsible in any way," Speaker said. "I have been active in discouraging my players from holding Mays responsible and in respect to Chapman's memory as well as for the good of baseball. I hope all talk of this kind will stop. I can realize that Mays feels this thing as deeply as any man could and I do not know what prompted the action of the Boston and Detroit players in wanting to ban him. For my part, I think it's deplorable."

Mays, the man who threw the pitch was grief-stricken.

"It was a straight fast ball and not a curved one," he said. "When Chapman came to bat I got the signal for a straight fast ball, which I delivered. It was a little too close and I saw Chapman duck his head in an effort to get out of the path of the ball. He was too late, however, and a second after, he fell to the ground. It was the most regrettable incident of my career and I would give any-thing if I could to undo what has happened."

Mays, however, was able to keep his concentration and focus as he went out and won his next game 8–0 and finished the season with a 26–11 record, leading the league in shutouts with six. The following year he was 27–9 as he and Babe Ruth led the Yankees to their first pennant. In 1921, Mays led the league in victories, games pitched, winning percentage—and even saves (7).

Mays had started with the Red Sox in 1915, twice winning 20 games for Boston, He was 2–0 in the 1918 World Series. That year he won both ends of a doubleheader against Philadelphia to clinch the American League pennant for Boston.

Former Red Sox teammates, outfielders Harry Hooper and Duffy Lewis, acknowledged Mays's morose personality but thought that shouldn't overshadow his achievements on the mound. Hall of Famer Hooper said, "Carl had an odd disposition, but he was a great pitcher and I have a warm regard for him."

Lewis said of the uncommunicative Mays: "Carl Mays wasn't very popular, but when nobody else could win, Carl could. He was a great stopper."

He was traded to the Yankees in one of Boston owner Harry Frazee's ongoing "fire sale" deals that also sent the likes of Babe Ruth, Everett Scott, Joe Dugan, Wally Schang, and pitchers Waite Hoyt, Herb Pennock, Bullet Joe Bush, and Sam Jones to form the nucleus of the first Yankee dynasty.

After his stint with the Yankees, Mays had several good years with the Reds, winning 20 games for the fifth time in his career in 1924. He narrowly missed a sixth 20-game season two years later with a 19–12 record, including a league-leading 24 complete games.

Mays, who was also one of the best hitting pitchers of all time with a .268 lifetime batting average, was continually passed over by the Hall of Fame, despite his 208–125 lifetime record and 2.92 ERA. He expressed his disappointment to *San Diego Union* sportswriter Jack Murphy in 1961 after the Veteran's Committee voted to enshrine Rube Marquard and Chick Hafey: "I think I belong," he said. "I know I earned it. They took in Marquard this year and that's fine with me. He was a great pitcher. But I deserve it, too. I won seven more games than Rube and I lost 51 less than he did. What's wrong with me?"

There is no question that Mays belongs in the Hall of Fame, but the combination of the fatal pitch and a sour public image were just too much for his sterling record to overcome.

Bobby Bonds

OF, 1968–1981, Giants, Yankees, Angels,
White Sox, Rangers, Indians, Cardinals, Cubs

Baseball history remembers outfielder Bobby Bonds as the father of future Hall of Famer Barry Bonds and as heir apparent to Willie Mays as the leader of the San Francisco Giants. Bonds should also be remembered as a player with one of the greatest combinations of speed, power, and defensive ability who ever played the game.

When he retired in 1981, Bonds was the only player to have hit at least 30 home runs and steal 30 bases in the same season five times. In 1973, he was one home run short of becoming the first man to hit 40 home runs and steal 40 bases in the same season, a feat that's rare even in today's game of missile ball.

From the beginning, Bonds was burdened by comparisons to his mentor, Mays. The high expectations were based on Bonds's terrific minor league record and his all-around athletic prowess. He had been a letterman in four sports at Riverside (Calif.) Polytechnic High School starring in football, track, and basketball in addition to baseball. He was the California state long jump champion and was named to the high school all-American track team in 1964, running a 9.5 in the 100 and a 21.0 in the 220. At 6'1", and a solid 190 lbs., you couldn't have asked for a more perfect outfield prospect. As Mays said when he watched Bonds play in his rookie year, "Bobby has it all . . . He's intelligent and he wants to learn."

The right-handed hitting Bonds quickly justified predictions for his success in 1968 when he hit a grand slam in his first big league game. Nobody had done that since 1898.

As Mays's career declined, Bobby assumed the leadership role in the Giants outfield. He led the Giants to the 1971 National League Western Division Championship over the Dodgers, with 33 home runs and 102 RBI, and he won a Gold Glove.

Bobby Bonds *at a glance*

- Five times in 30–30 club
- Three Gold Gloves
- Grand slam in first major league game (1968)
- Set major league record 11 game-leadoff homers (1973), including two games in a row
- Six times scored 100 or more runs, led NL in 1969 (120) and 1973 (131)
- Three-time All-Star

In 1973, Bonds had his career year, leading the league in runs scored with 131 and total bases with 341. He also hit 39 home runs with 96 RBIs. Batting mostly in the leadoff spot, Bonds set a record by leading off eleven games with home runs. He won the second of his three Gold Glove Awards and finished third in the MVP balloting.

Testimonials hailing Bonds as "the best player in baseball" were common over the next two years. Sparky Anderson, his manager in the 1973 All-Star Game said, "As of today, Bobby Bonds is the best ballplayer in America."

In an article in *Sports Illustrated* several of Bonds's contemporaries praised his ability as a "complete player." Oakland A's Sal Bando said, "He's the most dynamic hitter I've ever seen" And the Dodgers' Davey Lopes said, "Bonds is probably the best outfielder in the majors."

"With his individual skills, he can blow a game apart quicker than anyone," said Steve Garvey.

According to his Giants manager Charlie Fox: "Bonds can do anything required of a superstar. He really does it all. If he misses a fly ball, he'll make up for it with fifty good catches. At bat, there's absolutely nothing he doesn't do. He has cut down his strikeouts and increased his power. And then there's his great speed."

The knock on Bonds throughout his career was that he struck out too much, although he never came close to his record-setting 189 whiffs in 1970.

Bill Virdon, who was Bonds's manager with the Yankees, minimized the strikeout numbers. "That's the only bad thing he does," Virdon told *The Sporting News*. "He does everything else well. It seems that whenever we played against him, if he didn't strike out, he got a hit."

His hitting achievements obscured the fact that Bonds was a gifted and cerebral defensive player with an outstanding arm, twice leading National

League outfielders in double plays. While in his prime, he was considered the best right fielder in the game.

"He not only has speed but is an intelligent student of the hitters and of playing conditions," said Ron Fimrite in the *Sports Illustrated* feature. The same article quoted Bonds about his defensive preparation for a game: "I always walk my position to see if there are any irregularities in the ground, any wet spots or holes. You must find out how the ball comes off the turf, how it drifts in the air," Bonds said. "Your own speed and ability to go back on a ball have a lot to do with where you play a hitter."

In 1975, Bonds was traded to the Yankees for Bobby Murcer and hit 32 home runs and drove in 85 runs. He was traded to California in the offseason for pitcher Ed Figueroa and outfielder Mickey Rivers. Bonds bounced around after that, putting together productive years with several American League teams before retiring after the 1981 season, but never regaining the status he enjoyed as a Giant.

Bonds credits Mays with teaching him a great deal of what he learned about hitting and fielding. Mays was like an older brother and when Willie left, Bobby had to adjust to becoming the team leader. "I never thought of myself as another Willie Mays," Bonds said. "There was only one of him."

The two remained close friends when their playing careers ended—Mays is Barry Bonds's godfather.

Certain players seem destined to play for one team. That's just the way it is. Bobby Bonds was a San Francisco Giant. When he was traded in 1974, the baseball gods were rattled and he never equaled his early years in San Francisco. In that regard, his fate was similar to that of Cleveland's Rocky Colavito, who should have remained a Indian, and Vida Blue, who should have been declared a landmark before he was let go by Oakland.

Had Bonds been able to play out his career in San Francisco, who knows?

While his career numbers will never get him the attention he needs to make the Hall of Fame, his rare abilities earn him high placement on our list. For at least a few years, some experts regarded Bobby Bonds as the best player in the game.

Bert Blyleven

P, 1970–1992, Twins, Rangers, Pirates, Indians, Angels

When Bert Blyelven first heard he was on the list in this book, at number twenty-six, he had a request: "Can you drop me down two places so I can have my uniform number?" Whether he was kidding or not, that was typical Blyleven—always there with the quick one-liner.

He might have been joking about where he was in our book. But Blyleven wasn't in a joking mood after the 2000 Hall of Fame balloting was announced, as he spent another year *not* getting into the Hall of Fame.

He had gotten 121 votes, 31 more than the year before, but 266 shy of what he needed for induction.

"To see my numbers increase like that, I think it's a joke," Blyleven told the *Minneapolis Star–Tribune* when Kirby Puckett and Dave Winfield were announced as the new Hall of Famers. "The Hall of Fame is supposed to be about the numbers. It's a museum—it's about the history of baseball, a place to enshrine the all-time greats. You look at my numbers, and they're better than the numbers of a lot of the all-time greats, and now my vote goes up 23 percent?

"Now I'm supposed to go out and party? I wish they would just end it, give me less than the five percent (needed to remain on the ballot). I don't want to go through what Tony Oliva went through for 15 years."

Blyleven wasn't through—questioning how fellow near 300-game winners Tommy John and Jim Kaat could get more votes than he did: "This is a message to all writers," he said. "Don't vote for me at all." The next year, he received 124 votes.

Vote for him for the Hall of Fame or not, the native of Zeist, the Netherlands, certainly *belongs* in our club. The numbers are there. But, more importantly, so is the talent. Blyleven was a top-level pitcher for a long time.

Bert Blyleven *at a glance*

- 287 career wins
- Two-time All-Star
- 3,701 career strikeouts
- 5–1 in postseason play while winning two World Series
- 1989 AL Comeback Player of the Year

Sporting News writer Ken Rosenthal, speaking about Blyleven, said, "I think Blyleven is a stronger candidate than Tommy John and Jim Kaat, both of whom finished ahead of him. But he made only two All-Star teams in 22 seasons, and never finished higher than third in the Cy Young balloting." In 1991 John had 127 votes, Kaat had 109.

Rosenthal made valid points. But Blyleven, who pitched for five teams (six, if you count the Twins twice), did win 287 games and strike out 3,701 hitters in a career that went from 1970 (when he came up as a nineteen-year-old with 21 games of minor-league experience) to 1992. He also lost 250, but played for some bad teams.

Big games? Blyleven was 5–1 lifetime in the postseason, going 2–0 for the World Champion Pirates in 1979 and 3–1 for the winning Twins in 1987 (he had been traded back to the Twins and became the veteran leader of their pitching staff).

Blyleven led the American league with 17 losses in 1988 and was shipped to the California Angels—where he won 15 games and was named Comeback Player of the Year in 1989. He retired in 1993, after another try at making the Twins—and moved into the broadcast booth.

Speaking of broadcasting, one of the things people will remember most about Blyeleven is the name given to him by nickname-freak Chris Berman of ESPN—"Bert Be Home Bly-leven." The name stuck quickly and never really left the right-hander. Another thing that never left was the label of having as good a curve as anyone around.

"Bert Blyleven had the nastiest curveball I've ever seen," offers Willie Randolph. "I've seen some good ones . . . from a right-hander? None better. The ball would actually stop on you. You'd think it was there and all of a sudden it would fall off the table. Real old-fashioned with the old-fashioned drop. You know the drop—when we kids called it a drop—well he had a drop on your ass. And he had a fastball to go along with it—a high fastball pitcher who could throw the ball in the zone. And it was tough to hit him because his curveball would start up so high and then it would drop. And then the fastball would be up there and would be right by you.

"He was just one of those guys that was power and crafty at the same time. It's very rare to have a pitcher who can throw for power and get strikeouts but also spot the breaking ball the way he did. He was one of those guys that always gave you fits when you faced him."

Basically, Blyleven was a workhorse who threw strikes, which is probably why he gave up 430 career home runs—seventh on the all-time list—and yielded a big-league record 50 dingers in 1986.

"I don't see how you can not vote for this guy (for The Hall)," says Frank White, another member of our elite group. "This guy—I mean, he came to the big leagues when he was 19 years old with the Twins, had an excellent fastball, great curve ball, developed a changeup late in his career. He was a winner everywhere he went . . . he was just a guy that I admired an awful lot.

"In terms of being competitive and with his stuff and his resiliency, they don't come any better than Bert Blyleven. The wins and the stuff are two different things. Sometimes you get wins because of longevity, you get wins because you become a different type of pitcher [Kaat and John, whose mound styles were altered by injury], where Blyleven was pretty consistent his whole career—fastball, curveball, changeup."

Regardless, all three are on the outside looking in—out by a step.

Dale Murphy

C, OF, 1B, 1976–1993, Braves, Phillies, Rockies

Leo Durocher used to tell us "nice guys finish last." In the case of Dale Murphy, nice guys just sometimes don't make it to the Hall of Fame. "If it's possible to be overlooked because you're too nice a guy—maybe they figured they gotta spurn somebody and here's a guy who won't complain." That type of thing.

A humble, religious guy who made no enemies during his time but apparently had few friends among the Hall of Fame voters.

"I can't imagine Joe DiMaggio was a better all-around player than Dale Murphy," Nolan Ryan once said of the former Braves and Phillies center fielder.

The above quote was pulled from a web site touting Murphy, a two-time Most Valuable Player, for Cooperstown. But, as time wore on, it didn't look like this clean-living star would ever have a real shot. "I'd like to see him be in the Hall of Fame," says Joe Torre, his former manager. "He won back-to-back MVPs [1982 and 1983]—not too many people have done that."

Adds Paul Molitor: "He was one of the most dominant players for at least a five- or six-year period in the '80s." But Murphy got 70 votes on the 2001 ballot.

Ask Torre about Murphy—ask anyone about Murphy—and you get smile. You listen to some and he was almost too good to be true, especially as a human being. Leo would certainly call Murphy a nice guy. Says Torre: "If you're a coach, you want him as a player. If you're a father, you want him as a son. If you're a woman, you want him as a husband. If you're a kid, you want him as a father. What else can you say about the guy?"

Well, listen to lefty Terry Forster, an ex-teammate.

"Look at him over there," Forster once said. "Doesn't drink, doesn't smoke, doesn't take greenies, nicest guy you'd ever want to meet, hits the hell out of

Dale Murphy *at a glance*

- NL MVP in 1982 and 1983
- 398 career home runs
- Five straight Gold Gloves
- Once played in 740 straight games
- Seven-time All-Star

the ball, hustles like crazy, plays a great center field, and isn't trying to get anything from anybody . . . doesn't he just make you sick?"

Adds former manager Chuck Tanner: "I've never known anyone like him. God only makes one like Dale every fifty years."

Class—but so much more, in a career that produced a .265 lifetime batting average, 398 homers, 1,266 RBIs. Yes, there were a lot of strikeouts—1,748—but there were also 161 career steals and five consecutive Gold Gloves.

Granted, Murphy played in a couple of great hitters' parks—Fulton County Stadium in Atlanta and The Vet in Philadelphia. And he had only one brief postseason experience (3-for-11 in one playoff series). But look at the consistency, especially from 1982 to 1985, when he hit 36, 36, 36, and 37 homers (he led the league the last two years of that streak) and drove in 109, 121, 100, and 111 runs. He dipped in 1986 but then came back the next year with 44 homers and 105 driven in. He hit .300 in two of those years, which were also part of a run of Murphy playing in 740 straight games.

"Mr. Consistency," says Larry Bowa, a teammate in Philadelphia. "You didn't even know he was in the clubhouse but he put up numbers, got big hits, big home runs, and made himself a good outfielder."

"He ended up with 398 homers. I asked him about that—a lot of guys would want to get 400 but he said, 'I had a good career, I'm satisfied with what I did.' That tells you what kind of guy he is. Most guys, for selfish reasons . . . I mean, 400 is a big number . . . but he knew what he did and he knew what he brought to the table."

During his prime, *The Sporting News* polled one hundred pitchers on the most feared hitter in the National League. Murphy led with twenty votes. "He was wonderful, a very unselfish player, a player who was so devoted to . . . well, family, but his team was like his family," says Torre. "He was there for everybody. He was mild mannered and yet could be very ferocious when it came to holding up his end of the deal.

"I really liked him a lot. You had to push him a little bit to get the fire burning but once it was burning . . . he reminds me, personality wise of Bernie Williams, where you sorta had to stoke him a little bit to get him going."

Murphy began his career as a catcher, but had a mental block when throwing the ball back to the pitcher. He was moved to first base, and couldn't throw from there, either. Then, he went to the outfield, playing center and right, and there was never a problem.

"I used to kid with him," says Torre. "He couldn't play first base for the same reason [as catcher]. He couldn't throw to the pitcher, couldn't throw anyplace and I'd say to him, 'Hey, Murph, whattya say you play first base for me today?' He said, 'No, no, you don't want me to play first.' Then he'd laugh. Outfield? He was a Gold Glove outfielder, throws and the whole thing. It's funny how those things work." *Note*: it worked for Torre again in 2001 when he moved scattergun second baseman Chuck Knoblauch to left field for the Yankees and the throwing woes disappeared.

"He could play center field, right field, with the best of them," Torre said of Murphy, adding, "A lot of people struck out a lot that are in the Hall of Fame. He hit a lot of home runs but he wasn't a home run hitter. I think he did everything right to the edge but never got over the hump. I think Jim Rice is ahead of him in that regard [in terms of the Hall of Fame]."

Did Murphy hit the ball hard? Former long-time reliever Grant Jackson thought so, once saying, "When Murphy hits a ball in Georgia, I get the idea it might land in Florida."

Al (Flip) Rosen

3B, 1947–1956, Indians

When you make out your lineup card for the American League All-Star team of the 1950s, pencil in the name Al "Flip" Rosen of the Cleveland Indians at third base.

Yes, even ahead of Hall of Famer George Kell.

Without taking anything away from Kell, who certainly has the credentials for Cooperstown, Rosen was clearly a dominant force in the American League when he was healthy. No one will argue that Rosen belongs in the Hall, because his baseball prime was just too short, but he was a warrior, a team leader, and an intelligent student of baseball, who drove himself to become one of the best players in the game.

Ralph Kiner and Al Smith were among those who regarded Rosen, as the best all-around player they ever had as a teammate. A former amateur boxer and a four-sport star at Miami University, Rosen acquired his nickname "Flip" during his youth, when he was an outstanding softball pitcher.

The tenacious Rosen, whose nose was broken a dozen times during his athletic career, not only retired early, at age thirty-two, but he had to wait until he was twenty-six to succeed regular slick-fielding veteran Ken Keltner at third base. When he finally arrived in the majors to stay in 1950, Rosen made an immediate impact as a hitter, setting a rookie record with 37 home runs. He also drove in 116 runs.

The great Honus Wagner, watching Rosen take batting practice before a preseason exhibition game in Pittsburgh, remarked: "Now there's a hitter. Watch him whip into that ball the last second. That's where it counts. That snap in there, just when you connect."

Rosen, however, wasn't satisfied with his rookie season and always tried to improve by seeking the advice of the game's great hitters. Among his mentors were Hall of Famers Kiner, Ted Williams, and Hank Greenberg.

Al Rosen *at a glance*

- 1953 unanimous choice for AL MVP, with a .336 BA, .613 SA, 201 Hs, 43 HRs (led league), 115 Rs (led league), and 145 RBIs (led league)
- Missed 1953 Triple Crown by less then one percentage point in batting average to Mickey Vernon
- Five consecutive seasons with 100-plus RBIs
- Led AL in HRs in 1950 (37), a ML rookie record at the time, and in RBIs in 1952 (105)
- Four-time All-Star
- Hit two consecutive HRs in 1954 All-Star game

Indians manager Al Lopez said of Rosen: "He's the kind of fellow you love to have on your ball club. He works so hard. If everybody worked like that, managing would be easy."

Rosen's work paid off in 1953 when the baseball writers made him their unanimous choice for the American League Most Valuable Player award, when he came within one batting percentage point of winning the Triple Crown, losing the batting title to Mickey Vernon on the last day of the season. Rosen led the league in home runs (43), RBIs (145), runs scored (115) and slugging average (.613).

Snubbed by Yankees manager Casey Stengel when he chose the reserves for the American League All-Star team in 1950 and 1951, Rosen played in the mid-summer event every year between 1952 and 1955 (hitting two homers in the 1954 game), and Casey turned out to be one of his greatest admirers.

Rosen was the object of these typical Stengel compliments: "This fellow Rosen leads the Indians in just about everything. It's a shame, not for us but for Cleveland, that the other fellows haven't helped him. If he had some help the pitchers wouldn't all bear down on him so much.

"What I like about him is that he taught himself to hit to all fields. Makes it tough to put your man in the right place for him. He doesn't play too bad in the field either. That fellow doesn't get enough credit."

Former Cardinals pitcher Harry "The Cat" Brecheen was another Al Rosen fan. "He's a wonderful player, a great competitor. There's no one I'd rather have come to bat for me in a tight spot than Rosen. As a pitcher, I'd rather see anybody else in baseball but Rosen swing a bat at me. He's very hard to strike out. He almost always gets a piece of the ball and he hits with power to all fields. He doesn't have any real weakness and even his outs are well hit."

During his early years, Rosen's defensive play was quite another story. Considered a butcher at the hot corner when he arrived, Rosen was known to field grounders off his chest, arms, and face—anything to make the play. Again, through intelligence, toughness, and determination, he became one of the better third basemen, leading the league in assists and double plays for a third baseman in 1953.

"I've worked hard to improve my fielding," Rosen said. "I might get maimed out there trying to stop everything hit down third, but I'll knock them down or they'll knock me down."

He credits Cleveland teammate Joe Gordon with helping him improve in the field. "Joe helped me with my footwork and he was always reminding me to get down low on grounders," Rosen said.

This toughness and desire was best illustrated after Rosen's eleventh broken nose was caused by a line drive to the face off the bat of Red Sox first baseman Walt Dropo. He was led off the field with internal bleeding and swelling so bad that he could hardly open his eyes. The injury would have put most people on the shelf for at least ten days. Two days later, in Philadelphia, Rosen got to the ballpark early and the trainer worked on his eyes, reducing the swelling so that he could see well enough to play. Rosen proceeded to drive in four runs with a homer, a double, and a single to lead the Indians to an 8–6 victory.

Rosen, however, paid for his determination and ability to play hurt. A series of injuries, including whiplash and a broken finger that permanently affected his batting grip, diminished his abilities and forced him to retire after the 1956 season. He had a lifetime average of .285, two home run crowns and five, 100-plus RBI seasons.

After his playing days, Rosen put his business administration degree to work, selling stocks and bonds. He returned to baseball years later and had an outstanding career as an executive, serving as president of the Yankees and Astros and as president and general manager of the Giants.

Dick Lundy
(King Richard)

SS, 1916–1939, Negro Leagues: Bacharach Giants, Hilldale Daisies, Baltimore Black Sox

John Beckwith (SS, 3B, 1916–1938, Negro Leagues: Chicago American Giants, Baltimore Black Sox)

Dick **Lundy** was one of the greatest Negro League players of all time, a complete ballplayer, who was a natural leader and was personally admired by all those who knew him. Usually regarded as the premier shortstop in the 1920s between the eras of John Henry Lloyd and Willie Wells, there are many who rated him on par with or ahead of the two Hall of Famers.

Negro Leagues historian James A. Riley talked about Lundy's abilities in the *Biographical History of the Negro Leagues*. "A superb fielder with a wide range and an exceptionally strong arm that allowed him to play a deep shortstop, the graceful Lundy polished his skills with quiet professionalism," Riley said. "A great showman who thrived on pressure and performed the most amazing feats with ease in front of large crowds, the big, husky shortstop's sterling play made him one of the greatest gate attractions of his day. A switch-hitter who hit for average and with power, he was a smart base runner who posed a threat on the bases."

Although he played on a number of teams, the 5'11", 180 lb. Lundy spent his prime years with the Atlantic City Bacharach Giants (1918–1928) and the Baltimore Black Sox (1929–1932). A native of Jacksonville, Florida, Lundy began his pro career there with the Duval Giants, which moved north to

Dick Lundy *at a glance*

- Twice hit over .400 with the Atlantic City Bacharach Giants, eight out of nine years over .300 from 1921 to 1929
- Led Bacharachs to two pennants in 1926 and 1927
- In 1926 Black World Series had .325 BA, 6 RBIs, and 6 SBs
- Shortstop in "million-dollar infield" for 1931 champion Baltimore Black Sox
- Starting shortstop for the East in the first two East–West Negro Leagues All-Star Games
- Lifetime .330 BA in the Negro Leagues, .341 in Cuban Winter League, and .344 against Major Leaguers

Atlantic City to become the Bacharach Giants. His fame grew so rapidly that other teams began to covet his services and he spent time barnstorming with the strong Hilldale Club of New York. In 1920, Lundy signed three contracts and a court decided that he was legally bound to play for the New York Bacharachs. He stayed with the Bacharachs, in both New York and Atlantic City, for most of the 1920s, usually batting higher than .340.

In 1921, he led the team with an incredible .484 batting average. He led the Eastern Colored League with 13 home runs in 1924. Lundy, who had the respect of teammates and opponents alike, demonstrated a quiet leadership ability that earned him the team captaincy and the nickname "King Richard." At the age of twenty-seven, Lundy was appointed a player-manager. With Lundy as the skipper, the Bacharach Giants won the Eastern Colored League pennant in both 1926 and 1927. They lost in the Championship Series both years to the Chicago American Giants, but Lundy was outstanding in the 1926 series, hitting .325 with 6 RBIs, 4 runs scored, and 6 stolen bases. He hit over .400 in 1928, his last season with the Bacharachs.

In 1929, Lundy was traded to the Baltimore Black Sox, where he continued as field general and became the centerpiece for one of the great infield combinations ever seen in baseball. With the "million-dollar infield" of Lundy at short, Jud "Boojum" Wilson at first, Frank Warfield at second and Oliver "The Ghost" Marcelle at third, the Black Sox won the 1929 American Negro League pennant. Lundy hit well over .300 in all four seasons he played with the Black Sox.

In 1933 and 1934, Lundy put in a year each with the Philadelphia Stars and the Newark Dodgers and was selected as the East's starting shortstop in the first two East–West All-Star Games in Chicago. As his career wound down, Lundy coached and managed the Negro League team in Newark (first the Dodgers and then the Eagles) and is credited with having played an important role in the development of infielders Ray Dandridge and Willie Wells as Hall of Fame performers.

When Lundy retired after twenty-two years in the Negro Leagues, he had a .324 lifetime average. In addition, he had a .341 average in eight seasons in the Cuban Winter League and hit .341 in exhibition games against major leaguers.

John McGraw, who made several attempts to sign black ballplayers for the New York Giants, said that with the exception of Honus Wagner, Lundy was "the greatest shortstop to ever live."

John Beckwith was one of the great power hitters in black baseball. While not in the class with Dick Lundy as an all-around shortstop, we feel that John Beckwith deserves recognition here as one of the game's great hitters. He was a moody, hard-drinking, sometimes violent man, whose temperament caused him to jump from team to team throughout his career. Shortstop was his primary position during some of his best years, but this giant of a man (6'4", 230 lbs.) was versatile enough to play any position on the field. The *Baseball Encyclopedia* credits Beckwith with a .356 lifetime batting average. In 1930, he batted a documented .393 with the New York Lincoln Giants.

A right-handed pull hitter, Beckwith continued to hit home runs and post a high batting average, despite the fact that fielders always shifted toward left field when he came to the plate. He first starred with the Chicago American Giants, winning the home run crown twice, before having to leave Chicago because he ran afoul of the law. He later won or came in second in home runs as a member of the Baltimore Black Sox, Harrisburg Giants, and Homestead Grays. He was credited with 72 home runs in 1927 and 54 in 1928.

Like Mule Suttles and Cristobal Torrienti, Beckwith had legendary power. Some swear he was stronger than Josh Gibson. At the age of nineteen, he became the first man to hit a fair ball over the fence at Cincinnati's Redlands Field, and he also hit a home run in Griffith Stadium in Washington, D.C., that traveled 460 feet and hit an advertising sign that was 40 feet off the ground.

Tommy John (TJ)

P, 1963–1974, 1976–1989, Indians, White Sox,
Dodgers, Yankees, Angels, A's

Did Tommy John really cheat?

"Did he cheat? Yeah, he cheated—darn right he cheated," says Hall of Famer Rod Carew, with a touch of admiration in his voice. "It didn't bother me at all. That's something as a hitter you can't be concerned about. As much stuff as Gaylord [Perry] did, I never thought about that stuff—you know they're gonna do it."

Aside from Perry, a two-time Cy Young award winner, few did it as well as John, who pitched for twenty-six years in the big leagues—through seven presidents of the United States. Both are records.

If the word "crafty" was listed in a sports dictionary, you might find TJ's picture next to it for various reasons, like doctoring the baseball to make it do special things.

"I imagine he [cheated]; I thought he did," offers former catcher Buck Martinez. "But you know what? He perfected it."

John did a lot of things during a long, long career that left behind the legacy of 288 wins, a 6–3 postseason record—and an elbow surgery named after him.

TJ actually had two careers (three, if you count a late comeback after he'd apparently retired), the first with the elbow given to him at birth and the other with the new elbow built by Dr. Frank Jobe—in what was then an experimental surgery that goes on all the time now.

After finding out how severe the damage in John's elbow really was, Jobe transplanted a tendon from the pitcher's right wrist into his left elbow in what

Tommy John *at a glance*

- Pitched for twenty-six years in the majors
- Won 288 games
- 6–2 in postseason
- NL Comeback Player of the Year in 1976
- Won 20 games three of four years from 1977 to 1980
- Four-time All-Star

would become known as Tommy John Surgery. A return was a longshot—but it happened and it has happened to many other pitchers since that breakthrough surgery.

John, ever ready with the one-liners, said he told Jobe to "Put in a Koufax fastball" and added, "He did—but it was Mrs. Koufax."

TJ was 13–3 with a 2.59 ERA for the 1974 Dodgers (he came up with Cleveland and then went to the White Sox before Los Angeles, and he went there in exchange for Dick Allen, player number one in this book) when the elbow blew up. He missed the 1975 season—and it looked for all the world like his career may well end with a 124–94 record and a scrapbook full of what-ifs.

Remember, this was 1975, just before the big money really started. But TJ would make plenty of that money. The rehab lasted a year and a half. John returned with a 10–10 season in 1976—good enough for Comeback Player of the Year honors. He then won 20 games three of the next four years, once in two years with the Dodgers and then in 1979 and 1980 with the Yankees. He was 22–9 in 1980, when he was thirty-seven—but his pitching arm was only going on six.

"Tommy John never made it easy for you to hit," says Carew.

Adds Martinez: "Tommy John was a guy . . . you'd go up there and say, 'Man, I saw the ball pretty good,' and it felt like a shot put when it left your bat.

"He was never really a guy you felt uncomfortable against—but you just knew you were gonna have to battle your ass off all day long. Screwball down and away and that big, slow breaking ball inside. He had such a smooth delivery that the ball got on you and then disappeared.

"You never had a ball out over the plate to hit."

Jim Kaat's career mirrored John's in many ways—crafty pitcher who fielded his position well who didn't quite make it to the magic 300-win mark that means automatic Hall of Fame induction. Kaat was lucky enough to have avoided serious injury and the major surgery John had to endure—but the careers are close: Kaat winning 283 and losing 237 to John's 281–231.

On the whole, John played on better teams. But he never won a World Series.

"I would say when people ask me about my chances for the Hall of Fame," says Kaat, "if there's one guy who got in and the other guy didn't . . . if he got in and I didn't I'd be disappointed. If I got in and he didn't, he should be disappointed because our careers were so much alike."

John left the Dodgers for the Yankees as a free agent and was 21–9 in 1979 and 22–9 in 1980. In 1981, the year of the first big baseball strike, John's young son, Travis, was critically injured in a fall from a window and Tommy John had to endure yet another test.

The Yankees let him go during the 1982 season and John would pitch for the California Angels until he appeared to be done after the 1985 season (with a brief stop in Oakland). He returned to the Yankees, pitched a year and then became pitching coach at the University of North Carolina—for a month. The Yankees brought him back and TJ won 24 more games in the big leagues through 1989.

When he retired, Tommy John was forty-six years old, but his left elbow was only going on fifteen.

Minnie Minoso

OF, 3B, 1949, 1951–1964, 1976, 1980, Indians,
White Sox, Cardinals, Senators

Minnie Minoso put up Hall of Fame career numbers despite his late arrival as a full-time major league player at the age of twenty-eight. He was one of the most exciting and one of the best players in the 1950s and the cornerstone of the "Go-Go" White Sox teams.

A native of Matanzas Province in Cuba, Minoso worked in the sugar fields as a young man while playing semi-pro baseball. He joined the New York Cubans of the Negro National League in 1946 and the following year helped his team to the Negro National League pennant and a World Series victory over the Negro American League's Cleveland Buckeyes. He was the starting third baseman in both the 1947 and 1948 Negro League All-Star Game and was signed to a Cleveland Indians contract in 1949.

Minoso made brief appearances with Cleveland in 1949 and 1951 before being swapped to the White Sox in a three-team deal early in the 1951 season.

He became an immediate favorite in Chicago after hitting a home run over the left field fence in his first time at bat off Vic Raschi of the Yankees.

"From that first at bat we knew we had a ballplayer," said Billy Pierce, Minoso's White Sox teammate. "He gave 100 percent all the time whether he was hitting, fielding, or running the bases. He was the perfect number three hitter behind Nellie Fox. And he was outstanding in every facet of the game."

Eddie Robinson was the Sox first baseman when Minnie joined the team. "Minnie added so much to our team. He could run, throw, field, and he was a great hitter. He was also a great teammate who really loved playing baseball."

Minoso went on to hit .326 that year and he led the league in triples (14) and stolen bases (31) while shuttling between third base and the outfield. He was second in the league in batting and in runs scored. *The Sporting News*

Minnie Minoso *at a glance*

- Six-time All-Star
- One of only two five-decade players in Major League history
- Batted .300 eight times and had 100 RBIs four times
- Held record for being HBP most times in career with 189
- Led AL in stolen bases first three full years in majors
- Three Gold Gloves
- Led AL in triples three times and in doubles in 1957

---

named him AL Rookie of the Year, although the baseball writers gave the award to Yankee Gil McDougald.

Minoso, who became a full-time outfielder in his second season, hit .300 eight times, drove in 100 or more runs four times, and scored 90-plus runs nine times. He led the American League in stolen bases in his first three years, was the league-leader in triples three times, doubles once, and hits once—and he smacked 186 home runs.

He was named to the American League All-Star team six times and, proving that he was one of the great all-around players of his time, Minoso also won three Gold Gloves.

"He was a great hitter who often hit bad balls for base hits," recalled longtime White Sox center fielder Jim Landis. "Minnie had one philosophy: 'I see the ball good, I swing.'"

Minoso's batting style gave him another offensive weapon that could have gotten him killed in the days before batting helmets. Minoso crowded the plate with his shoulder in the strike zone, practically daring pitchers to throw at him. He set the major league career record by being hit by pitches 189 times, leading the league in that category a record ten times.

Minnie believed, as did other early black major leaguers, that the color of their skin had something to do with the frequency with which they were hit or brushed back by pitches.

"I stood close to the plate, but that's not the reason I was hit by the pitch so often," Minoso said. "At the beginning, the pitchers tried to push me off the plate or hit me. That was before there was any protection. They wanted to see if I was scared. If they had me scared, I knew I'd never succeed in major league baseball. But I wasn't scared and didn't move away from the plate. That's why I would set records for being hit by the pitch."

Minoso and Luke Easter, his teammate in Cleveland, developed a method for dealing with the frequent "purpose pitch." "They'd throw at us, but neither of us got frightened and neither of us tried to fight," Minoso said. "We just got back up and tried to pay the pitcher back with our bats. If we got hit, we were happy to get on base. Sometimes I would then steal second and they would realize that when they walked me or hit me, it was like giving up a double."

After the 1957 season, Minoso was traded to the Indians for Early Wynn and Al Smith. He hit .302 in both years at Cleveland and ironically missed his "Go-Go" Sox's first American League pennant since the Black Sox of 1919.

The following year, Bill Veeck got Minoso back and the thirty-seven-year-old outfielder had one of his best seasons, hitting .311 with 105 RBIs. He also led the league in hits with 184.

Contemporary Jim Piersall, who was Minoso's teammate in Cleveland, believes Minnie belongs in the Hall of Fame.

"He came to play every day and he could beat you in many ways," Piersall said. "There was no one more exciting or more aggressive than Minnie in hitting and running around those bases."

Sox owner Bill Veeck felt so badly that he traded Minnie away before the pennant-winning season that he gave him an honorary World Series ring.

Veeck also gave Minoso the opportunity to become the second five-decade player by activating him briefly in 1976 and then at the age of fifty-seven in 1980.

After his major league career ended, Minoso spent nine more productive years in the Mexican League, playing mostly at first base. In his first two years with Jalisco he hit .360 and .348.

For many years since, Minoso has worked in community relations for the White Sox, becoming as much a part of the Chicago scene as the Sears Tower and Lake Shore Drive.

"I would love to see Minnie in the Hall of Fame," Landis said. "He was a great player and he's always been a great ambassador for the game. And he's a lovable person. I was privileged to be his teammate."

Davey Concepcion

SS, 2B, 3B, 1B, 1970–1988, Reds

J oe Morgan's view may be a bit slanted, but the Hall of Fame second
baseman thinks his Cincinnati double-play partner should be right
there in Cooperstown with him. "I've long said that Concepcion
belongs in the Hall of Fame," Morgan states in his autobiography, talking about
Davey Concepcion.

He also says Concepcion was *not* the greatest defensive shortstop he'd ever
seen—he was *only* second to Ozzie Smith, marvelous company for this unsung
cog in the "Big Red Machine," a guy people tend to overlook when talking about
those great teams—and those great names—of Sparky Anderson.

Concepcion, the pride of Venezuela, batted .267 with 101 home runs in his
major-league career. He hit .351 in fifteen playoff games (over .400 in both the
1975 and 1979 League Championship Series) and .266 in twenty World Series
Games. He had 2,326 hits in a nineteen-year career. But he also won five Gold
Gloves and provided the glue on some of the best teams of his time.

Anderson remembers, "Concepcion was really a key" and notes how amazing
it was for a young kid to come to a strange country and step into a spot like he did.

Concepcion won his starting job in 1972, when he turned twenty-four, and
was the Reds' captain by the next year. He passed the torch to a pretty fair
shortstop who would be around for a long time, too—a guy named Barry
Larkin—and even played as a utility player after Larkin arrived in 1987.

"Davey Concepcion was a guy that probably played like these shortstops
are playing now," offers Buck Martinez, alluding to the likes of Alex Rodriguez,
Nomar Garciaparra, and Derek Jeter. "He had speed, a little bit of power, a
strong arm, knowledge of the game. From what I understand, he patterned
himself after [Luis] Aparicio because both were Venezuelan.

"He gets overshadowed because of all the great teams he played on and
because they had so many great players."

Dave Concepcion *at a glance*

- Hit .351 in 15 NLCS games
- Hit .266 in 20 World Series games
- 2,326 career hits
- Five Gold Gloves
- Reds captain at age twenty-five
- Nine-time All-Star

Concepcion was not overshadowed within the game. Like so many others in this book, he was appreciated as being a talented leader on great teams. It may not be good enough to get a player into the Hall of Fame, but it's plenty to get recognized on these pages.

"He's another guy, who, without him on that team in Cincinnati, they're not what they were," says contemporary Larry Bowa, who played against Concepcion in so many big games and who also has a spot in this text. "There were so many integral parts on that team. They had so many great players. You take away any one of those guys and who knows what would have happened. Each guy was valuable on that ballclub."

Adds former Tiger shortstop Alan Trammell: "I was with Sparky for a number of years [in Detroit] and we had a lot of conversations about the Reds guys. He told me Davey Concepcion hit left-handed pitching as well as anybody he'd ever seen. He said he just feasted on left-handed pitching—and he grew into a good player, when he started off kind of like myself, kind of underweight, didn't mature physically yet, very gangly, skinny. With the players we both had on our teams, that allowed us to develop at our own pace. He was a cornerstone of that club, an unsung hero but he was more than an unsung hero.

"Of course you talk about [Johnny] Bench and [Pete] Rose and [Joe] Morgan, [Tony] Perez and those guys, but Davey Concepcion was very instrumental on that ballclub. And he was the start of the production guys at shortstop—and the next era came in with [Robin] Yount, myself, [Cal] Ripken. Now, it's a productive position."

Says Bowa: "He and I were constant rivals. I tell you what—in his own way, he's the guy that pushed me as hard as anybody. I always wanted to stay up with him. Obviously, he was hitting more home runs than I was but everything else—our batting average, our hits—it was like a friendly competition. It got so that when we were going through the prime of our careers, I'd get up in the morning and just check out what he did just to see where I was because at the time he was as good as anybody."

In 1978, Concepcion became the first Reds shortstop in sixty-five years to hit .300—something that might get lost considering what Larkin has done since. In 1980, an elbow injury forced Concepcion to perfect the artificial turf throw—a quick release and a bounce to the first baseman, who would always handle the ball cleanly because of the perfect bounce you'd get off the carpet. "I'd say, 'your arm's not that weak, now,' " says Bowa. "As he got older, he'd say, 'I just have to get rid of it.' "

But just like everything else he did during his proud major league career, he got rid of it well.

Billy Pierce

P, 1945, 1948–1964, Tigers, White Sox, Giants

When baseball people talk about the Chicago White Sox left-hander, they remember him as a great pitcher . . . but always add something about his personality or character. He was "a great teammate"; "a wonderful human being"; "a class act."

Pierce joins Andre Dawson, Gil Hodges, Ken Boyer, Elston Howard, and a few others on this list as that rare breed of baseball player who is remembered equally as a great player and a great guy.

"Billy is a gentleman, a decent, polite person, and he was a true leader on our team," said former White Sox center fielder Jim Landis, who was quick to add: "But he was the greatest little competitor on the mound. He was all business and a great battler."

Former opponent Jim Piersall addressed Pierce's character and his pitching ability in a recent interview. "Billy should be in the Hall of Fame. He was a tough competitor who pitched in the real big games, and he never broke down," Piersall said. "He's also a class act who did a great job for baseball in the way he conducted himself."

But let's not get too carried away about the fine human being. Billy Pierce also has a resume that should be good enough for the Hall of Fame. However, he had the misfortune of being "the other" crafty little lefty in the American League during the 1950s. Billy Pierce was always "not Whitey Ford."

The White Sox and Yankees aces faced off in many key games throughout the decade.

"Every time we played the Sox," said the Yankees' Bill Skowron. "It was Pierce against Ford on Friday night to begin the weekend series. Those were great battles. It seemed like they were always pitching against each other."

Surprisingly, in their head-to-head games in which they both got the decision Pierce held an 8–6 career advantage over Ford.

Billy Pierce *at a glance*

- Led league with 1.97 ERA in 1955, lowest in the Majors in the 1950s
- Had 8–6 career record against Yankee rival and Hall of Famer Whitey Ford
- Twice a 20-game winner (lifetime 211–169, 3.27 ERA)
- Tied for AL lead in complete games three years in a row (1956–1958)
- In 1953 led league in strikeouts (186)
- Seven-time All-Star and AL starting pitcher three straight years

And, while nobody is claiming that Pierce was Whitey's equal, most who remember the amiable White Sox southpaw, including Ford, believe that he belongs in Cooperstown.

"I don't know why Billy isn't in the Hall of Fame," Ford said recently. "He was a great pitcher. He had a good fastball, slider, and changeup. He had good control and he knew how to pitch. He just wasn't with great clubs like I was."

Former White Sox and Yankees first baseman Eddie Robinson agreed.

"Billy won a lot more than he lost and if he were with the Yankees, he might be in the Hall of Fame," Robinson said. "Being on a good team that scores a lot of runs could be the difference between a pitcher having a great record rather than a good record."

In order to win for the light hitting "Go-Go Sox" Pierce had to be nearly perfect and was frequently involved in low-scoring, one-run decisions.

One time when teammate Nellie Fox scored to make the score 1–0, he half-jokingly told Pierce "Here's your run, now go out there and hold it."

While Ford went to the World Series eleven times, Pierce only pitched in the postseason twice and had to wait until he joined the San Francisco Giants in 1962 to gain his one and only World Series victory. However, in his eighteen years in the big leagues, the Detroit native won 211 games and carved out an impressive place in major league history.

As a teenager, Pierce gained the attention of major league scouts when he was named Most Valuable Player in *Esquire*'s all-American boys game. He passed up a scholarship offer to the University of Michigan to sign with the hometown Tigers. The Tigers were bringing him along slowly but then let him go to the Sox in a trade and in 1949, his thirteen-year career in Chicago began.

The twenty-two-year-old Pierce showed promise in posting losing records (7–15, 12–16) his first two seasons, but was wild in his early years. With the help of new manager Paul Richards and pitching coach Ray Berres he became a control pitcher, developed a slider and topped the .500 mark with a 15–14 record in 1951 and went 15–12 with a 2.57 ERA in 1952.

By 1953, Pierce was clearly established as the White Sox ace and one of the most respected pitchers in the league. He was usually the starting pitcher in the first game of a crucial series, often going against aces such as Ford, Bob Lemon, and later, Jim Bunning.

Pierce finished the 1953 season with an 18–12 record, a 2.72 ERA, and led the league in strikeouts with 186. He threw seven shutouts and at one point didn't give up a run in 51 straight innings.

He also made his first of three-straight All-Star Game starts (he was an All-Star seven times) and pitched three scoreless innings, as did his opponent, Robin Roberts.

In 1955, he really came of age, posting a 15–10 record with a league-leading 1.97 ERA.

It was the only time in the 1950s that a pitcher allowed fewer than two earned runs a game, and it is the achievement that gives Pierce the most pride.

Pierce posted 20-win seasons in both 1956 and 1957 and led the league in complete games in 1956, 1957, and 1958. And in 1958 he just missed a perfect game when, with two outs in the bottom of the ninth, Washington pinch-hitter Ed Fitzgerald hit a single down the right field line.

"Playing behind Billy Pierce was such a great thing," said Landis. "When he pitched it was a quick ball game. He pitched strikes. Everyone played harder and better because of the tempo of the game."

Pierce's big career disappointment came in 1959. After going 14–15 on the season, he was used sparingly by manager Al Lopez in the World Series, a move that was criticized by vocal Sox fans.

He had the chance for redemption in 1962 as a member of the Giants. At the age of thirty-five, the little lefthander had one good year in him and went 16–6. He shut out the Dodgers in the first game of a best-of-three playoff and went on to pitch a three-hitter against the Yankees in game three of the World Series.

Pierce retired after the 1964 season with a record of 211–169, 38 shutouts and an ERA of 3.27. He had a successful business career in his post-playing days and as a beloved Chicago hero, he makes appearances at many special White Sox events and nostalgia conventions.

In summing up his career, Pierce said recently, "I showed up and pitched hard every day. That's what you did in those days," he said. "To me it was a thrill pitching in the major leagues and it was especially thrilling pitching in an All-Star Game or a World Series."

Marty Marion

SS, 1940–1953, Cardinals, Browns

The man had three nicknames—Slats, Octopus, and Mr. Shortstop. That alone should qualify him for the Hall of Fame. Though often a candidate before the Veteran's Committee, the lanky Cardinals infield leader of the 1940s has yet to be granted his proper place in Cooperstown. For many years, Marion was the standard against which all shortstops were measured. Those who were tall and lean bore the extra burden of being hailed as "the next Marty Marion."

With the 6'2", 170-lb. Marion at shortstop, the Cardinals won four pennants and three World Championships. Old-timers will usually bring his name up when talk turns to "best shortstop of all-time." Cardinals manager Billy Southworth said that Marion "represented everything a shortstop should be."

"He's the best ever," Southworth said. "He anticipates plays perfectly, can go to his right or left equally as well and has a truly great arm. Some of the things he does have to be seen to be believed. And he's just as grand a person too, as he is a player."

With long, gliding strides and tremendous reach, Marion covered more ground than any shortstop in the game. He had tremendous leaping ability that enabled him to snare line drives that robbed many enemy batters of base hits. He played closer to the plate than most, which gave him a great advantage on slow rollers past the mound and his superb reflexes allowed him to get a fast jump on the ball.

And if that wasn't enough, Marion was a keen student of the game, who knew where to play every batter. He was usually in the right place when the ball was hit between second and third.

Marion, who was selected for seven All-Star Games, was chosen the National League's Most Valuable Player in 1944, and his stellar defensive play

Marty Marion *at a glance*

- 1944 NL MVP as shortstop and leader on three Cardinals World Champions (four pennant winners).
- Cards never finished lower than second when he was in his prime
- Regarded as the greatest shortstop of his time, and by some as the greatest ever
- Seven-time NL All-Star
- Batted .357 in 1943 World Series

was instrumental in the Cards victory over the cross-town rival, the St. Louis Browns in the World Series.

Satchel Paige once told sportswriter Milt Richman: "Marty Marion plays shortstop just like Duke Ellington plays the piano.

"Man, I've been in this game a lotta years, but I ain't seen a better shortstop than Marty . . . He's so good that all the other players stop what they are doing to watch him. I mean it. They just sit back and enjoy the show."

During his career, Marion, who won four fielding titles, was regarded as the greatest shortstop since Honus Wagner, although he wasn't in a class with the Flying Dutchman as a hitter. When asked to make a comparison, Wagner said it was hard to compare because "you must remember that I've never watched myself play ball."

Wagner admired Marion, complimenting him for his intelligent play and for "putting everything into his work."

"I've seen him make many of the most difficult plays, some of them seeming next to impossible," said Wagner, who was at Ebbets Field in Brooklyn in 1945 to present Marion with the 1944 National League Most Valuable Player Award.

Even though he was considered a cool, "loosey-goosey" type of player, between pitches Marion was perhaps the most fidgety fielder in the game. One sportswriter watching Marion at shortstop likened him to an industrious housekeeper.

"He's constantly tidying up the place, reaching down for pebbles, lumps of dirt specks invisible from the stands. He goes through the motions of throwing them back of him toward left field, but never do you see anything leave his hand," said Ed Pollock of the *Philadelphia Bulletin*.

Decades later, when St. Louis baseball aficionados were claiming that Ozzie Smith was the best Cardinals shortstop of all time, former Cardinals outfield great Terry Moore came to the defense of his teammate's reputation.

"People always ask me what I think of Ozzie in comparison to Marty," Moore said. "I tell 'em I'd give Ozzie the nod as the best shortstop I've ever seen on Astroturf. But if you put Ozzie on the fields that Marion played on and put Marion on the fields that Ozzie played on, then I don't think you could compare them. I don't think Ozzie would have been the shortstop that Marion was in Marion's conditions."

He wasn't a great hitter, only .263 lifetime, but always seemed to be there with the clutch hit when the Cardinals needed it most. His highest average was .280 in 1943 and he led the league in doubles in 1942.

Those great Cardinals championship teams included such lethal offensive weapons as Stan Musial, Enos Slaughter, Harry "the Hat" Walker, and Walker Cooper and great pitchers such as Harry "the Cat" Brecheen, Mort Cooper, and Johnny Beazley, so timely hitting was all that was needed from Marion. His consistent fielding made him the most essential player on one of the most consistently strong teams in National League history.

A great team player, when discussing his greatest thrills in baseball, Marion always put the Cardinals championships ahead of his individual achievements.

St. Louis sportswriter J. Roy Stockton called him one of the most modest stars the game has ever produced.

"Each stop he makes is 'lucky.' He 'just happened to be there.' If you tell him he made a terrific play, he'll smile and thank you, but insist that he just happened to be moving in that direction," Stockton said.

A chronic back injury forced Mr. Shortstop into an early retirement and he managed the Cardinals in 1951. The following season he replaced Rogers Hornsby as the Browns manager and played sparingly over the next two seasons before retiring for good.

One of the early organizers of the Players Association, he was the driving force behind improved player/management relations and drafted major leagues baseball's first pension plan, known as "the Marion Plan."

Ballplayers, writers, and fans who saw Mr. Shortstop, the Octopus, and Slats play say it's a crime that they aren't in the Hall of Fame.

Cristobal Torrienti

OF, 1913–1928, Negro Leagues:
Cuban Stars, Chicago American Giants

He was called "the Babe Ruth of Cuba" because he had the power. According to many, he also had the Bambino's charisma. On his native island and in many Negro League cities, Cristobal Torrienti was worshiped by several generations of ballplayers and fans.

The New York Giants wanted to make Torrienti the first black ballplayer in the major leagues since the color line was drawn in 1877. But before you think there was any serious effort to integrate baseball in the 1920s, understand that Torrienti was a light-skinned Cuban, whom John McGraw wanted to pass off as a white man. This particular experiment never got much beyond the talking stage.

As Torrienti's teammate Floyd (Jelly) Gardner reported in Robert Peterson's *Only the Ball Was White*: "The New York Giants had a scout following us to Kansas City, St. Louis, and Indianapolis. He was watching Torrienti. He hit a line drive in Indianapolis that hit the top of the right-field wall and the right fielder threw him out at first base. That's how much power he had." Gardner said the Giant scout liked Torrienti and would have signed him were it not for his hair. "He was a light brown, and he would have gone up to the major leagues, but he had real rough hair."

So the legendary superstar labored for two decades in the Negro Leagues, Cuban winter ball, and in exhibition games against white teams. Everyone who saw him, including many major leaguers who faced him, knew that Torrienti would have been an outstanding major leaguer, "one of the all-time greats," if only he had been given a chance to play in the majors.

Torrienti's career began with the New York Cubans in 1913 and ended in 1934, but in the United States he is best remembered for his years (1919–1925) with Rube Foster's Chicago American Giants, which dominated the Negro

---

Cristobal Torrienti *at a glance*

- Led Chicago American Giants to first three Negro National League pennants, 1920–1922, hitting .411, .338, and .342
- Won league batting title in 1920 (.411 BA) and in 1923 (.412 BA)
- In 1926 led Kansas City Monarchs to first-half league title with .381 BA and hit .407 in playoff against Chicago American Giants
- Lifetime .333 BA in Negro Leagues
- Lifetime .381 BA in Cuban winter league, included two batting titles
- Hit .318 against Major League competition

National League. The 1919 American Giants outfield, which consisted of Torrienti, Hall of Famer Oscar Charleston, and Jimmie Lyons, is regarded as the fastest and best defensive outfield in Negro Leagues history.

With Torrienti leading the way, Foster's Giants won the league championship three years in a row. Torrienti won the batting title in 1920 with a .411 average, and followed that up with averages of .338 and .342 in the next two championship years. The team also featured such all-time greats as Lyons, Gardner, pitcher Dave Brown, second baseman Bingo DeMoss, and third baseman Dave Malarcher.

The left-handed Torrienti could spray the ball to all fields but was known as the lone true power hitter in the strong Giants lineup. Bobby Williams, who played shortstop on the Chicago American Giants remembered one home run that contributed to the legend of Torrienti.

"We were playing in Kansas City," Williams recalled, "Torrienti hit a line drive that cracked a clock that was located beyond the center field fence, and the hands just started going round and round."

Torrienti put together two more great seasons after the championship years, hitting .412 in 1923 for another batting crown and .336 in 1924, but then he faded to .240 the following year. It is believed that Foster became fed up with Torrienti's love of the nightlife, and finally had had enough when the outfielder's production dipped in 1925.

In his first year with the Monarchs, Torrienti was instrumental in their winning the league title for the first half of the season. He hit .381 the first half, but once again his temperamental personality got in the way and he left the team in August, costing the Monarchs the second-half pennant. The Monarchs were defeated in the nine-game playoff by Torrienti's ex-mates, the Chicago

American Giants. On the final day of the playoff, Kansas City's pitcher, Hall of Fame member Willie Foster, defeated fellow Hall of Famer Bullet Joe Rogan in both games of a doubleheader.

The muscular, 5'9", 190-lb. Torrienti, whose lifetime batting average in the Negro Leagues was .339, was an amazingly versatile athlete. He was a great fielder and had a strong arm. He was sometimes used as a left-handed second baseman and even took the mound on a number of occasions. His lifetime record as a pitcher was 16–5.

In the Cuban League, he ranks with the great Martin Dihigo and pitcher Jose Mendez as the all-time stars. He was the Cuban batting champion three times, usually hitting greater than .360. He won four home run crowns and led the league in a number of other categories including stolen bases. His lifetime average in Cuban League competition was .352. In the winter of 1920, the New York Giants visited Cuba with Babe Ruth joining them for the tour. Torrienti out-hit Ruth .378 to .345 as the Cuban team won the Series, five games to four. In one game, Torrienti hit three home runs to Ruth's zero. To be fair, one of Torrienti's homers was hit off Ruth, who was by this time a full-time outfielder, and two were against Giants' first-baseman George Kelly, who was filling in on the mound. But the day that Torrienti hit three homers in competition against Ruth (The Torrienti of the United States?) was talked about for years. Through the years, Torrienti hit .313 in exhibition games against major league competition.

Toward the end of his career the years of fast living took their toll on Cuba's greatest slugger. He became an alcoholic and lived out his life in poverty and obscurity. He died of tuberculosis in 1938.

Torrienti's abilities and impact on the game were best summed up by Indianapolis ABCs manager C. I. Taylor who said: "If I should see Torrienti walking up the other side of the street, I would say, 'There walks a ball club.'"

Urban Shocker

P, 1916–1928, Yankees, Browns

The St. Louis Browns, who were to many a symbol of baseball futil-
ity, actually had a heyday. It was a briefly open window during
which they were first in the division three years in a row (1920–1922)
and almost stole a pennant from the Yankees in 1922. The team was led by the
great George Sisler at first base and a hard-hitting outfield of Jack Tobin, Baby
Doll Jacobson, and Ken Williams, and one of the great pitchers of the day—
Urban Shocker.

Acquired in a trade with the Yankees before the 1918 season, Shocker,
who never had a losing season, remains one of the best-kept secrets in baseball history. Many believe that he ranks as the top American League hurler in
the first half-dozen years of the hitters' era that was ignited by Babe Ruth. He
is regarded to this day as one of the Hall of Fame oversights from the
pre–World War II period.

Born Urbain Shockcor in Cleveland, Ohio, Shocker started his career as a
catcher, which didn't get him to the major leagues, but did get him a broken finger on his right hand that left him with a hook on his last joint. The injury proved
to be a blessing when he became a pitcher, because it added one more effective
pitch to a repertoire that already included a sharp fastball, a variety of curves,
and a spitball, which Shocker used "just enough to keep the batters off-balance."

"That broken finger may not be pretty to look at," Shocker said, "but it has
been very useful to me. It hooks over a baseball just right so that I can get a fine
break on my slow ball and that's one of the best balls I throw. If the finger was
straight I couldn't do that. As it is, I can get a slow ball to drop just like a spitter
and as I occasionally use a true spitter, you will find players all over the league
talking about my slow spitter, which isn't a spitter at all, but a slow ball with a
freak break thanks to that crooked finger. Perhaps if I broke some of my other
fingers I could get the ball to roll over sideways or maybe jump up in the air."

Urban Shocker *at a glance*

- Regarded as the most knowledgeable pitcher in baseball and as one of the best fielding pitchers of his time
- Four-time 20 game winner for St. Louis Browns (1920–1923)
- Never had a losing year in thirteen-year career
- Lifetime 187–117 record, 3.17 ERA, and .617 winning percentage
- Led AL in saves (5) in 1920, wins (27) in 1921, and strikeouts (149) in 1922
- 19–11 for Yankees pennant winners in 1926 and 18–6 for World Champions in 1927

Shocker was the ace of the "Golden Age" Brownies staff, winning 20 games four years in a row and even leading the league with five saves in 1920 (times have really changed!)

He was known to many of his contemporaries as Professor Urban Shocker because he was a fine student of the game who always studied the strengths and weaknesses of the opposing hitters. He was especially tough on the great hitters and took particular delight in beating his old team, the Yankees. During his career with the Browns he won 24 percent of the team's victories and in all but one year in his career he had a better winning percentage than his team.

Pitcher Carl Mays said Shocker was the best in the game at finding batters' weaknesses.

"He was the best pitcher in the game against dangerous batsmen," Mays said. "He didn't fear the dangerous, the big hitters. That's when he was at his best."

Ruth found it especially aggravating to hit against Shocker, who once struck him out three times in one game. Shocker believed he was Babe's master and usually struck him out once or twice a game.

Wally Schang, who caught Shocker and batted against him, thought he was the best pitcher in the American league at the time. "To me the best pitcher means the one I found toughest to hit," Schang said. "And that would be Urban Shocker. Shocker had everything—change-up, spitter, fastball, and curve. He struck me out four out of four in a big game in 1922 when I was with the Yankees."

Yankees manager Miller Huggins coveted Shocker throughout the pitcher's St. Louis days and the team finally swung a trade for him in 1925, though they didn't know at the time that Shocker was ill with the heart disease that would kill him just three years later.

Despite his health problems, which caused him to sleep while sitting up through most of the later years of his life, Shocker went on to have a great run with the Yankees. He went 12–12 in 1925, the year that the Yankees sank to seventh in the standings. The following year, with the Yankees winning the pennant, he was 19–11 with a 3.38 ERA. Then with the 1927 Yankees, the famed "Murderers Row" team, a deteriorating Shocker went 18–6 with a 2.84 ERA (third best in the league), but he did not pitch in the World Series due to his health.

By Christmas he was down to 115 lbs., but made a brief comeback the following year, pitching two scoreless innings in one game before he was forced to retire. Shocker died before the end of the 1928 season at age thirty-eight. His career record was 187–117, (.617 winning percentage) and an ERA of 3.17.

In a 1996 column in the *Oneonta Star*, baseball historian Jim Hamilton advocated Hall of Fame admittance for the pitcher, cited four reasons why Shocker has been, thus far, ignored.

"1) He was seven years in his grave when the first Hall of Fame election was held; 2) he didn't win 200 games, which seems to be a big hang-up with the writers; 3) he spent much of his career with the St. Louis Browns (nobody in the Hall of Fame except George Sisler and Rick Ferrell spent a major portion of his career with the Browns); and 4) a lot of people tend to get him confused with his former teammate, Bob Shawkey, a quality pitcher in his own right, but not in Shocker's class."

We agree with Hamilton and do our own small part to preserve the memory of Urban Shocker by naming him one of Baseball's underrated 100.

Ted Simmons
(Simba)

C, DH, 1B, 1968–1988, Cardinals,
Brewers, Braves

All things considered, Ted Lyle Simmons probably came along at the wrong time.

"I would think in his era, he was overshadowed by [Johnny] Bench, overshadowed by [Carlton] Fisk, possibly even [Thurman] Munson." Lou Piniella says of the former, catcher, designated hitter, first baseman, and major-league executive.

Simmons was never considered the top catcher of his time. And there was a knock on his defense. But he was a player—and many wonder why he's not alongside Bench and Fisk in the Hall of Fame. "Why is Fisk a shoe-in and Simmons wasn't?" asks Tom Grieve, making a pretty good point.

Simmons, a line-drive hitting machine, came up with the St. Louis Cardinals at a time when Bench and the Big Red Machine were making headlines. Bench hit more home runs than Simmons and some considered Bench the best catcher of all time. The comparisons always hurt Simmons, who also never played on a World Series winner—and certainly never hit a remembered homer like the one Fisk hit to win Game Six of the 1975 World Series.

"I don't think there were ever very many catchers who could hit like Ted Simmons," Sparky Anderson says. "He wasn't like Bench. John was death and destruction. For pure hitting, though, Simmons was the best catcher I ever saw."

He hit .285 lifetime, with 2,472 hits—many thinking he would have reached the magic 3,000 had it not been for all those years of catching on the

Ted Simmons *at a glance*

- Eight-time All-Star
- Seven times batted .300
- Eight times hit 90 or more RBIs
- .285 lifetime batting average
- 2,472 career hits

St. Louis turf (120–140 degrees in summer). He batted .300 seven times, had 90 or more RBIs eight times. He was an eight-time All-Star. He also set a modern record for career passed balls and was never a thrower, becoming a designated hitter during his days with the Milwaukee Brewers, but there are many who feel the rap on his defense was a bad one.

"He called a great game, he really did," says Piniella. "I remember when I played, being a guess hitter the way I was, that you really had to think with this guy behind home plate. I mean, things weren't automatic, things didn't fall into pattern. He had a good baseball mind and it's shown—he's gone and done some real, real nice things in the front office for a few teams.

"When you look at his career, and the length of it and how he produced, he probably hasn't gotten in because of the fact that in his era there were three or four great names that made it to the Hall of Fame."

"People knock his defense but he was a lot better defensive player than he got credit for," says former fellow catcher Randy Hundley.

Says Rusty Staub: "People have a tendency to label players. He wasn't a bad defensive catcher. I've seen some bad defensive catchers and Simmons wasn't one of them. And he could hit with anybody. He was a grinder."

Adds fellow former catcher Buck Martinez: "Pete Vuckovich swore by Teddy Simmons. He'd have done anything—if Ted says, 'turn around and throw the ball into center field,' Pete would have done it because Teddy had a reason for it. He was that good."

But Joe Torre, who came to the major leagues as a catcher, says, "Teddy wanted to be a hitter. He used to do some things—he used to wear this leaded vest taking batting practice. He made everything geared toward his hitting. Catching just got in the way for him.

"He was a DH. He worked at everything he did but for a time there, Ted Simmons was the best hitter in baseball. I remember putting him on base as the winning run when I was managing the Mets, to pitch to Bobby Bonds, in the ninth inning. He was scary because everything was a line drive. Then he started hitting home runs, but everything was a line drive that he hit—both ways, righty, and lefty.

"Bench was that good but [Simmons] wasn't a good catcher. He wanted to be because he was very proud but hitting . . . that was his life."

But there was a lot more to this guy. Talk to teammates and opponents about him and they remember a leader on the field—and one who sat in front of his locker, smoking cigarettes, doing crosswords and using the big words he might have found in them. "He didn't sound like a baseball player," Dan Quisenberry once said. "He said things like 'nevertheless' and 'if in fact.'"

His former teammate, Paul Molitor, said Simmons' intelligence is probably what got Molitor started on what would be a long-term activity with the Players Association. Recalling a speech Simmons gave at one winter meeting session during one of the early labor battles, Molitor said, "He used so many big words we missed quite a bit of it. It was impressive." Basically, when Simmons talked, people listened. "He commanded attention when he spoke," Molitor said.

And that carried over to his handling of his pitchers.

Simmons was traded by the Cardinals to the Brewers during Whitey Herzog's serious trading period and wound up in the World Series against his old team and boss in 1982. The Brewers led that Series, 3–2, before losing the last two games and leaving Simmons without a World Series ring.

"Simmons could do everything," says Rod Carew. "I think he was very underrated. Everyone talked about Johnny Bench but they should talk about this guy."

Vada Pinson

OF, 1958–1975, Reds, Cardinals, Indians, Angels, Royals

Style. Grace. Talent. Three words so often used to describe Vada Pinson.

"When I came to the majors, and for a long time after that, Vada may have been the best hitter in the National League," says Maury Wills, another member of our elite "Out by a Step" club. "He and Frank Robinson made up as good a 1–2 punch as there was."

Ahhh, that last thought right there might be the thing that has kept Vada Pinson from at least some of the credit he deserves—Frank Robinson. The silly people who left Robby off the greatest team of all time omitted one of the game's greats—and Pinson played in the shadow of that greatness. It started in high school, when the pair and Curt Flood were all produced by the same school in Oakland in the same era.

"No question," says Joe Torre. "Overshadowed by Frank because Frank was a mountain of a guy."

"I don't know that he lived in his shadow but perhaps if he were solitarily recognized, if he played by himself, he would have stood up and stood out a little bit more than when he played with Frank Robinson." says Tim McCarver, who, like Torre, played against and with Pinson. "There were very few players that could stand out with Frank as a teammate."

The recognition from this center fielder's peers has always been there. The Hall of Fame voters were a different story—almost completely overlooking a man who collected 2,757 hits, stole 305 bases, and smacked 256 home runs while driving in 1,170 runs and scoring 1,366 times. Pinson, who also had 485 doubles, died in 1995.

Vada Pinson *at a glance*

- 2,757 career hits
- .286 lifetime batting average
- Two-time All-Star
- 1961 Gold Glove
- Four-time .300 average for a season
- Hit 20 homers seven times

"Of all the people who aren't in (the Hall), he's certainly in the class of the elite," adds McCarver. "Living in someone's shadow is never a reason not to vote somebody into the Hall of Fame. That's ridiculous. Players like that should be taken out and looked at from an individual standpoint, but human nature being what it is—whatever human nature is—from that standpoint it's difficult to do."

But it seems to have happened—Vada Pinson has been ignored.

"Vada was just a steady ballplayer and sometimes the steady ballplayers— even Hank Aaron, who was just so steady and not flashy—who are not in a big media market, get overlooked, even though their numbers are there," says former teammate Tommy Harper. "Vada played for a long time, but if you would ask anybody about the Cincinnati Reds, they immediately go to the Big Red Machine and they're always gonna go 'Pete Rose, Frank Robinson.' Or 'Frank Robinson, Pete Rose.'

"There were a lot of great players who played there . . . and Vada Pinson is another name. And people know Vada was a good ballplayer. Being in Cincinnati, not a big media market, and having Frank on the same team [hurt him]."

"Vada was just a person I always considered to be Hall of Fame caliber because the way I look at it, he has longevity, being steady, and putting up good numbers for a number of years," Harper says. "He came up short of 3,000 hits. As far as a center fielder in his day, he was considered one of the best. He was fast. He didn't run a lot, he didn't steal a lot of bases because he just didn't run a lot."

"Vada was a five-tool guy," adds McCarver. "Real quiet. He didn't get a lot of attention but the guys on the field knew how good he was. Ask any player in the years that he played and they'll tell you he was one of the best."

Pinson had a .286 lifetime batting average with the Reds, Cardinals, Indians, Angels, and Royals. He hit .300 four times, drove in 100 runs twice, and hit 20 homers seven times. His big year was 1961, when he finished second in the National League in batting at .343 and stroked 208 hits, one of four 200-hit seasons. Playing that funky center field incline at Crosley Field, Pinson also won his only Gold Glove that year. However, he had a poor World Series in his only visit to the postseason, going 2-for-22.

"Vada could beat you in a lot of ways," says McCarver. "He could beat you with his arm or his legs or his power or his average. Vada Pinson was one of the more underrated players in my day. He was similar to Curt Flood, but Vada had a stronger arm than Curt. They played in the same outfield in high school—Robinson, Pinson, and Flood. Vada and Curt were similar; Vada had more power and a stronger arm and was perhaps a little bit faster.

"Vada did things so effortlessly that a lot of times it looked like he was on cruise control when he wasn't at all—one of the great guys I thought."

That class is often talked about. "We were teammates in St. Louis in '69," says Torre. "When [Roger] Maris retired, they traded [Bobby] Tolan for Vada. He could do everything—he could run, he ran in an unusual style, flat-footed, had base stealing ability, played the outfield real well. Very smooth, looked good in the uniform, and was a good hitter."

Looked good in the uniform. Former friend and foe Tony Cloninger takes that a step further when talking about Pinson.

"I remember what a jump he got on the ball in center field, what a clutch hitter he was and what a class person he was," the former pitcher says. "He was a great ballplayer. And he could shine those shoes. You don't remember that, do you? Vada Pinson was one guy who always had his shoes spiffy shined. A clean, classy person."

Clean, classy—and talented enough in the minds of many to *not* be left out of the Hall of Fame by a step.

Joe Torre

C, 3B, 1B, 1960–1977, Braves, Cardinals, Mets

J oe Torre will go into the Hall of Fame some day—and when he does, he'll go there largely because of what he has done managing the New York Yankees. When he gets to Cooperstown, when he finally has that big day, he might have to fight the urge to grab the microphone and make a statement about Joe Torre—the player.

"My brother Frank, every time somebody gets voted into the Hall of Fame, he says, 'you know, your stats match up with his.'" Torre says. "I say, 'Frank, don't bother me.' I've never been a fan of people who have politicked to get into the Hall of Fame.

"I remember telling Enos Slaughter one time because he bitched for the longest time about having to be in the Hall of Fame [and attend the yearly functions]. We were playing in an old-timer's game at Buffalo, New York, and he's complaining because of how he's going to have to drive from Buffalo to Cooperstown and I said, 'Enos, you bitched long enough to get in the Hall of Fame and now you're complaining about driving there.' I just always felt uncomfortable with people who did that."

Torre was not complaining about anything. But you know when you talk to him he feels a bit slighted by the way his numbers as a player have gone pretty much overlooked. Winning four World Series in a five-year span gets you noticed as a manager—but doing what he did as a player is pretty special, too, and deserving of some attention. Hey, maybe that's why we did this book.

"My numbers are pretty good, and when Frank pointed it out to me then I would look at it and I'd see my numbers did match up," Torre says, adding, "plus the fact that I played three positions and I think I was the first player to have 500 games at three different positions."

"What he's done as a manager has given him a little more, I guess you'd say, visibility toward becoming a Hall of Famer," says Jim Kaat. "I don't think

Joe Torre *at a glance*

- 1971 NL MVP
- 1971 NL batting champion
- Nine-time All-Star
- 1965 Gold Glove
- First player to play 500 games at three positions
- Drove in 100 runs five times
- .297 career batting average

he would have gotten in just on his playing. But talk about a pure hitter—he was an RBI guy, a production guy, almost like Cepeda."

Strangely enough, Torre and Hall of Famer Cepeda were traded for each other prior to the 1969 season—Torre going from the Atlanta Braves to St. Louis, where he would be the National League Most Valuable Player and batting champion in 1971. "When he played for the Braves, he was an average catcher, he wasn't a great catcher," says former National League shortstop Bobby Wine. "When he went to St. Louis, he lost 40 pounds and played third base."

Torre played third base in high school, but became a catcher after signing with the Milwaukee Braves (his brother's team)—moving behind the plate because the Braves had a guy named Mathews playing third base for them. Torre's time in the minors was brief—a batting title in A-ball in 1960 and a brief stay in triple-A before Del Crandell got hurt in 1961. He would go on to become a nine-time All-Star who, despite what Wine said, would win a Gold Glove in 1965. He hit .300 four times, drove in 100 runs five times.

Torre hit .325 with the 1970 Cardinals, with 21 homers and 100 RBIs. Then came 1971, when he hit the league-best .363 and also had 24 homers and 137 RBIs.

Some things you have to remember when looking at Torre's career—his career-best 36 homers came in 1966, the Braves' first year at tiny Fulton County Stadium in Atlanta, his power numbers should have dropped dramatically at spacious Busch Stadium—and his .297 career batting average was achieved with legs that gave him very few infield singles.

"That great year he had when he hit .363 was amazing," says Tom Grieve, who played for Torre with the Mets in 1978. "And you think about the way Joe ran, he sure didn't get any bunt hits or infield hits—he earned every bit of that."

The lack of speed was evident as Torre led the league in hitting into double plays in 1964, 1965, 1967 and 1968. Late in his career, he set a modern record with the Mets by grounding into four double plays in a nine-inning game—and he ranked ninth all-time in that category. Basically, he hit balls hard and when they went right at people, Torre was in trouble.

But no one will forget 1971. Adds Sparky Anderson, who was managing the Cincinnati Reds in those days: "Joe Torre showed me a lot by winning a batting title there. It's hard to hit home runs there so he became a line drive hitter. He learned to use the middle and not try to do what can't be done."

Torre managed the Mets and Braves, became a broadcaster and returned to manage the Cardinals—actually managing three teams he played for. His arrival in New York was met with skepticism, as people thought George Steinbrenner was just hiring another guy he could push around for awhile and then dump. It didn't work out quite that way.

"Joe's going to the Hall of Fame," says Don Zimmer, his bench coach with the Yankees. "There's no doubt—managing has really, really helped him. So he's actually going to go in both ways. He's a cinch now after what he's done as a manager."

Ted Kluszewski

1B, 1947–1961, Reds, Pirates, White Sox, Angels

Ted Kluszewski was a genuine marquee player for the Cincinnati Reds in the 1950s. He was a name-above-the-title guy. It was " 'Big Klu' and the Reds are coming to town for a three game series." He was one of the premier sluggers of his day and was generally considered the most likely to break Babe Ruth's record of 60 home runs in a season.

A 6'2", 235-lb. tower of bulging muscle, the left-handed hitting Klu was renowned for smashing scorching line drives that put fear in pitchers and fielders alike. One coach claimed facetiously that Kluszewski's bat even endangered pedestrians walking in the street beyond the right field wall at Crosley Field.

Big Klu presented a truly menacing sight at the plate, his biceps accentuated by his habit of cutting off his uniform sleeves at the shoulders. Though everyone thought that was done to intimidate the opposition, Klu claimed that the standard uniform was too tight and prevented him from moving his arms freely. One day he just took scissors and cut off the sleeves.

As the story goes, Leo Durocher, then manager of the New York Giants, was asked whom he thought was the strongest man in baseball. Without hesitating "The Lip" replied Gil Hodges. "What about Kluszewski?" he was asked. "Oh, I thought you were asking about human beings."

Veteran baseball observers compared him to Lou Gehrig, because of his physical strength—and because he was a truly gentle man. Like Gehrig, when Klu arrived in the majors he was a terrible fielder who worked hard to make himself into an above average first baseman.

Kluszewski, grew up in Argo, Illinois, outside of Chicago and went to Indiana University on a football scholarship. The Reds signed him for $15,000 and sent him to Columbia, South Carolina, in the Sally League where he won the batting title, hitting .352 in 1946. The following year he did the same for Memphis in the American Association, hitting .377.

Ted Kluszewski *at a glance*

- Led NL in HRs (49) and RBIs (141) in 1954
- Seven-time .300 hitter (lifetime .298)
- Five 100 RBIs seasons (career 1,028)
- Three-times in a row hit 40 HRs (career 290)
- Four-times in a row was NL All-Star (1953–1956)
- Never struck out more than 40 times in a season

In 1948, he was in a Reds uniform full time hitting .274 and later .309 but without true home run power. And his fielding was atrocious.

"He was like Gehrig all over again," one observer said. "Big and strong and clumsy, but tripping over his own feet and messing up plays that would be routine for an experienced first sacker."

However, the Reds saw his potential as a great hitter and did everything imaginable to make him adequate in the field. They brought in retired first basemen such as George "Highpockets" Kelly and Johnny Neun to coach him. The great Bill Terry came out of retirement to serve as Klu's fielding instructor. When he first saw Kluszewski play, Terry said the young player could never hit enough in the majors to compensate for his poor fielding.

The extra work paid off because Kluszewski became a good first baseman, leading the league in fielding average five years in a row, and in double plays four years in a row.

But it was at the plate where the "Big Klu" legend was made. A free-swinger with a good eye, Kluszewski was not someone who waited for his pitch or tried to figure out what the pitcher was trying to do. He just gripped the bat and swung from the heels.

The one criticism that dogged Klu throughout his career was that he wasn't aggressive enough. The curmudgeonly Rogers Hornsby, the Reds' manager in 1952 and 1953 told *Sport Magazine*: "You wouldn't want to meet a more pleasant or a finer-type young man. And he swings a pretty good bat . . . But he doesn't always go up there with the same determination. I kept trying to tell him that he could take over from Stan Musial as the best hitter in the league if he'd only push himself a little harder."

Criticism notwithstanding, Kluszewski developed into one of the National League's most dominating players. He hit over .300 in seven of his nine full seasons with the Reds, compiling a .298 batting overage over a fifteen-year career. He slugged 40 home runs or more three years in a row. He drove in more than 100 runs five times, four in a row. In 1954 he led the league in home runs with 41, RBIs with 141, and finished fifth in batting with a .326 average. Klu was second in the MVP voting to Willie Mays. He batted .500 and fielded flawlessly as the National League's All-Star first baseman from 1953 to 1956.

He was certainly on the road to Cooperstown when his career was derailed by a slipped disc late in 1956. He finished that season at .302, with 35 homers and 102 RBIs, but the chronic back problem diminished his power and restricted his movement. Klu was never the same again. In 1958, he was sent to Pittsburgh, where he became a part-time player. The White Sox traded for him in 1959 and, at thirty-five, the great slugger had one more encounter with glory as he hit .297 down the stretch in the Pale Hose' first drive to the pennant since 1919. And, in a losing effort against the Dodgers, Klu, in his only World Series, batted .391 with 10 RBI (a record for a six-game Series) and three home runs, two of them in a Game One 11–0 White Sox victory.

"It really meant a lot to me to play in that Series, even though we lost," Klu said in Rich Westcott's book *Diamond Greats*. "I had been around [pro baseball] for fourteen years, and I hadn't played in one. I was really happy to get the opportunity when it finally came,"

Kluszewski played one more year with the White Sox and ended his career as a member of the expansion Los Angeles Angels in 1961.

He later returned to the Cincinnati organization where he served as hitting coach for "The Big Red Machine." Many members of that team, including Dave Concepcion, Pete Rose, George Foster, Johnny Bench, Ken Griffey, Joe Morgan, and Tony Perez, credited "Big Klu" with improving their batting skills and helping them out of hitting slumps

Ted Kluszewski is remembered as the strongest man in baseball. People used to say that it's a good thing that he never gets mad because if he did "it wouldn't be safe for the rest of us."

When his career was over Big Klu confided that he was happy that no one ever challenged him because frankly "I wasn't much of a fighter."

Cecil Travis

SS, 3B, 1933–1941, 1945–1947, Senators

A very unfunny thing happened to Cecil Travis on the way to the Hall of Fame—Word War II.

Travis was twenty-eight years old and just had his best season for the Washington Senators when the war broke out. As one of the top hitters in the American League, he was in his prime and looking forward to improving on a career that had already seen him hit over .300 in eight of his nine seasons (.292 in an injury-plagued 1939).

In the recently ended 1941 season, Travis was in great company as one of the American League's top offensive threats. He batted .359, second in the league to Ted Williams's .406 (the last time that a major leaguer hit .400) and two points ahead of Joe DiMaggio in the year of the Yankee Clipper's legendary 56-game hitting streak.

Travis missed most of the next four years serving his country, suffering severe frostbite in his feet during the Battle of the Bulge. When he returned to baseball, he never regained his pre-war form. Observers blamed it on the frostbite, but Travis refused to alibi, claiming he had just "lost it" after the four-year layoff.

Travis, who grew up on a farm in Riverdale, Georgia, was discovered at a baseball school in Atlanta run by old-time major league infielder Norman "Kid" Elberfeld. "The Tabasco Kid," one of the more colorful turn-of-the-century ballplayers, recommended Travis to the Chattanooga minor league team. Tavis had three outstanding seasons and was called up to the Senators in 1933 when third baseman Ossie Bluege was injured. Cecil broke in with 5 hits in his first major league game and hit an impressive .302 in an 18-game major league trial. He became the Senators starting third baseman in 1934.

Manager Joe Cronin called Travis "one of the most natural hitters I ever saw come into the big leagues.

Cecil Travis *at a glance*

- Eight-time .300 hitter (lifetime .314 average)
- Hit .359 in 1941 (second in league) and led AL in hits (218) with 101 RBIs
- Five hits in his first Major League game (1933)
- Three-time All-Star

"No pitcher of reputation will disturb his calm . . . he is picture perfect at the plate. It makes no difference if the ball comes in high or low, inside or out."

Travis developed into one of the most consistent hitters in the league producing averages of .319, .318, and .317 in his first three seasons, getting most of his hits to left field early in his career.

A notorious plate-crowder, in 1936 Travis was hit on the head by a fastball thrown by Cleveland pitcher Thornton Lee and spent three weeks in Georgetown Hospital for observation and treatment. Everyone feared that he would be plate-shy when he returned. But fear wasn't in Travis's batting vocabulary. Coincidentally, the first pitcher he faced was Lee, and he lined the first pitch into right-center for a triple.

Manager Bucky Harris said: "He's so plate shy, he's crowding the plate again." Travis continued to lean over the plate and throughout his career was one of the league's most hit batsmen.

Travis was also a good third baseman with a strong, accurate arm, but for the good of the team, he moved to shortstop in 1936. He was a pretty good shortstop with one notable weakness. Shirley Povich of the *Washington Post* observed: "Travis knew his limits. He could go get a ground ball with the best, and his throwing arm was wonderful, but he couldn't scramble like a good shortstop should to protect himself from base runners around second. He didn't have the nimbleness or the reflexes to get out of the way, so he took many a beating." Trainer Mike Martin used to call him Kid Bandage because he was the most spiked infielder in the league.

Never considered among baseball rowdies, the favorite of the Washington fans didn't smoke, drink, or chew tobacco and steered clear of the nightlife. In the offseason he went back to work on his farm.

During his career year of 1941, Travis led the league in hits with 218 and drove in 100 runs. At twenty-eight, a more muscular Travis was now hitting to all fields, hitting lefties and righties with similar results. He was looking forward to many years as one of baseball's premier hitters. And then the war broke out.

When it was announced that the tall, left-handed hitter with the sweetest swing in baseball was going into the army, Yankees pitcher and resident wit Lefty Gomez said, "Now isn't that just too bad. I doubt if the pitchers in this league will ever console themselves. This is breaking our hearts, but not very much."

Travis returned in 1945 but never regained his pre-war eminence, and after two unproductive seasons decided to hang up his spikes at the end of the 1947 season.

In August of 1947 they held "Cecil Travis Night" at Griffith Stadium. He was showered with gifts, cash, an automobile, and equipment for his Georgia farm. One of the great tributes came when it was announced that the American League umpires chipped in for a gift to Cecil Travis. Umpire Bill McGowan, a Hall of Famer, said of Travis, "He's the favorite player of the umpires. He hasn't squawked yet on a called strike or any decision against him anywhere. He's the only ballplayer I ever felt sorry about calling out."

Cecil Travis was one of the most quietly efficient ballplayers of the pre-war era. His .314 lifetime batting average was third among shortstops behind Honus Wagner (.327) and Arky Vaughan (.318). Experts say that he would have received more Hall of Fame consideration if he had played in a World Series or if there was still a team in Washington so fans and beat writers could have served as vocal supporters who remembered the tall, lean lefty.

The selection of Travis for the Hall of Fame is long overdue.

Curt Flood

OF, 1956–1969, 1971, Reds, Cardinals, Senators

History remembers Curt Flood as the crusader who challenged baseball's reserve clause and lost. His suit, however, eventually paved the way for free agency and the tremendous (some say outrageous) salaries that are being paid to today's athletes. Flood is recognized for his courage and the sacrifice he made for his principles when he was traded to the Phillies in 1969 but refused to report because "I do not feel that I am a piece of property, to be traded irrespective of my wishes."

The historical court case may obscure the memory of Curt Flood, the seven-time Gold Glove winner, consistent .300 hitter, and Cardinals center fielder in three World Series.

A native of Houston, Flood grew up in Oakland, California, and followed two other hometown outfielders, Frank Robinson and Vada Pinson, into the Cincinnati Reds organization. The Reds tried to make him a third baseman, but with little success. "The manager used to beg me to throw to second anytime I got my hands on a ground ball," Flood said. "That way we can hold it to a single."

After a cup of coffee in 1956 and a free refill in 1957, Flood was traded to the Cardinals and he played semi-regularly until 1960 when manager Johnny Keane made him the starting center fielder. Flood became a student of the game who always went to the best mentors for advice. For fielding instructions he approached Cardinals coach Terry Moore, who in his day was considered the best in baseball.

"Terry helped me with the biggest thing a center fielder needs—getting a good jump on the ball," Flood said. "I can almost always tell whether the batter is going to pull the ball, so I shift my weight accordingly. Sometimes the difference in making the play or not is in going in the right direction before the ball is hit."

> ### Curt Flood *at a glance*
>
> - Won seven Gold Gloves (1963–1969)
> - Six-time .300 hitter (lifetime .293)
> - Led NL in hits (211) in 1964
> - Played NL record 226 errorless games (568 errorless chances) 1965–1967
> - Three-time NL All-Star

He must have learned well because he won the Gold Glove award every year from 1963 to 1969. This included a string of 226 errorless games from September 2, 1965 to June 4, 1967. He fielded 1.000 for all of 1966.

Lou Boudreau called Flood the most underrated outfielder in the game. "I haven't seen a thing that Flood can't do. He gets as good a jump on the ball as Mays does. He has absolutely no fear of the walls."

Roger Maris, who played alongside Flood in the Cardinals outfield said: "His swiftness is sometimes amazing. When I first played beside him in the spring he really surprised me. I'd think to myself 'that one's in there.' But Curt would catch it. He has to be the best."

After the errorless streak was broken, Bill Virdon, a great center fielder himself, and then a Pirates coach said: "When you have a man who can play center field the way Flood does and can get 200 hits a season, you've really got something."

Despite his reputation as a fielder, Flood took some time to develop as a hitter. He was determined to improve his hitting and spent many hours observing the best in the game and seeking advice from coaches and players.

Coach Harry Walker advised him to keep a little black book on strategy to use against pitchers because you can't keep mental notes on ninety hurlers in the league. George Crowe, first baseman and teammate, suggested that Flood take a shorter stride and a level swing. "He said whatever else happens, those two things would compensate for them," Flood said.

Dick Groat, one of the great place hitters, advised Flood to give up the illusion of being a home run hitter and learn to hit to all fields.

"I thought I had to be Babe Ruth. Dick Groat taught me there were eighteen other places to get a safe hit besides in the seats," Flood said. "The pitch that used to give me the dickens was the ball low and away. I'd try to pull it too often. And when I start hitting homers, I'm in trouble."

Pitcher Larry Jackson, who claimed he owed many victories to Flood's great fielding and timely hitting, saw Flood's intensity and determination, even in batting practice as the key factors in his the improvement over the years.

Flood topped the .300 mark six times and was usually the leadoff man in the Cardinals World Championship lineup of 1964, which included Hall of Famer Lou Brock, Ken Boyer, Dick Groat, and Bill White. He was also the center fielder on the championship team of 1967 and again when the Cardinals went to the World Series against the Tigers in 1968.

The one negative on his outstanding record was a misplay that lost the Series for St. Louis. The teams were tied 0–0 in the seventh inning of Game Seven with Bob Gibson facing Mickey Lolich. With two out and two men on in the seventh, Jim Northrup hit a hard drive to center, which Flood lost sight of momentarily. He took a couple of steps in toward home plate, reversed direction, and slipped. The ball carried over his head for a triple and two runs. The Tigers won the game 4–1 and took the Series.

The Cardinals weren't in contention in 1969 and owner Gussie Busch cleaned house, dealing Flood, Tim McCarver, and Joe Hoerner to Philadelphia for three players, including Richie Allen. But Flood refused to report and instead sued for his freedom from the "reserve" system that bound players to their teams forever. Flood compared the system to slavery, which the public found difficult to understand, because he was making $90,000 a year at the time.

He eventually lost the suit, but the Players Association continued to challenge the reserve clause and years later won the current system of free agency. Flood sat out the 1970 season but signed with the Washington Senators in 1971 and played for two months before retiring.

Curt Flood, the first man to challenge baseball's reserve clause, died of throat cancer in 1997 at the age of fifty-nine.

45

Don Newcombe

P, 1949–1951, 1954–1960, Dodgers,
Reds, Indians

"**B**ig Newk," the ace pitcher for the "Boys of Summer" Brooklyn Dodgers is the only man in history to win the Rookie of the Year, Cy Young award, and Most Valuable Player awards.

The 6'4", 240-lb. right-hander, with a fastball that was compared to that of Bob Feller, was the first great black pitcher in the major leagues. He was a 20-game winner three times, has a lifetime winning percentage of .623 and was also one of the best hitting pitchers in the game.

Yet circumstances—and some of his own human flaws and professional disappointment—prevented him from being officially recognized in Cooperstown as a great pitcher on one of the greatest teams in history.

"Newk was a dominant pitcher who put up big numbers," said longtime Dodgers teammate Carl Erskine. "He won every award that recognizes greatness. He had all the Hall of Fame qualities. Our team was one of the best there ever was and it's a shame that one of our pitchers isn't in Cooperstown. Newk should be that person."

Newcombe's 149 lifetime victories didn't get much attention from the voters, but how many more games would Newk have won had it not been for the gradual nature of integration that probably kept him in the minor leagues for an extra year or two? Or how many victories might be added if he hadn't spent two years in the Army right after his first 20-game season

And, finally, how many victories could have been added had Newcombe not lost the battle of the bottle in the mid-1950s, a loss that ruined his career, and eventually threatened his life, after he had one of the greatest seasons by any pitcher—ever.

Former Dodgers general manager Buzzie Bavasi thinks Newcombe would be in the Hall of Fame, if he just had the numbers he lost to the two Army

---

Don Newcombe *at a glance*

- 1956 NL MVP with a 27–7 record
- First Cy Young award winner (1956) for all of Major League Baseball
- 1949 NL Rookie of the Year
- Three-time 20-game winner
- Four-time NL All-Star
- Hit .359 with NL record for a pitcher 7 HRs in 1955

---

years. "I have no doubt that if Newk didn't lose those two years to the service right in the prime of his career, he would have been in the Hall of Fame a long time ago," Bavasi said.

Because of several unfortunate late season and postseason failures, Newcombe was labeled as someone who "couldn't win the big one."

Let's not forget that in many cases it was Newcombe who got the Dodgers to the big one, and even in some of the memorable losses, he had pitched excellent ball games.

A native of Staten Island, Newcombe grew up in New Jersey, and starred for the Newark Eagles of the Negro Leagues in 1945. The following year Newcombe and Roy Campanella were signed to Brooklyn Dodgers contracts by Branch Rickey, who intended to move them to the majors in the years after Jackie Robinson broke the color line. Newcombe had two great seasons at Nashua, New Hampshire, and was 17–6 at Montreal in 1948.

He was promoted to the Dodgers early in 1949, went 17–8 and led the league with five shutouts, becoming the first pitcher to win the Rookie of the Year award.

In each of his first three seasons, Newcombe was named to the National League All-Star team but each year brought a crushing late season disappointment.

He started Game One of the 1949 World Series and engaged in one of the great pitching duels in Series history against Allie Reynolds of the Yankees. Newcombe struck out 11 batters and took a 4-hitter into the bottom of the ninth with the score tied 0–0. Tommy Henrich hit a home run in the bottom of the ninth to give Newcombe his first big game disappointment.

"Newk pitched a great game that day," Erskine said. "If Henrich doesn't hit that home run. Who knows?"

The following year Newcombe went 19–11 and was the starting pitcher on the last day of the season with the Dodgers trailing the Phillies by one game and needing a victory to force a playoff. Newcombe pitched another gem that should have been his twentieth victory of the season, but again it wasn't to be. In the tenth, with the score tied 1–1, he gave up a three-run homer to Philadelphia's Dick Sisler and the "Whiz Kids" went to the Series.

In the 1951 season, Newk went 20–9, but is remembered more for the third game of the playoffs against the Yankees. The Dodgers were leading 4–1 going into the ninth behind a great game by Newcombe, who was beginning to tire. He gave up 3 hits in the ninth and was relieved by Ralph Branca who gave up *the* home run to Bobby Thomson.

The next two years were spent serving Uncle Sam. After returning from the army, Newcombe suffered a down year in 1954, but rebounded to go 20–5, for the first Dodgers World Championship team in 1955. That year, he established himself as one of the greatest hitting pitchers in baseball history. Newcombe hit .359 with 7 home runs and 23 RBIs. He was 8 for 21 as a pinch hitter. He had a .271 lifetime batting average.

In 1956, Newcombe was the best pitcher in baseball. He went 27–7 with a 3.05 ERA, struck out 139, and walked only 46 in 268 innings while throwing five shutouts. He was the first player to win both the MVP and Cy Young awards in the same season, at a time when they awarded only one Cy Young for all of major league baseball.

"Throughout his career Newcombe was a great pitcher," Bavasi said. "He was consistent and he was dominating. But in 1956 he was the best I ever saw."

However, the postseason brought more World Series failure and a devastating game seven defeat to the Yankees. Newcombe a sensitive man, who took each crucial loss harder than the last, went spiraling down hill. After the 1956 World Series, his drinking got totally out of control.

Carl Erskine remembers the circumstances of the seventh game in which Yogi Berra smacked a two-run homer off Newk. "Campy had a bone spur in his hand and he was dropping pitches because he couldn't grip the ball," Erskine said. "Newk actually struck out Berra, but the ball popped out of Campanella's glove and the ump signaled a foul tip. Then Yogi came back and put it over the Ebbets Field screen. Newk lost it that day."

He had a bad year, going 11–12 in 1957 and after a bad start in 1958, the team's first year in Los Angeles, the Dodgers traded him to Cincinnati, He made a brief comeback with the Reds, going 7–7 and 13–8, but alcohol was just too much to overcome and he was out of the majors by 1960.

After a prolonged period of darkness after he left baseball, Newcombe kicked his drinking habit and joined the Dodgers community relations staff and has for many years lectured and counseled others about the dangers of alcoholism.

Sherwood (Sherry) Magee

OF, 1B, 1904–1919, Phillies, Braves, Reds

S herry Magee was a superstar of baseball's dead-ball era, a player "who ranked among the mightiest hitters of the game when the rabbit ball was yet unborn and a .300 hitter was the exception and not the rule." However, the hot-tempered Phillies outfielder has been virtually forgotten by all but the most attentive followers of baseball history, and he has been virtually ignored by the Hall of Fame.

Magee was a solidly built switch-hitter whose career numbers include a .291 batting average, 2,169 hits, 83 home runs, 1,182 RBIs, 1,112 runs scored—all in an era when good pitching dominated the game. In 1910, he led the National League in batting (.331), RBIs (123), runs scored (110), and slugging average (.509). He led the league in RBIs four times, the only player to have accomplished that who is not in the Hall of Fame. His record of 55 stolen bases in a season is still in the Phillies record book.

As Jack Ryder of the *Cincinnati Enquirer* wrote during Magee's playing days: "To my mind, Sherwood Magee is one of the best all around players the game has ever seen."

The *Biographical Dictionary of American Sports* called "the smart aggressive Magee, a fast, excellent fielder with a strong accurate throwing arm, a superior base runner who hit sharp line drives to all fields."

Why has history paid so little attention to this outstanding career?

The reasons given for Magee's rejection by Cooperstown vary, but together they may present an accurate picture of why a man who seemingly has all the qualifications, is unlikely to join his peers in the official shrine of baseball immortality.

Sherry Magee *at a glance*

- 1910 NL Batting Champion with .331 BA
- In 1910 led league in SA (.507), runs (110), and RBIs (123)
- Four-time NL RBI leader
- In 1914 led NL in hits (171), SA (.509), RBIs (103), and doubles (39)
- Five-time .300 hitter (lifetime .291)

First of all, Magee had the misfortune of dying young. He succumbed to pneumonia in 1929, almost a decade before the first class of Hall of Fame inductees took their rightful place in history.

The first few Hall of Fame elections focused on the easy choices—Babe Ruth, Ty Cobb, Walter Johnson, and the like—which was understandable. Voters in succeeding decades probably overlooked him in favor of more recent heros as they became eligible.

The explanation for his rejection by the Veteran's Committee may be found in Magee's personality. Although he was, by all reports, a temperate good citizen and likeable family man away from the game, his on-field and clubhouse behavior, which received a great deal of publicity in his day, were often deplorable.

The fiery Magee was often suspended for his run-ins with umpires. In one memorable confrontation on July 10, 1911, he knocked out and bloodied umpire Bill Finneran with a punch to the jaw over a disputed called third strike. For this Magee was suspended for the rest of the season, but the suspension was eventually lifted and the Phillies left fielder returned to the lineup after five weeks.

A perfectionist, he had no inhibition about speaking his mind about the imperfections of less talented teammates, especially younger players. He was blamed for breaking the spirit of more than one young Phillies hopeful.

His impatience with the limitations of others was sometimes regarded with respect. One sportswriter compared Magee to Johnny Evers, who was so infamous for riding his teammates that he was nicknamed "The Crab."

"Magee, like Evers, has an unusual amount of baseball gray matter and spirit. The spirit plays for victories and is easily upset when 'bones' are pulled. Both men are continually bawling out their fellow players for bad play. They just can't help it. They don't mean to hurt anyone's feelings and are sorry after it is all over," he said.

In contrast, another scribe who followed his career observed: "Off the field, Sherry was a gentle, warm person who exhibited much wit and humor, abstained from hard liquor, and remained extremely popular."

Jim Hamilton of the *Oneonta Star* thought the Veteran's Committee members may have confused Sherry Magee with a contemporary player of lesser quality named Lee Magee, who was banned from baseball for life in 1919 for betting against his own team. Hamilton reported that for years it was thought that Sherry Magee was the banished player. (The memory of his run-ins with teammates and umpires probably reinforced that impression).

During Magee's tenure with the Phillies (1904–1914) they were usually a first-division team but never won the pennant, which was one cause of his frustration. Several observers credited him with keeping the Phillies from being "a hopeless tail-ender."

After the 1914 season, a year in which Magee, who served as team captain, led the league in runs batted in, hits, doubles, and slugging percentage, he was traded to the Boston Braves. The "Miracle Braves" had won the National League pennant in 1914 and went on to sweep Connie Mack's Philadelphia A's in the World Series. This looked like a great opportunity to finally get to the World Series. With typical Magee luck, the Braves finished second that year, seven games behind—of all teams—the Phillies.

As a reserve outfielder for the victorious Cincinnati Reds in the 1919 World Series that was tainted by the Black Sox scandal, Sherry Magee finally made his first and only appearance in the Fall Classic, getting a single in two pinch-hit appearances. That was his last year in the majors.

In 1928, the man who, along with John McGraw, was known as the most obnoxious umpire baiter in the game returned to the majors as, of all things, an umpire.

Philadelphia reporter Bill Dooly said: "His appointment at the time brought a reflective smile to the fans and players that recalled his ancient feuds with the umpires, but Sherry surprised the old-timers by his cool decisions on the field, the manner in which he ran his ball games, and the cleverness of his work."

When he died at age forty-four, a Philadelphia paper had this tribute to Sherry Magee: "He was one of the greatest natural hitters in the game. Magee was a past master of judging fly balls, a fine base runner, and full of so called 'inside baseball.'"

Elston (Ellie) Howard

C, OF, 1955–1968, Yankees, Red Sox

I f you want an idea of just how good a catcher Elston Howard really was, all you have to do is ask some of the guys who worked with him.

"Unless you pitched to him, you didn't know how good he was . . . how agile he was behind the plate," former reliever Hal Reniff says in *Baseball: The Biographical Encyclopedia*. Adds ex-lefty Yankee Bobby Shantz in the same book: "He got more strikes for his pitcher than any catcher I ever saw. When the ball hit his glove, it didn't move. His glove stayed right there. Most catchers give a little . . . the umpires can tell the difference between great ones and not-so-greats. They gave him the call. He was a pitcher's best friend."

And he meant so much to Yankee history. Elston Gene Howard, the first black to play for that great franchise that took too long to integrate, was also the first black to win the American League Most Valuable Player Award, which he did in 1963. Oh, for good measure, he was also the first black coach in the American League. Most people felt he was managerial material, but that crowning moment to his career never took place—a big-league career that began eight years after Jackie Robinson had broken the color barrier, in the same city.

"The Yankees claimed they were waiting for the right man," said former Yank Norm Siebern. "In retrospect, you'd have to say they couldn't have done better. He had great morals, personality, and character. He was an outstanding individual."

He wasn't a bad player, either.

Howard, who played the outfield for the Kansas City Monarchs in the Negro Leagues (his roommate was Ernie Banks) before the Yankees made him a catcher (Hall of Famer Bill Dickey was assigned to work with him in the minor leagues), got to the majors in 1955, at age twenty-six. He played fourteen

Elston Howard *at a glance*
• Nine straight All-Star selections
• Two-time Gold Glove winner
• AL MVP 1963
• 1958 World Series MVP
• 167 HRs, 762 RBIs in fourteen seasons

years, batted .274, with 167 homers and 762 RBIs—but those numbers don't really tell the story about Howard.

He made the All-Star team nine straight times from 1957–1965, won two Gold Gloves and followed the 1963 MVP by finishing third in the voting the following year—all while playing different positions on a Yankee team that also had a fella named Berra behind the plate. In 1958, Howard won the Babe Ruth Award as the Most Valuable Player of the World Series win over the Milwaukee Braves—one of his four Series titles.

Howard was a four-time All-Star before he became the Yankees regular catcher. There are stories out there he was a master at supplying the nicks on Whitey Ford's special pitches by making sure the baseball happened to hit the buckle on his shinguard as it was being returned to the Hall of Fame lefty.

"He was a steady player," recalls Jimmy Piersall. "He was older when he became a full-time catcher, but he was the best in the league. You feared Ellie when he came to the plate. He could hit to all fields and you didn't know where to play him."

Former reliever Dick Radatz, who didn't have trouble with a lot of hitters—especially right-handed ones—calls Howard "one of my toughest outs," and also talks of the power to all fields. Ex-reliever Bill Fischer says, "Ellie Howard was a good player—he was a star. He was a winning player, an All-Star. He was probably overlooked because of those great Yankee teams he played on. He was a leader; he took charge."

Howard, who played 54 games in ten World Series—the last with the Red Sox in 1967—hit .348 with 21 homers, 77 RBIs on that great 1961 Yankee team. In 1963, he batted .287 with 28 homers and 95 RBIs and earned that MVP honor. The following year, Howard hit .313, with 15 homers and 84 RBIs as the Yankees won the final pennant of the great run before the franchise began to go downhill.

In 1967, Howard was shipped to Boston for the final 42 games of the season. He only hit .147 for the Sox and went just 2-for-18 in the seven-game World

Series loss to the Cardinals. But his leadership was invaluable to a young team that came from nowhere to win the American League pennant. "I don't think I ever saw a pitcher shake off one of his signs," said Tony Conigliaro. "They had too much respect for him."

When Howard died in 1980 at just fifty years old, he was remembered fondly in a *New York Times* obituary. "Ellie was a permanent fixture in the Yankee picture," said former Yank executive Cedric Tallis. "He was one of the popular Yankees of all time." Added owner George Steinbrenner, who had brought Howard back to the Yankees as an administrative assistant after Howard's long coaching tenure with the team was interrupted by a year away: "We have lost a dear friend and a vital part of the organization. If indeed humility is the trademark of many great men, with that as a measure, Ellie was one of the truly great Yankees."

The late Dick Howser, the Yankee manager at the time of Howard's death, and a teammate and fellow coach with the team, may have said it best when he offered: "Elston exemplified the Yankee class of the 1950s and 1960s. Class was the way to describe the guy. He epitomized the Yankee tradition. Everybody in baseball respected the guy."

By the way, some of the Hall of Fame voters must have read the above obituaries and other tributes when Howard passed away. At the end of that year, he jumped from 29 Hall of Fame votes from the previous year to a high of 83—clearly becoming a better player in death than he was in life.

Wes Ferrell

P, 1927–1941, Indians, Red Sox, Senators,
Yankees, Dodgers, Braves

The melodrama that was Wes Ferrell's career had one of the most exciting and promising first acts in the history of baseball.

In 1929, the year stock market crashed, the Cleveland Indians pitcher exploded onto the baseball scene with a blazing fastball, Hollywood good looks, and a renowned temper that led to a career sprinkled with rebukes, fines, and suspensions. Ferrell remains today the only pitcher in the history of baseball to win at least 20 games in his first four full years in the majors. In 1929, he pitched a no-hitter against the St. Louis Browns and in 1930, he won 13 games in a row, then lost one, going on to win 7 more. He was also one of the best hitting pitchers of his time, a lifetime .280 hitter, he set the major league record with nine home runs in one season and 38 in his career. Ferrell had won two minor league batting championships as an outfielder.

In his early years with Cleveland, Ferrell, one of seven baseball-playing brothers who grew up in North Carolina, was the biggest gate attraction in the league besides Babe Ruth. Sportswriters said that his easy delivery and his command of a variety of pitches reminded them of Christy Mathewson. He possessed a self-confidence that bordered on arrogance, he was an intensely fierce competitor and he had a raging temper.

Ferrell hated losing more than most players. When he lost a game, he was likely to go into the clubhouse and tear his mitt to shreds. One time he had a new mitt he couldn't pull apart, so he ordered the batboy to get him a pair of scissors, and then he cut his mitt up into little pieces. One teammate estimated that Ferrell went through about ten mitts a year. His low boiling point led him to argue violently with anybody about anything, often with little or no provocation.

Wes Ferrell *at a glance*

- Six-time 20-game winner (including first four Major League seasons)
- No-hitter vs. Browns (1931)
- Led AL in victories (25) in 1935
- Led league in complete games four times and innings pitched three times
- .280 lifetime BA and 9 HRs in 1931, most by a pitcher (38 HRs lifetime)

When it was suggested to Yankees pitcher Lefty Gomez that Ferrell was temperamental, Gomez said: "I'd say he was 99 percent temperament and 1 percent mental."

Ferrell's career was also punctuated by conflicts with management and he came to be known as the perennial holdout. In 1931, when the Philadelphia A's were in the midst of a three-year run as the dominant team in baseball, Ferrell held out for six weeks demanding $8,000 more than the A's were paying their ace Lefty Grove (whom some experts believe was the greatest pitcher of all time). The following year, Ferrell refused to leave a game and was fined $1,500 and suspended for ten days by manager Roger Peckinpaugh for insubordination.

Prior to the 1933 season, after four consecutive 20-win seasons, Ferrell held out for $15,000, which management termed "preposterous." He finally signed a contract with performances clauses, which he didn't reach because he had injured his arm during the season and finished with an 11–12 record, his first non-20-win season. At mid-season, however, he was named to the American League team in the first All-Star Game held at Comiskey Park in Chicago.

When his next spring contract holdout lasted into the 1934 season, he was suspended and on May 25 he was traded to the Red Sox. Still under suspension, he had to be reinstated by Judge Landis in order for the trade to be completed. In Boston, he was united with his older brother and catcher, Rick. In 1984, Rick Ferrell was selected to the Hall of Fame by the Veteran's Committee, prompting several baseball historians to write that the wrong brother is in Cooperstown.

With Boston, Wes had a comeback season with a 14–5 record, though the sore arm had taken its toll on his fastball. He reinvented himself as a "junkball" pitcher, getting by on curves and assorted medium speed pitches. In 1935, he went back to his typical winning ways, posting a 25–14 record and leading the league in victories, games started, complete games, and innings pitched. Rick was more mild-mannered than his younger brother, and was somewhat of a calming influence on Wes, who needed calming because he could no longer rely on his trusty fastball.

Ferrell's temper, which had gotten him suspended and fined by Cleveland Manager Roger Peckinpaugh in 1931, once again erupted in 1936. This time it was Boston Manager Joe Cronin who fined him $1,000 and suspended him indefinitely for walking off the mound during a Yankee rally.

"I don't care if I never see Ferrell again," said Cronin.

Predictably, Ferrell was furious when told of the manager's remark and promised "I'm going to punch Cronin in the jaw as soon as I can find him."

Though he finished the year with a 20–15 record, the press paid more attention to his temper tantrums, which included thumbing his nose at the fans and kicking over water buckets in the dugout and dressing room.

During the 1937 season, the brothers Ferrell were dealt to the Senators for Bobo Newsom and Ben Chapman, and it didn't take long for Wes Ferrell to run afoul of manager Bucky Harris. After he said the "club was so cheap it wouldn't pay cab fares, the Senators released Wes Ferrell, even though his record was 13–8 at the time. After short stays with the Yankees and Dodgers, Ferrell's career ended with the Boston Bees (Braves) in 1941.

Later, as a minor league manager, showing that he hadn't lost his form, Ferrell slugged an umpire over a questionable decision and was suspended for a whole season.

Lew Burdette

P, 1950–1967, Yankees, Braves, Cardinals,
Cubs, Phillies, Angels

Hoo boy, did Lew Burdette ever make the Yankees sorry they gave up on him. Six years after they traded him to the Boston Braves for Johnny Sain, Burdette, as a member of the Milwaukee Braves, demolished the Yankees with one of the top pitching performances in World Series history.

Burdette won the 1957 World Series MVP award after tossing three complete-game victories, two of them shutouts, to lead the Braves to a 4–3 Series triumph. He beat the Mantle-Berra Bronx Bombers 4–2 in Game Two, pitched a 1–0 shutout against Whitey Ford in Game Five, and won Game Seven 5–0 to clinch the championship. In each outing, Burdette gave up seven hits. His Series ERA was 0.67.

Burdette claimed after the Series that he didn't get any particular satisfaction in beating his old team. "I can't go along with that revenge motive stuff," Burdette said at the time. "Because I'm the kind of guy that likes to beat anybody so much that there's no difference in what kind of letters they have on their uniforms or where they came from."

Even though Burdette had a brilliant career with the Braves, the trade has to go down in history as one that helped both clubs because Sain played a key role in three-straight Yankees championships.

In recalling his days in Yankees pinstripes, Burdette said, with some humor, that manager Casey Stengel didn't even know his name. "Whenever he wanted me, he'd yell over: 'Hey you, you, get in there and warm up.' It was always 'Hey you'; he never knew my name."

When he first arrived in the National League, Burdette was still a "hey you" for a while, but emerged as a reliable starting pitcher when the Braves moved

Lew Burdette *at a glance*

- 1957 World Series MVP (3 wins, 0.67 ERA, 2 shutouts)
- Two-time 20-game winner
- No-hitter vs. Phillies in 1960
- Led NL with 2.70 ERA and 6 shutouts in 1956
- Led NL with 21 wins, 39 games started, and 4 shutouts in 1959

to Milwaukee in 1953. In his first season in the midwest, "Nitro Lew," as he was called after his hometown of Nitro, West Virginia, established himself as the number two man on the staff behind Warren Spahn. In 1953, Burdette compiled a 15–5 record as the Braves developed into one of the great teams of the decade, with an offense that featured Hall of Famers Hank Aaron and Eddie Mathews. For the next decade, the lefty-righty duo of Spahn and Burdette formed the number one pitching tandem in the game.

During his time in Milwaukee, Burdette twice won 20 games and he had nine seasons of 15 or more victories. He led league with a 2.70 ERA in 1956, and was the league leader in complete games twice and in shutouts once. In two All-Star Games, Burdette allowed only one run in seven innings. In 1960, Burdette pitched a no-hitter against the Phillies.

A fine all-around athlete, he could be counted on to move the runners up with a bunt, was a swift base runner, and a pretty good hitter. Burdette was also known as a good team man because of his wit and penchant for practical jokes. Dick Groat, his teammate with the Cardinals in the 1960s, remembers Burdette affectionately as "wacky as a bedbug."

"Life was great to Lew Burdette. He just had fun," Groat said.

Groat was quick to point out that on pitching days Burdette was all business.

"He was a great, great competitor. He was a marvelous pitcher who won big game after big game," shortstop Groat said. "It was fun to play behind Lew. He knew how to pitch everybody and he wouldn't beat himself with bases on balls. He also pitched the way he said he was going to pitch before the game and made us better infielders because there were never any surprises. We knew how to position ourselves."

Burdette, who could get batters out with a variety of fastballs, screwballs, curves, sliders, and sinker balls—thrown at different speeds, overhand, three-quarter arm, and sidearm—was also accused of being one of the game's most notorious spitball pitchers. That suspicion was fueled by his habit of constantly fidgeting when he pitched. He had a full routine of mannerisms on each pitch and he kept up a steady stream of chatter—to himself, to his teammates, to the batter. According to former teammate Gene Conley in *The Ballplayers*, Burdette sometimes even talked to the ball.

Burdette was always cagey when he answered questions about his alleged spitter.

"I think there's a lot of psychology going for me," he said. "I fidget when I'm getting ready to pitch. Batters get it into their heads that I'm doing something tricky to the ball. So, they're more than half convinced that I'm throwing a spitter or something like that. The result is I get guys out on balls that merely may be rather ordinary sinkers."

One person who disagreed was Dodgers great Jackie Robinson: "He's got the best spitter I ever saw," said Robinson. "They call it a sinker, but I never saw a sinker act like that. Why, he struck me out once on a pitch that must have broken a foot. I missed it by eight inches."

In 1959, Burdette was the winning pitcher in one of the most storied games of all time when the Pirates' Harvey Haddix pitched a perfect game against the Braves for 12 innings, but lost on a Joe Adcock home run in the 13th.

When he was negotiating his 1960 contact, Burdette joked with the press that he was the greatest pitcher who ever lived.

"The greatest game that was ever pitched in baseball wasn't good enough to beat me, so I've got to be the greatest," he said.

Burdette retired in 1967 with a record of 203–44. He received some Hall of Fame support from the baseball writers, getting more than 80 votes five times, with a high of 97 in 1984.

We say he belongs in Cooperstown. Having Burdette join teammates Spahn, Mathews, and Aaron would be a fitting tribute to his career and appropriate recognition for the Milwaukee Braves, one of the great teams of its era and one of the most beloved teams of all time.

Alan Trammell

SS, DH, 1977–1996, Tigers

Alan Trammell admitted he was "somewhat disappointed." It's not that he expected to join Ozzie Smith in the Hall of Fame's class of 2002—but the former Tiger shortstop had trouble dealing with getting only 74 votes in his first year on the ballot. "Certainly, he should have been elected," Trammell said of Smith. "But I'm somewhat disappointed with the percentage I got [15.68]. It'll keep me on the ballot, but I was thinking that if I started with a base of about 40 percent, maybe I could work up from there. At 15 percent, it's not looking too good."

Simply speaking, Trammell is probably being overlooked in the Hall of Fame voting the way he was as a player—an underrated player in a career that saw him hit .285, with 185 homers and 1,003 RBIs. Solid numbers for a guy who made all the plays—and did so much more for a team, the only team he ever played for during a twenty-year career.

"I don't like to go just by the numbers," his old manager, Sparky Anderson, states in his autobiography. "I've seen some great shortstops—Dave Concepcion, Ozzie Smith, Cal Ripken, just to name a few. I'll take Trammell because of everything he can do.

"Smith is a wizard in the field and can do more with the glove; Ripken is stronger and hits with more power. But Trammell does everything. Trammell hits 15 homers a year, knocks in 90 runs a year, and plays around the .300 mark. In the field, he never botches a routine play."

And, teamed with second baseman Lou Whitaker for most of his career, he always did what Sparky needed him to do. "Trammell is not a home run hitter but because we were desperate for a cleanup hitter, I had to put Trammell there—and he came through all year long," Anderson says, looking back at 1987. "He finished with 28 homers and 105 RBIs. When it got down to nitty-gritty time in September, Trammell was there. He batted .416 for the month and knocked in 17 runs. We won the division on the last day of the season."

Alan Trammell *at a glance*

- .285 lifetime batting average
- Six-time All-Star
- Four-time Gold Glove
- 1984 World Series MVP
- 3 homers, 9 RBIs in eight postseason games
- Seven-time .300 season average

"I've watched this man for eleven years. I saw him when he earned $50,000 a year and now he earns $2 million a year—and he hasn't changed one bit. That's remarkable. That's the sign of a true pro."

Adds former Texas general manager Tom Grieve: "When I think of Alan Trammell, I think of a very steady player, a very dependable player, not a spectacular player, the kind of guy that makes all the routine plays. The kind of guy you would expect to be the captain of a team. The kind of guy that if there's a man on third base and less than two outs, you know he's gonna put the ball in play somewhere and get the run in.

"Maybe not the guy that's going to hit the three-run homer to win the game. Maybe not the guy that's going to go in the hole and come up and fire a rocket across the infield to get the guy, but the guy that will always make the double play, never boots a routine grounder, hits behind the runner, sacrifices the runner when he needs to.

"In other words, Alan Trammell, to me, is the kind of guy that you take for granted sometimes. A manager would absolutely love to have this guy because you pretty much, at the beginning of the season, you pencil him into the lineup, you bat him second, and you forget about him. He's going to play every day and you're always going to be happy with what he does.

"If you had to compare Trammell to [Smith and Ripken], I guess what kinda comes through is he wasn't as stylish and flashy as Ozzie, maybe couldn't make quite as many plays as Ozzie, but when there was a play he should make, I think he makes it just as much as Ozzie. With Ripken, he probably didn't have the power numbers that Ripken did.

"There's not one thing on the field that he didn't do well. He was an excellent base runner, he could steal a base. He's a manager's dream, without the gaudy stats. He probably never knocked in 90 runs, probably never hit 25 home runs, I couldn't even tell you how many times he hit .300 . . . he's not like a mediocre player, he's better than that. He's a frontline, star player."

Trammell, who hit .300 seven times, really did have only one big power year—that 1987 Anderson was talking about, which happened to be the year of the lively ball. Trammell also had 205 hits that year—and a .551 slugging average, finishing second to Toronto's George Bell in the Most Valuable Player voting. Trammell's Tigers nipped Bell's Blue Jays on the final day of the season for the AL East crown, then lost to the Twins in the playoffs.

In 1984, Trammell, a six-time All-Star and four-time Gold Glover, hit .314 with 13 homers and 60 RBI during the regular season and then went 13-for-31 with 3 homers and 9 RBI in eight postseason games, winning the World Series MVP award as the Tigers won it all for the first time since 1968.

"He was your typical, non-flashy, just get the ball and throw you out shortstop," says fellow shortstop Bucky Dent. "He just made all the plays, he had great hands, he had a real good throwing arm, as he got older he turned out to be a real outstanding offensive player. Defensively, he was very, very steady.

"He became a big offensive force. He was a tough out, he'd hit the ball all over the place, he'd hit for power and as he got older he just became an outstanding hitter. He and Whitaker came up together and they turned into an outstanding double play combination."

Johnny Sain

P, 1942, 1946–1955, Braves, Yankees, A's

I n recent years, there's been a groundswell of support for Johnny Sain's election to the Hall of Fame for his outstanding career as a pitching coach. Some regard him as the greatest pitching coach of all time. The legend of coach Johnny Sain, however, should not obscure the memory of Johnny Sain, the curveball pitcher of the Boston Braves and New York Yankees who won 20 games four times and played a key role on four pennant-winning teams.

After his great post–World War II seasons as a starting pitcher in Boston, the Havana, Arkansas, native reinvented himself as a reliever and spot-starter for Casey Stengel's Yankees dynasty teams of the early 1950s.

In 1948, the rallying cry for the pennant-winning Braves was "Spahn and Sain, then Pray for Rain." While Warren Spahn is deservedly honored as a member of "the Team of the Century," it was Johnny Sain who was the Braves ace that year. Sain led the league in victories (24), games started (39), complete games (28), and innings pitched (315).

He was also third in winning percentage (.615), ERA 2.60, and strikeouts (137). During the pennant drive, Sain, sometimes pitching on two days rest, tossed nine complete games in twenty-nine days, for a 7–2 record. The two games he lost were by scores of 2–1 and 1–0. Sain finished second to Stan Musial in the MVP voting that year.

The season was capped by a four-hit, Game One 1–0 shutout against the Cleveland Indians' Bob Feller in one of the great pitching duels in World Series history. The immortal Cy Young, who was in the stands that day, praised Sain's control and the variety of speeds and deliveries he showed the American League Champions.

"I think Sain is wonderful . . . He's a lot like some of us old-timers," said Young.

According to Hall of Famer Tris Speaker, Bob Feller's two-hitter was a masterpiece and would be "good for a victory 99 times out of 100." Speaker said

---

Johnny Sain *at a glance*

- Four-time 20-game winner
- In 1948 led NL in victories (24), games started (39), complete games (28), and innings pitched (314.2)
- Led AL in saves (22) in 1954
- Pitched 4-hit shutout over Cleveland (Bob Feller) in Game One of 1948 World Series
- Three-time All-Star
- Great hitting pitcher (.346 in 1947)

---

that Sain's assortment of curves and his control (he didn't walk a single man) reminded him of Christy Mathewson.

Sain subsequently lost Game Five by a score of 2–1 to Steve Gromek, but finished the Series with a 1.06 ERA and did not allow a single walk.

Although Cleveland went on to win the Series, that opening game victory remains one of the highlights of Johnny Sain's career. "I always try to minimize the importance of a game," he said. "But it was a thrill of a lifetime to beat a guy like Bob Feller."

To appreciate Sain's greatness, you must look beyond that one game or one season.

In 1946, Sain won 20 games (leading the league with 24 complete games) and he won 21 in 1947 (his 22 complete games tied Spahn, one behind league leader Ewell Blackwell). In three seasons, Sain completed 64 of his 65 victories. He pitched for the National League in both the 1947 and 1948 All-Star Games.

In 1949, he paid for the heavy workload of the pennant-winning season and slumped to 10–17, but rebounded with his fourth 20-victory season in 1950. After hurting his shoulder in 1951, Sain was given a new baseball life when Boston traded him to the Yankees for Lew Burdette. He rejoined Stengel, his manager in Boston in 1942.

"I told Casey that I'd do anything—spot start, relieve, pinch-hit," Sain said. "Casey and I had a great relationship. In later years he would tell everyone about how I carried the Yankee pitching staff in those years. I appreciated that, but remember, that staff had people like Ford, Reynolds, Raschi, and Lopat."

In his American League debut, Sain threw a five-hitter over Philadelphia. He went 2–1 down the stretch and his new teammates voted him a full World Series share.

In the offseason John went to Dallas for X-ray therapy (a never-before-used experimental remedy for major league pitchers) on his arm, a procedure he credits with extending his career.

"The therapy relieved the soreness in my shoulder and I was able to throw free and easy in Spring Training of '52," Sain said. He later recommended the treatment to Yankees teammates and several pitchers he coached.

He had three outstanding seasons with the Yankees, often winning key games against top contenders. He pitched in the World Series in both 1952 and 1953. His league-leading 22 saves in 1954 made him the only pitcher in history to lead one league in victories and the other in saves.

Sain finished his career in 1955 with Kansas City.

When his friend Ralph Houk took over the Yankee reins in 1961, he brought John along as his pitching coach.

Sain loves to talk about pitching, but he is especially proud of his record as a "good hittin' pitcher." His lifetime batting average is .245, with a high .353 in 1954. He is one of a handful of pitchers who have hit .300 and won 20 games in the same season. He led the National League with 16 sacrifice bunts in 1948 and struck out only twenty times in a career of 774 official at bats.

"I set a goal one year to go through an entire season without striking out, but I struck out once," he said, his disappointment undiminished by time.

Another source of great pride for Johnny Sain is his role as a footnote in baseball history. "I was the last one to pitch to Babe Ruth [in an exhibition game in New York in 1943] and the first one to pitch to Jackie Robinson," Sain said.

Sain was the Braves pitcher in Jackie's historical debut with the Dodgers in 1947. Robinson grounded out on his first at-bat. People often ask Sain if there was a great deal of excitement surrounding Robinson's first game.

"It was opening day, so there was excitement because of that, but I treated Jackie just like Pee Wee Reese and Pete Reiser and the rest of the Dodgers," Sain said.

Does Sain think he would have been given greater Hall of Fame consideration (he received a high of 153 votes in 1975) if he hadn't lost three years to World War II?

"The years in the service helped me become a pitcher," Sain said. "I played baseball wherever I went. I worked hard during those years and that's why I was ready to go in 1946."

Johnny Sain was one of the great control pitchers of his time; he knew how to work a hitter and win in the clutch. There's no reason why the Veteran's Committee can't look at his record as a player and combine it with his legacy as a pitching coach and grant him his deserved spot in Cooperstown.

George (Mule) Suttles

1B, OF, 1918–1944, Negro Leagues:
St. Louis Stars, Newark Eagles

Mule Suttles is a Negro League legend of Paul Bunyanesque proportions. The passing years enhance the legend and the cries of "Kick, Mule, kick!"—the chant that met Suttles each time he stepped to the bat—echo across the decades. Many Negro League players had vivid memories of Mule's epic home runs.

Buck O'Neil, who named Suttles the right fielder on his all-time Negro Leagues All-Star team, said: "Every team needs a long ball hitter and my team has Mule Suttles. When I say long ball, I mean *long* ball. In Havana one time Mule hit a ball that was measured at 600 feet, and they put a marker there to commemorate it."

Other former Negro Leagues greats recalled their favorite Suttles distance shots. Leon Day remembered Suttles hitting one over the fence in center field in Washington's Griffith Stadium. Ray Dandridge saw Mule hit one 500 feet to dead center in Memphis only to have the ball caught by the outfielder. There were several eyewitnesses to the time Suttles hit three home runs in one inning against the Memphis Red Sox.

O'Neil said that the biggest home run Suttles hit was in the 1935 East–West All-Star Game in Chicago, off Hall of Fame member Martin Dihigo.

The score was tied 8–8 in the bottom of the eleventh inning with two out and two men (Cool Papa Bell and Josh Gibson) on base. The right-handed hitting Suttles, who had been walked intentionally his first three times at bat, smashed a hard line drive that cleared the fence in right center field, giving the West team the victory, 11–8.

William G. Nunn, writing for the *Pittsburgh Courier* called the shot "one of the greatest in baseball." He said cheering momentarily stopped as the fans

George Suttles *at a glance*

- Five-time selection to Negro League East–West All-Star game
- Led St. Louis Stars Negro National League championship teams in 1928, 1930–1931
- Won Negro League batting title and home run title
- .329 lifetime BA
- .412 BA in All-Star Games
- Hit first All-Star Game home run (1933)

watched to see if it would clear the fence. When it bounced off an empty seat well beyond the fence "pandemonium broke loose." Players and fans mobbed Suttles as he completed his home run trot.

It was the second time in the three summer classics held up to that date in which Suttles had demonstrated his heroics. In the first game played in 1933, Suttles hit the first home run in All-Star Game history, a mighty fourth inning blow off Sam Streeter of the Pittsburgh Crawfords to give the West an 11–7 victory.

Suttles, who swung a thick forty-ounce bat, played in five East–West Games and hit for a .412 average, with the highest slugging average in the game's history at .882.

Chico Renfroe of the Kansas City Monarchs, who later worked as sports editor of the *Atlanta Daily World*, said Suttles had the most "raw power" of anyone he had ever seen.

"He went after the ball viciously," Renfroe said. "He wasn't a finesse player at all. He just overpowered the opposition."

Suttles grew up in Birmingham, Alabama, and worked in the coal mines as a young man while playing semi-pro ball on mining teams. In 1923, the muscular Suttles who stood over six feet tall, was signed by the Birmingham Black Barons. He was with the Black Barons, mostly as an outfielder, until 1926 when he went to play for "Candy" Jim Taylor's St. Louis Stars, teaming with Cool Papa Bell. Suttles walloped 27 home runs in his rookie year, a league record. He is also credited with league home run titles in 1937 and 1938. He helped lead the team to Negro National League pennants in 1928 and 1930, before the league had to be disbanded when the Great Depression hit.

For three years, Suttles and many other Negro National League veterans barnstormed with various teams, and then in 1933 he joined the Chicago

American Giants, playing for "Gentleman" Dave Malarcher, one of the fine third baseman and most successful managers in black baseball. Malarcher, who was a great teacher, helped Suttles shorten his swing, which improved Mule's batting average without sacrificing his electrifying power. As he got older, Suttles played more first base than outfield. Though he had above average quickness and agility for a man his size, Suttles was only an average fielder.

In 1936, Suttles came east to play for the Newark Eagles. He was the first baseman in the "Million Dollar Infield," with Dick Seay at second and Hall of Famers Willie Wells at shortstop and Ray Dandridge at third. Suttles had several of his most productive years in Newark and stayed with the Eagles until 1941.

Suttles was often recruited for barnstorming tours, many against teams made up of white major leaguers. Records show that he had a .374 lifetime batting average in these exhibition games.

In one game, Suttles hit a single, double, and triple off Cubs pitcher Jim Weaver. When he came up to the plate for the fourth time, Weaver asked shortstop Leo Durocher for advice on how to pitch to him. Durocher answered "Just Pitch and Pray."

Suttles was a friendly, gentle man who could tell a good story and had a positive outlook on life. As he got older and the press began to question him about retirement, Suttles said: "Don't worry about the Mule going blind, just load the wagon and give me the lines."

Suttles retired as a full time player in 1941 with a .329 batting average and 190 recorded home runs, the highest of any Negro League player. He was named manager of the Eagles in 1943 and stayed in that position for several years. He was regarded as a fine leader and a patient batting instructor.

The memories of Suttles are dominated by stories of his tremendous power. Hall of Fame first baseman Buck Leonard of the Homestead Grays summed it up when he named Suttles the hardest hitter he had ever seen.

"In my opinion, Mule could hit the ball just as far as anybody—Josh, John Beckwith, or Babe Ruth—or anybody," Leonard said.

Cesar Cedeno

OF, 1B, 1970–1986, Astros, Reds,
Cardinals, Dodgers

Legendary manager Leo Durocher once predicted Cesar Cedeno would be "the next Willie Mays," even saying Cedeno was "better than Willie Mays at the same age." And while it's true Leo had a tendency to overstate his case on certain things, talent-wise he wasn't far off on this one.

Others hailed Cedeno as a new Clemente, prompting a young Cedeno to say, "Harry [Walker, his first big-league manager, with the Houston Astros, before Durocher took over] told me I might be Clemente some day. So I told him, 'That might be hard to do. I know Clemente, I might be something like him, but, ha, not like him. There is only one Clemente.'"

As it turned out, Cedeno, a Dominican signed by the Astros at age sixteen, had enough trouble just being Cedeno.

You wouldn't know it by his career numbers, and the general consensus is Cedeno wasn't, to borrow a phrase, all he could have been. But he was a true athlete who could do some very special things on a baseball field.

"He was an electric player," says fellow "Out by a Stepper" Joe Torre. "He could do it all. He had all the tools of Mays—he could run, he could throw people out, he could hit a home run."

But he just never achieved what he could have achieved.

"You look at him and you look at [Dave] Parker and you look at [Darryl] Strawberry, Richie Allen—they just found the life a little too tough," says Rusty Staub, also a member of this list. "Whether it was this temptation or that temptation, he did not end up as great a player as everyone thought he should have been. It's like [Mickey] Mantle—the secret is to grind every day and when you finish to know you did not shortchange yourself or your teammates."

Cesar Cedeno *at a glance*

- Five straight Gold Gloves
- Four-time All-Star
- 550 stolen bases
- Had back-to-back .320 seasons, hitting 47 homers, stealing 111 bases
- Just 9-for-51 with no homers, one RBI in seventeen postseason games

"He left a lot on the field. The potential that was there was awesome. He certainly had Hall of Fame potential. But this is life and nothing works out perfect in life."

"He had every tool there was," says former teammate Art Howe. "He could beat you in any way—defense, speed, hitting, hitting with power. He had it all—as gifted a player as I ever played with.

"And a great guy. I thought the world of CC. CC was kinda misunderstood by a lot of people, I think, but when he put the uniform on, he played hard."

Cedeno hit .285 with 199 homers and 976 RBIs during a seventeen-year career that actually ended with stints in St. Louis and Los Angeles. (He played the bulk of his games with Houston before moving on to Cincinnati.) He had back-to-back .320 seasons with the Astros in 1972 and 1973, hit 47 homers (in a ridiculously tough home park, the Astrodome, which people were calling "Cesar's Palace" back then), and stole 111 bases over those two seasons—111 of the 550 he swiped in a career that included five Gold Gloves in center field.

It was after the 1973 season that Cedeno got into trouble—serious trouble. His girlfriend was shot and killed during a struggle with Cedeno for a gun she asked to see in a hotel room in Santo Domingo. Cedeno was first charged with voluntary manslaughter but it was later found that nineteen-year-old Altagracia de la Cruz had pulled the trigger. Cedeno paid a fine and was free but the incident scarred his entire career.

Through it all, through people always saying he should have been even better, Cedeno was a special player to watch.

"He was a great athlete," says Larry Bowa.

"He didn't hit that many home runs but the Astrodome was enormous," offers Torre. "Then he got that second life with the Cardinals and did a hell of a job for them."

Torre was talking about a twenty-eight-game stay with the Cardinals at the end of the 1985 season, during which Cedeno hit a sizzling .434 and helped St.

Louis into the postseason. But Cedeno went just 2-for-12 in the National League Championship Series and 2-for-15 in the World Series as the Cards came up short in a seven-game Series loss to the Kansas City Royals (Cedeno played one more year with the Dodgers after that).

The poor postseason capped an inauspicious playoff and World Series career for Cedeno, who went just 9-for-51 with no homers, one run batted in, and one run scored in seventeen postseason games—another thing that didn't endear him to those evaluating his overall career performance.

"Unfortunately, for people who want to look back on your career, everyone has to say [with Cedeno], 'gee, he should have been a better player for a longer period of time,'" says Staub. "He was a very, very good player for a shorter period of time."

No, he wasn't Clemente. There was only one Clemente. And, in many ways, there was only one Cesar Cedeno.

(Pistol) Pete Reiser

OF, 1940–1942, 1946–1952, Dodgers, Braves, Pirates, Indians

"P istol Pete" Reiser, the Dodgers' center fielder in the 1940s, might have been the equal of Mays, DiMaggio, or Musial. However, Reiser's career was severely shortened by the cumulative effect of numerous injuries, many resulting from violent collisions with outfield walls.

Pee Wee Reese thought that if the supremely aggressive Reiser "didn't get hurt, he was as good as Musial."

Former Dodgers' vice president and general manager Buzzie Bavasi claimed that Reiser was the greatest he ever saw. "Pete might have been the best of all of them, including DiMag," Bavasi said. "He could do it all, a true five-tool player. Joe couldn't run with him. Reiser had more power and he hit from both sides of the plate and could throw equally well with both hands. He was the fastest and the strongest guy in the game. The only trouble is, he didn't do it long enough. He was more than aggressive. He was reckless."

Anyone who saw Reiser as a rookie for the 1941 pennant-winning Dodgers would agree with these evaluations. On a Dodgers team that Larry McPhail loaded with stars, Pistol Pete was the brightest. He won the batting crown, hitting (.343), had the top slugging average (.558), and scored the most runs (117). He also led the league in doubles (39) and triples (17).

Originally property of the St. Louis Cardinals, Reiser was one of the minor league players set free when Commissioner Landis decided that Branch Rickey was stockpiling players in the Cardinals system.

Reiser was signed by the Dodgers and brought up at the end of the 1940 season as a third baseman. Manager Leo Durocher recognizing Pistol Pete's talents, made him his regular center fielder the following spring.

Pete Reiser *at a glance*

- Youngest ever NL batting champion in 1941 with .343
- In 1941 led NL in SA (.558), doubles (39), triples (17), and Rs (117)
- Two-time NL stolen base leader (1941–1942)
- Stole home seven times (set major league record)
- Three-time All-Star
- Three-time .300 hitter, lifetime .295 BA

Even Reiser's spectacular rookie year was interrupted by injuries. In April, he was hit in the face by a pitch thrown by Ike Pearson of the Phillies and was carried unconscious from the field. He missed just a week with a concussion.

A little more than a week after his return, Reiser injured his back leaping against an iron-door exit, to rob Enos Slaughter of an extra-base hit. That injury put him down for five games.

But his recklessness and misfortune were just getting started.

The following season Pete was atop the league with a .361 average at the All-Star break and for the second year in a row started for the National League in the mid-summer classic.

Then nine days later, he crashed into the concrete wall in St. Louis, again chasing an Enos Slaughter shot. As Reiser lay on the field unconscious, Slaughter circled the bases for an inside-the-park homer. Reiser woke up the next day in the hospital and had no recollection of the play. He suffered from dizzy spells for the remainder of his career.

Against doctors' orders, Reiser was back in the lineup less than a week later, but he continued to suffer from headaches and nausea. The Dodgers were leading the league by ten games in early August, but the Cardinals were coming fast. By the end of the month he again missed about a week as the Cardinals moved into first place and their catcher Walker Cooper took over the league lead in batting. The Cards won an amazing forty-three of their last fifty-one games to win the pennant.

The following year, despite headaches and dizziness, Reiser was drafted and played baseball in the Army for three prime years of his career. Playing ball in the service, he suffered several injuries including a damaged right shoulder chasing a ball through a hedge and into a gully.

After the war Reiser was never the same, the injuries had turned him into a part-time player. He lasted three years with the Dodgers, leading the league in stolen bases in 1946 with 34, and hitting .309 the following year, but he continued to be dogged by the injury jinx.

In June of 1947, Reiser went after a fly ball, and once again his head crashed violently into the concrete wall. Again, he was carried from the field on a stretcher. In the clubhouse, the injury appeared so serious that a priest gave Pistol Pete last rites of the Catholic Church.

There was no fracture, but an increasingly dizzy and groggy Reiser soon returned to the Dodgers lineup. But, the calamities continued. He was injured in an outfield collision during fielding practice and was also forced to miss a few days when he dislocated his left shoulder trying to make a shoestring catch.

Reiser started in center field in the 1947 World Series against the Yankees. In the third game he walked in his first at-bat and then broke his ankle sliding into second base. Later in the Series, with his ankle taped, Reiser made an appearance as a pinch hitter, was intentionally walked and removed for a pinch runner.

Before the next season, the Dodgers covered the outfield walls with foam rubber, and that year teams began laying down dirt warning tracks for the protection of outfielders headed for the wall. Padded walls and warning tracks are Pete Reiser's legacy.

By 1948, at just twenty-nine-years-old, Pete Reiser was a shadow of the player who broke in so spectacularly seven years earlier. His skills were severely eroded by the numerous injuries, and he bounced around the majors, playing for the Braves and Pirates and finishing his career with the Indians in 1952.

Leo Durocher said of Reiser, "If he hadn't been hurt you'd probably be talking about him the rest of your natural born life. I think Willie Mays was the best I ever saw, but Pete might have been better. He hit from both sides like Mickey Mantle and had the same kind of power. He fully flew down to first base. He had everything but luck."

Bavasi said that if they had padding on the walls in those days "Pete Reiser would not be forgotten; he'd be in the Hall of Fame."

Al Oliver

OF, 1B, DH, 1968–1985, Pirates, Rangers, Expos, Giants, Phillies, Dodgers, Blue Jays

When the Los Angeles Dodgers acquired thirty-eight-year-old Al Oliver prior to the 1985 season, there was no way for Tommy Lasorda to know how much the veteran with 2,676 hits had left in the tank. "We know one thing for sure," Lasorda said at the time, "the guy can hit."

As it turned out, there were only 67 hits left in Oliver's bat, leaving him at 2,743 lifetime to go with a .303 average. And now, all these years later, you ask people about Oliver, and they say what Lasorda did. "He could hit. Excellent hitter, really excellent hitter," says Lou Piniella.

Adds Joe Torre, "Boy, Al Oliver could hit!"

And Cito Gaston? "Great hitter."

Yet this man who finished 257 hits shy of that magic 3,000 mark isn't really remembered for being as good as he really was. Maybe it was the shadow of Roberto Clemente and Willie Stargell in Pittsburgh, or hitting only 219 homers in a power position. Or his poor defense. Whatever it was, people tend to shrug off what Oliver did as a three-decade player—people outside the game, anyway.

"He could hit!" recalls Tom Grieve. "Al Oliver is a guy that deserves [recognition] . . . he had, what, 2,700, 2,800 hits? Nobody ever talks about this guy. He didn't have the power but you want to talk just as a hitter—man, that son of a gun was a good hitter. He was one of the best hitters that I played against."

"When I saw him with the Pirates, he was a tremendous player," says Cookie Rojas. "If he would have gotten those 3,000 hits, he definitely would have been in the Hall of Fame."

Torre says 3,000 hits would have meant "All of a sudden, people perceive him differently. It's like the 300 wins. You have pitchers that go in automatically

---

Al Oliver *at a glance*

- Hit .300 for the season eleven times, including nine-straight years
- NL batting title 1982
- 2,743 career hits
- .303 lifetime hitter
- Made 139 errors in back-to-back minor league seasons, earning nickname "Scoop"

---

with 300 wins but if you're short, all of a sudden they're gonna say all the reasons that you shouldn't be in—well, you lost so many games, this and that. Three thousand hits—he would have had to be in the Hall of Fame."

As a hitter. His nickname, "Scoop," was given to him after he made 139 errors in two minor-league seasons. "He was more of a one-dimensional guy, more of an offensive player than an all-around player," Torre says. "His numbers were great but never to the point (of being Hall of Fame material). He was a terrific hitter and could run.

"He was part of the Lumber Company—that whole group. I don't think they ever worried about taking ground balls or fly balls because they scored so many runs."

Oliver hit .300 or better nine-straight years from 1976 to 1984 and had a .300 batting average eleven times. But he hit 20 homers only twice in his career and also drove in 100 runs but twice en route to 1,326 lifetime RBIs. He also didn't hit much in the postseason, batting .228 in 28 games—albeit with 17 RBIs in those games and a big three-run homer in the 1971 NLCS win over San Francisco. He had two game-winning hits for the Blue Jays in the 1985 ALCS, but retired after that season when the Jays released him—after Bobby Cox pinch-hit for him in the fifth game of that series, which hurt a proud hitter like Oliver.

His only World Series was 1971, when he went 4-for-19 for the Pirates as they won the Series over Baltimore.

His best year was 1982, when he won a batting title by hitting .331 with 22 home runs and 109 RBIs for the Montreal Expos, who picked him up from Texas and played him at first base (the Rangers had moved him from left field to the designated-hitter spot). The 109 RBIs tied Dale Murphy for the National League lead.

"Playing against him, I thought he was going to kill a pitcher sometime because he hit the ball up the middle as much as anybody I'd ever seen," says fellow Out by a Stepper Alan Trammell. "He'd hit line drives that would whiz by the pitcher's head—I thought one day he might hurt somebody because he hit the ball so hard."

"He had a really, really good swing," says Piniella. "He could hit the ball left-center, right-center, with power as well as anybody. He had that unique hitting style with a little leg kick—one of the first that really brought that front leg kick into play. He had no particular weaknesses at home plate—he'd hit left-hand pitching and right-hand pitching and early in his career he was a fairly adept outfielder.

"You look at the numbers and what he's done, he's another guy that needs to be considered—but you look at that era and there were a hell of a lot of out-fielders that were big names."

Gaston remembers another side of Oliver. "He certainly believed in himself," he says. "Once in a while I'll use Al as a great example for some of these guys about believing in yourself. If you don't believe in yourself, who's gonna believe in you? I see a lot of great players that talk about themselves and believe in themselves and Al was that way. When he walked to that plate, he would prove it. If he told you he was going to do something, it would happen."

Adds Trammell: "He was very confident. It's no coincidence when you talk to good hitters, not only are they good but they have the confidence."

J. R. Richard

P, 1971–1980, Astros

Art Howe didn't get to play all that much when he was backing Richie Hebner up in Pittsburgh. But Howe always knew there was at least one game he'd get to play.

"Hebner was a left-handed hitter and J. R. [Richard] was a right-handed pitcher," Howe says, looking back. "[Hebner] didn't want to face him. I'm a right-handed hitter and that was one of the games I got to play.

"I said, 'Hack [Hebner's nickname], what's the deal, man?' He said, 'I ain't facing that son of a bitch.' He'd say a couple of days before, 'I think my back's hurting a little bit, I'm not gonna be ready to play.'"

"That wasn't fair of Hebner—he should leave those bad backs to right-handed hitters," says old right-handed hitter Joe Torre.

But that's the way people felt about James Rodney Richard, the enormous righty many hitters felt was the most dominating pitcher of his time—a time that included Nolan Ryan.

"He had the ability to throw a no-hitter every time he walked out to the mound," says former outfielder—and right-handed hitter—Tom Paciorek. "You thought he would [throw a no-hitter] because you knew you weren't going to get a hit off him. You just maybe hoped he walked you or didn't hit you. The main thing you didn't want to get was hit by him.

"He got great control as he got older. He became one of the really great pitchers in the game. It's just a shame he didn't last longer. He'd have had to win 30 games a couple of times with that kind of stuff. He was scary."

Pitching for the Houston Astros, Richard never won 30 games. He won 20 once and then had three-straight 18-win seasons, becoming the first National League pitcher of the century with 300 strikeouts in a season in 1978, and then doing it again in 1979 (when he also led the league with a 2.21 ERA). That was before a stroke almost killed him in 1980. Richard, who stood 6'8" and was

J. R. Richard *at a glance*

- Led NL in strikeouts 1978–1979
- 107–71 lifetime record
- Career ended by a stroke 1980
- 84–54 over his last five years
- All-Star in 1980
- Led NL in ERA 1979

listed at 222 pounds, was 10–4 after 17 starts in 1980 when his world came tumbling down in his tenth year in the majors.

"Oh wow! Who knows what that could have been?" says Torre. "He was [Bob] Gibson. He was very intimidating as a pitcher. When you looked at the upcoming assignments, if you were going in there to play, you wanted to see if you missed him or not."

"That was shame that his career was cut short because he certainly was one of those pitchers that would sell tickets."

Before he was diagnosed—before he almost died on the Astrodome turf—Richard was accused of all kinds of things, because, frankly, people didn't think there was anything wrong with him. He was winning. But there was something very wrong. It almost took his life. As it was, it ended his baseball career (he later wound up homeless) at 107–71, with 1,493 strikeouts in 1,606 innings.

But look at his last five years—an 84–54 record with 1,163 Ks in 1,239 innings. He was thirty when it all ended.

"When I faced him, he was wild," says Howe, who became Richard's teammate. "You didn't dig in against him. It took him several years to corral all that. The last couple of years I played with him he was the most dominant pitcher in our league. I was glad I was on his side."

Richard combined a devastating fastball with a slider that was even tougher—a pitch that ate you up because the big frame looked like it was so close to home plate—like Randy Johnson is today, from the other side.

"I've seen Nolan, I've seen [Tom] Seaver, I've seen Gibson; I've never seen a slider as hard as he threw," says Larry Bowa. "Pete Rose, who I admire a lot as a hitter, told me he was thinking of hitting right-handed against him because that slide just ate him up. [Mike] Schmidt and [Greg] Luzinski were [Phillies] power hitters who wanted no part of him. I mean, they played, but they said, 'this guy's unbelievable!'"

Howe bristles at the theories that were being tossed around when Richard went down. People questioned whether Richard wanted to pitch, and they did not understand what was wrong with him (no one really knew what was wrong as a blood clot threatened his life). "I can't understand why they'd even think that because he was there through the lean years—he'd never missed a start and he always wanted to battle when he was with a lousy team. Finally, we had a good team [with Ryan in the same rotation] and he wanted to be part of it because he was our top pitcher. Even counting Nolie.

"He would come out in the fourth inning and say, 'my arm is dead.' But he had just thrown a 94-mile-an-hour slider. Guys would look at the velocity and say, 'how can there be anything wrong with your arm if you're throwing the ball that hard?' But he could feel something that was wrong. There was numbness in his arm."

Richard finally collapsed on the field. "Fortunately, we had our trainer there or he would have been gone," Howe says, shaking his head.

The whole thing was sad—but not as sad as Richard being discovered living on the streets of Houston years later. We are reminded of what might have been, of how we were deprived of the chance to see where this big guy would have wound up among the all-time greats of this game.

Bob (Indian Bob) Johnson

OF, 1933–1945, A's, Senators, Red Sox

Who knows? If the stock market hadn't crashed in 1929, Indian Bob Johnson might be in the Hall of Fame. How can we make this claim? Let's go back to the beginning.

It's part of baseball lore how Connie Mack, in his fifty years of running the Philadelphia A's, twice assembled teams that are rated among the best in American League history, and twice he had to dismantle these multi-pennant-winning teams for financial reasons.

First there was his 1910–1914 club that won four pennants and three World Series and featured Hall of Fame pitchers Eddie Plank and Chief Bender and the "$100,000 Infield" with Home Run Baker and Eddie Collins. When the Federal League came into existence and players' salary demands became too much for "the Grand Old Man's" purse, he promptly unloaded most of his players and finished rock bottom in 1915, remaining in the cellar until 1922 when the A's leaped to seventh place.

Then there was a gradual improvement through the decade as he acquired future Hall of Fame material and in 1929 replaced the Yankees as the juggernaut atop the league's standings. The great A's teams that featured Lefty Grove, Jimmie Foxx, Mickey Cochrane, and Al Simmons won three-straight pennants and two out of three World Series. In 1932, the A's finished second, but the country was so far into the Depression that Mack couldn't compete financially and once again started selling his players. This time the decline was more gradual—third place in 1933, fifth place in 1934, and by 1935 the Athletics were back as perennial residents of the low-rent district.

Mack always managed to make his money, if not from gate receipts and World Series shares, then from the sale of ballplayers. The traded athletes also

---

Bob Johnson *at a glance*

- Seven-straight seasons with 100 RBIs (eight career)
- Five-time .300 BA
- Nine-straight seasons with 20 HRs
- Ten seasons with 90-plus runs scored
- Seven-time All-Star
- 6-for-6 in a game (1934)
- 6 RBIs in one inning (home run and double) in 1937

---

did well with their new ball clubs. Who then, besides some heartbroken Philly fans, suffered from Connie Mack's Depression-era business dealings? Indian Bob Johnson, that's who. The sturdy Oklahoman who toiled in the Philadelphia outfield for a decade, rarely seeing first in the division, was the victim of history and economics.

Indian Bob (or Cherokee Bob, even though he claimed to be only one-thirty-second, Native American) arrived on the scene in 1933 and made an auspicious debut, hitting .290 with 21 homers as the team finished third. Al Simmons, Jimmy Dykes, and Mule Haas had already been dealt to the White Sox for $100,000. Before the 1934 season, Mickey Cochrane was the player-manager of Detroit and Lefty Grove and second baseman Max Bishop were sent to Boston, a pair of trades that netted Mack $225,000. As they always say, that was big money in those days. Finally, after the A's sunk to last place in 1935, the great slugger Jimmie Foxx was sent to the Red Sox for a couple of marginal players and $150,000. The dismantling of the great powerhouse A's was complete. What could have been a dynasty wasn't, and Bob Johnson, who could have been a key batsman in one of baseball's most feared lineups, labored impressively but in relative obscurity for the remainder of his career.

As it was, Johnson, whose older brother Roy was also a major league outfielder, put together impressive numbers and was respected by his peers and by A's fans ("both of them," as someone said). He had a .296 lifetime batting average (five times over .300), 2,051 hits, 1,283 RBIs (seven-straight seasons over 100), 1,239 runs scored (six times over 100 and four more over 90), 288 homers (nine times over 20), a slugging average of .506, and an on-base percentage of .393. Johnson was also walked about 90 times a season because opposing pitchers could easily pitch around him. Although he never led the league, he was usually near the leaders in the offensive production categories. Johnson was also regarded as a good runner, and an above average fielder with a strong arm. He was chosen for eight All-Star Games in his career.

His career highlights also included a 26-game hitting streak in 1934, the same year that he went 6-for-6 in a game with 2 home runs and 2 doubles. In 1937, he set a major league record with 6 runs batted in in one inning on a grand slam and a double.

Washington Manager Bucky Harris once said of Johnson, who got the only hit in three one-hitters: "That guy should have led the league both in hitting and runs batted in. But with the A's there was rarely anybody on base to drive home, and because there was nobody behind him in the lineup with any batting power, Bob had to keep hitting at bad balls. Connie Mack always figured there was more percentage in letting Johnson hit at a bad ball then letting the next batter hit at a good one."

According to sportswriter Shirley Povich, Johnson "used to go back to his outfield job and seethe at the spectacle of the bums in the A's infield, giving back to the opposition some of the runs he had slugged home."

After ten years with the A's, Johnson had a falling-out with Mack over (what else?) money, and was shipped to Washington. He spent one year in the nation's capital and, at age thirty-seven, was sent to the Red Sox, where he would have finally had the opportunity to bat in a lineup of good hitters. Except the war was on and regulars Ted Williams, Dom DiMaggio, and Johnny Pesky were serving their country, soon to be joined by Bobby Doerr and Jim Tabor. The team finished fourth in 1944 with Johnson hitting .324 and driving in 106 runs (second in the league behind the Browns' Vern Stephens). The following year his abilities diminished. Indian Bob was sent packing, but again the timing was awful. In 1946, everyone returned from the military and the Red Sox won the pennant.

Because the reserve clause shackled him to the lowly Athletics for his best years, Johnson, who was one of the great players of his time, missed out on the glory and the financial rewards that would have come his way had he played for winners. While he never pitied himself, he sometimes wondered how it could have been.

"If I'd played with stronger teams, I might have left some real records," he told *Baseball Digest* near the end of his career. "I'd like to have played for the Yankees when they were on top. Pitchers couldn't have concentrated on me so much."

Dave Stewart

P, 1978–1995, Dodgers, Rangers,
Phillies, A's, Blue Jays

No one has to tell the Boston Red Sox how good Dave Stewart was—especially in big games.

"In a four- or five-year period, he was as good as anybody that's ever played the game," says Wade Boggs, whose teams were swept out of the American League playoffs in 1988 and 1990, with Stewart going 3–0 in those two Series. "When you needed the big game won, he did it.

"He was probably the Bob Gibson of his era—the intimidating look, the focus, and if it's a playoff game, he just stepped it up. We played against him in '88 and '90 and he beat Roger [Clemens] four times [actually three, and Clemens was only 0–1 in those decisions]. It was lights out!"

For his career, Stewart, who also handed Clemens his second-straight loss after "the Rocket" started 14–0 in 1986 (the very first of Stewart's 124 Oakland wins [counting postseason] coming just after the Phillies had released him and he was a twenty-nine-year-old pitcher with no future), was 10–6 in the postseason. But that record doesn't show his dominance as the 1980s gave way to the 1990s. Stewart lost his first two postseason decisions, as a reliever with the Dodgers in 1981. He then went 10–4 the rest of his postseason career, was twice named ALCS Most Valuable Player, and also was MVP of the 1989 World Series. Oh, and he was 8–0 with a 2.03 ERA in five American League Championship Series in ten starts.

"I had the pleasure to play with Dave in the 1990 World Series," says Willie Randolph. "To me, there was no better big-game pitcher. You're talking about focus, you're talking about just being able to lock into your situation and your job and wanting the ball.

Dave Stewart *at a glance*

- Two-time ALCS MVP
- World Series MVP in 1989
- 10–6 postseason record
- 8–0, 2.03 ERA in five ALCS
- 1989 All-Star

"It's been well-chronicled, his stare, his zone—and he was the best at that. He came a long way—he wasn't a great pitcher all through his career, he made himself what he [became]."

Randolph's right. The Dodgers, Rangers (twice), and Phillies all saw Stewart come and go, much of that time spent as a reliever who also had some off-field trouble. He wound up in Oakland in 1986 and went 9–5 working with new pitching coach Dave Duncan. Then came a four-year stretch as good as any you'll find: 20–13, 21–12, 21–9, and 22–11. It all just clicked—Stewart (93) trailing only Clemens (100) in AL wins from 1986 to 1990. Stewart, who threw a no-hitter in 1990, began to wind down after that and finished 168–129 lifetime, but he could still pitch in the big games right down until the end.

"When we got Dave, of course he didn't have the same stuff he had in Oakland," says Cito Gaston, his manager with the champion Blue Jays in 1993. "But he pitched with a lot of heart, a lot of guts, and he'd battle you every day out there.

"He's certainly a Hall of Fame candidate for me, just the fact, his makeup. He's a winner . . . I'm a big fan of Dave Stewart."

Gaston was still playing when Stewart, who would go on to become a coach and executive, arrived in the National League. The book said the guy always had a good arm but it never worked until, Gaston says, "It clicked."

And he always had that look.

"He had that intimidation on his face all the time which I think really helps a pitcher," says Lou Piniella. "Very serious, get-in-your-face-type pitcher. In the years that he really came into prominence in Oakland . . . what people don't realize is that he could hit a gnat's ass with a fastball and with a slider at the same time—and then have the ability that if he fell behind in the count he could throw the ball by you because he threw the ball 94–95 miles an hour.

"Tremendous competitor, tremendous stuff. It wasn't a comfortable four at-bats off him. He could pitch and he could think out on the mound. He knew what he wanted to do with the baseball."

Adds long-time pitching coach Bill Fischer: "For five years, he was probably the best pitcher around. And those were good clubs he pitched for. Roger
couldn't beat him—he beat Roger every time in the big games. Roger's record
against Oakland was pretty good except for Stewart. [Stewart] was a dominant
pitcher there for five years."

Clemens, interviewed for this book, really didn't have much to say, basically using the "I don't face the opposing pitcher" angle—but anyone who
knew him during that time knew how frustrated Clemens was with losing to
Stewart and the A's all the time.

"For the years he had in Oakland, he had as good a stuff as anybody I've
ever seen," says former infielder turned scout and coach Cookie Rojas.
"Tremendous forkball, he had a good fastball, a good slider. When he was with
Texas and the other clubs, it seemed like his control was not there. When he
came to Oakland, it seemed like he finally found himself, then had great command of that strike zone—up, down, in, and knew the hitters very well."

Says Randolph: "He was one of those guys who when you want to get that
one win—when you needed that big, big win, you felt comfortable with the ball
in his hands. I mean, he was pitching against guys in that era, Clemens and
those guys who were supposed to be the real big dogs, but he always seemed
to beat them. They had some great teams back then but Stew was the kind of
guy a lot of people feared because he was such a hell of a competitor and a
good athlete. For one game, you might have given the ball to him."

It would be hard to argue with the selection.

6 Ron Santo

Ron Santo. Courtesy of George Brace

7 Dave Parker

Dave Parker. Courtesy of Topps Company, Inc.

9 Maury Wills

Maury Wills. Courtesy of George Brace

10 Jack Morris

Jack Morris. Courtesy of Ron Vesely

12 Ken Boyer

Ken Boyer. Courtesy of George Brace

13 Goose Gossage

Goose Gossage. Courtesy of New York Yankees

14 Raleigh Mackey

Raleigh (Biz) Mackey. Courtesy of Negro Leagues Baseball Museum

15 Joe Gordon

Joe Gordon. Courtesy of George Brace

16 Ron Guidry

Ron Guidry. Courtesy of New York Yankees

18 Thurmon Munson

Thurmon Munson. Courtesy of New York Yankees

19 Luis Tiant

Luis Tiant. Courtesy of Boston Red Sox

20 Roger Maris

Roger Maris. Courtesy of New York Yankees

22 Andre Dawson

Andre Dawson. Courtesy of Ron Vesely

24 Dom DiMaggio

Dom DiMaggio. Courtesy of Boston Red Sox

26 Carl Mays

Carl Mays. Courtesy of Boston Red Sox

27 Bobby Bonds

Bobby Bonds. Courtesy of Topps Company, Inc.

30 Al Rosen

Al Rosen. Courtesy of George Brace

33 Minnie Minoso

Minnie Minoso. Courtesy of Chicago White Sox

35 Billy Pierce

Billy Pierce. Courtesy of Chicago White Sox

39 Ted Simmons

Ted Simmons. Courtesy of Milwaukee Brewers

42 Ted Kluszewski

Ted Kluszewski. Courtesy of George Brace

47 Elston Howard

Elston Howard. Courtesy of New York Yankees

51 Johnny Sain

Johnny Sain with Hall of Fame pitcher Warren Spahn. Courtesy of Mary Ann and John Sain.

52 George Suttles

George (Mule) Suttles from 1928 St. Louis Stars team photo. Courtesy of Negro Leagues Baseball Museum

53 Cesar Cedano

Cesar Cedano. Courtesy of Houston Astros.

73 Dick Groat

Dick Groat. Courtesy of Topps Company, Inc.

76 Cecil Cooper

Cecil Cooper. Courtesy of Milwaukee Brewers

79 Bob Boone

Bob Boone. Courtesy of Topps Company, Inc.

82 Reggie Smith

Reggie Smith. Courtesy of Boston Red Sox

88 Vida Blue

Vida Blue. Courtesy of Topps Company, Inc.

Johnny Kling

C, 1900–1908, 1910–1913, Cubs, Braves, Reds

The Chicago Cubs teams that won four National League titles in the first decade of the twentieth century put four of its members in the Hall of Fame—pitcher Mordecai "Three-Finger" Brown and the famed double play combination of Tinker to Evers to Chance. But, many would have told you that the most important player on that team was the catcher: Johnny Kling.

The Kansas City native, who once retired over a contract dispute to spend a year defending his pocket billiards title, was the "brains" of the team from his position behind the plate. Kling was generally regarded as the best full-time catcher of the decade, and he was a pretty fair hitter, especially in the clutch.

The Cubs pitching staff of the Kling years is usually included on "best of all time" lists, and with good reason—they won four pennants and led the league in ERA almost every year. From 1905 to 1907, the team's ERAs were 2.04, 1.76, and 1.73. Pitchers such as Brown, Ed Reulbach, Orvie Overall, and Jack Pfiester (all 20-game winners) often credited Kling with a great deal of their success.

"Tinker, Evers, and Chance were great in the infield, but Kling deserved plenty of credit," said Brown. "I'm not ashamed to admit that I was just a so-so pitcher before I teamed up with Kling. A pitcher can always tell you how good a catcher is, and take my word, Johnny Kling was the best."

Kling came up to the Cubs in 1900 and competed with Chance for the starting catcher's spot. In 1902, he became a fixture. Chance moved to first base and the team that would dominate the second half of the decade began to take shape.

In 1906, everything came together. The Cubs won 116 games (still a National League record) and the pennant. In what might be considered a harbinger of the Cubs' future misfortune, they lost the World Series to their crosstown rivals, the "Hitless Wonders" White Sox. They bounced back to win the

Johnny Kling *at a glance*

- Best defensive catcher of his time
- Handled great pitching staff on Cubs pennant winners in 1906, 1907 (World Champions), 1908 (World Champions) and 1910
- Deadly arm nailed 7 base runners at second in 1907 World Series and didn't allow Ty Cobb to steal a base
- Batted .312 in 1906
- Led NL catchers in fielding four times, putouts six times, assists twice, and double plays once

World Series in both 1907 and 1908, twice defeating Ty Cobb and the Tigers. That makes Johnny Kling the catcher on the last Cubs World Championship team, maybe forever.

Kling was the total package on defense. He was smart and rugged (part of his career was spent before the use of shin guards), a fine receiver, a great handler of pitchers—and he had the best throwing arm of any catcher in the league.

His teammate for many years, Johnny Evers, known for being one of the smartest players of all time, regarded Kling as the "brainiest" player in the game. Evers said that Kling was "born knowing baseball. He was aware of all situations and had complete knowledge of all pitchers and hitters in the league."

When he was asked to name the greatest players of that era, Evers put Kling and Pittsburgh's Tommy Leach on the list with Hall of Fame immortals Honus Wagner, Christy Mathewson, Ty Cobb, Tris Speaker, and Mordecai Brown.

"He was a holler type guy and expert at the 'snap' throw from the crouch," Evers said. "In the particular of catching runners in crucial moments of games, John Kling was the best in the business. His ability and his coolness in that style of play alone was enough to stamp him the best of catchers."

Kling was nicknamed "Noisy" for his constant chatter directed at his team, opposing batters, and umpires. Like many great catchers who came later, such as Yogi Berra, Roy Campanella, Biz Mackey, and Gabby Hartnett, he was a friendly guy who talked constantly to hitters, trying to break their concentration. Kling also talked to umpires, flattering them, telling them they were right about certain calls. He would even tell the umpire when a curve ball was coming. He was also expert at framing pitches in order to get umpires to call strikes.

In evaluating the great Cubs pitching staff, John McGraw said: "they are all very good pitchers, but the man who makes them go is Kling."

His only competition as the best catcher in baseball was Giants Hall of Famer Roger Bresnahan, and he spent as much time as an infielder and outfielder as he did behind the plate.

But baseball wasn't Kling's only talent. After the 1908 season, Kling won the pocket billiards championship of the world. When he and Cubs' owner Charles Murphy got into a dispute over his 1909 contract, Kling retired from baseball to defend his billiards championship.

After three-straight pennants, without Kling in the lineup, the Cubs finished second in 1909. Kling returned the following year, paid a fine to get reinstated, and the Cubs won again in 1910. Murphy was always bitter toward Kling and held him responsible for the team's failure to win five pennants in a row.

Kling went on to play briefly for Boston and Cincinnati, but it was as a Chicago Cub that he's remembered.

Kling led National League catchers in fielding average four times and putouts six times. When he retired he held a number of World Series defensive records for catchers including:

Most chances accepted in a six-game Series (56)

Most players caught stealing in a five-game Series (6)

Most assists in a nine-inning game (4)

When his playing days were over, Kling became an astute businessman. He operated several pool halls and a hotels in the Kansas City area. He was also the owner of the Kansas City minor league team, which he sold to the Yankees at a huge profit. Kling retired to a farm outside Kansas City and raised cattle. He was ahead of his time as one of the first of the millionaire ballplayers though his fortune was made when his playing days were over.

Rusty Staub
(le Grand Orange)

OF, 1B, DH, 1963–1985 Astros, Expos,
Mets, Tigers, Rangers

When people talk about Rusty Staub, they talk about a hitter who took it a step further than most players.

"You talk about the student of hitting, with Rusty there was no question, this was a science for him," former teammate and fellow "Out by a Stepper" Joe Torre says of the former left-handed RBI man. "He was a good hitter. He was a very studious hitter. When he was young and had a lean body [he's listed at 6'2", 200 lbs. in various publications but got much bigger than that with time], he was scary."

Daniel Joseph Staub became Rusty Staub at just about the earliest age possible, his mother relating how the nurse at the hospital saw his red, fuzzy hair, and nicknamed him Rusty, the only name he would ever know in sports. Rusty Staub wound up having a twenty-three-year career and turning into one of the true professional hitters of his time—in addition to becoming famous for off-field culinary and charitable endeavors.

"Rusty was just a good all-around player for four different teams," says Tim McCarver. "He was a very good offensive player when he was older and a very good defensive player when he was younger.

"Rusty knew how to play the game. That's something that some Hall of Famers never knew how to do. All they knew how to do was hit home runs. That's a nice thing but as far as playing the game and the other facets."

Staub, a six-time All-Star who started his career as a Houston Colt-45 bonus baby and ended it by settling as a popular figure in New York, thinks his career

Rusty Staub *at a glance*

- Six-time All-Star
- First player to log 500 games with four teams
- 292 career homers, 1,446 RBIs
- Batted .300 five times
- 2,716 career hits
- Hit 3 homers in only NLCS and then .423 with 1 homer and 6 RBIs in only World Series

achievements have been largely overlooked, that his numbers rank right up there with anyone of his day and with people in the Hall of Fame. Some agree. Others don't.

"I think he's gotten the recognition that he deserves," offers McCarver. "Rusty was a very, very good baseball player and I think he's been recognized as that."

Torre thinks the Hall of Fame may have driven Staub in his later years—and caused bitterness since. "This was a goal of his," he said. "This was no question, I remember when he was at the end of his career, he had this all mapped out. He wanted this many hits . . . that's a shame. That would make you bitter when that's your life's ambition when you get to a certain age.

"You don't think about it when you first start out but when you get up there and you realize that you're in that rarified air where you're a stone's throw away, that would be frustrating."

As frustrating as it was for many pitchers who had to deal with the man who became known as "le Grand Orange" during his days in Montreal—a name that stuck even after he was traded to Houston and kept moving on.

Staub, who became the first player to record five hundred games for four different teams—the Astros, Expos, Mets, and Tigers—batted .279 during a 2,951-game career. He hit 292 homers, drove in 1,466 runs. and struck out more than 58 times in a season only once. Staub batted .300 five times and twice walked over 100 times while collecting 2,716 hits.

Basically, if his team had a man on third, Staub knew how to get that man home. He had 105 RBIs with the Mets in 1975 (a team record until Howard Johnson broke it in 1991), 101 with the Tigers in 1977, and a career-high 121 with Detroit the following year.

"I remember when he came to the Detroit," says former righty Rich Gale. "I was a hot-shot young guy [with Kansas City] and I see this guy up there, holding the bat way up here [choking up] and he's overweight, I'm like, 'he's not gonna hit me.' But he did."

He always hit.

"He was a situational type hitter that knew what to look for, when to look for it, how to look for it in situations," says former teammate Lee Mazzilli. "When I played with Rusty and then when I played against him, I always felt that . . . I wasn't too sure he was going to get a hit every time, but I always felt he was going to hit the ball hard somewhere—like hard contact and be a tough out. No one can predict he can get a hit every time up—but good hard contact—and if you needed a home run to beat you, he could do that, too."

In addition to being disappointed with his place in history, Staub also didn't get a chance to do much in the postseason—which could have hurt his historical perception, too. He only played once in the postseason, hitting 3 homers in the 1973 Mets NLCS win over Cincinnati and then batting .423 with a homer and 6 RBIs in the seven-game World Series loss to Oakland. He led both clubs with 11 hits in that Series and tied Reggie Jackson for the Series lead in RBIs. All that while playing with an injured shoulder.

Staub would actually end his career with the Mets after going to Detroit, briefly back to Montreal and Texas (he batted .300 in 1980). He became an outstanding pinch hitter on his second tour with the Mets, collecting 24 pinch hits (one shy of the record) in 1983 before going on to become the eleventh player to record 100 in a career.

In 1986, Staub and Bud Harrelson were the first players inducted into the Mets Hall of Fame, and the Expos retired Staub's number 10 in 1992.

When he retired, Staub remained a part of New York, as a broadcaster, restaurateur, chef—and his name burst back into the news after the World Trade Center tragedy as he continued his charitable endeavor of taking care of the families of lost police and firefighters.

Rocky Colavito

OF, 1955–1968, Indians, Tigers, A's, White Sox, Dodgers, Yankees

I n Cleveland in the 1950s, Rocky Colavito was part baseball player, part folk hero and part what they called in an earlier age, a "matinee idol." The handsome, curly-haired home run hitter with the rifle arm was beloved by fans and imitated by young ballplayers on the sandlots. Teenage girls and young women adored Rocky and squealed when he came to bat in the same way females screamed for Sinatra, Elvis, and the Beatles.

As broadcaster Nev Chandler said in Terry Pluto's book about the Indians' thirty-year post-Colavito slump, *The Curse of Rocky Colavito*, "As a kid, my favorite player was Rocky Colavito. Just about all the kids loved Rocky. All the kids imitated Rocky's batting stance. Before he'd step into the box, Rocky would lift his bat over his head and put it behind his shoulders. Then he'd stretch, left, stretch right, then bend around. As he stepped into the box, he would meticulously adjust his cap so it was right above his eyes. For his practice swing he would point the head of his bat right at the pitcher, as if he were aiming a rifle. You watch kids and they'd be pointing the bat just like Rocky. He was young, handsome and hit a lot of home runs. They talk about M. J. today. In Cleveland in 1959 it was 'be like Rocky.'"

The Bronx, New York, native, who grew up idolizing Joe DiMaggio, emerged as one of the top players and great attractions in baseball in 1958, despite a lack of speed caused by a pair of incredibly flat feet. In fewer than 500 at bats, Rocky hit 41 home runs, knocked in 113 runs and hit .303, with a .620 slugging average. He was third in the Most Valuable Player balloting behind Red Sox outfielder Jackie Jensen and Yankee hurler Bob Turley.

Colavito was especially hard on his hometown Yankees, blasting seven of his homers off their championship pitching staff. Turley observed: "There isn't

Rocky Colavito *at a glance*

- 1959 AL home run champ with 42
- AL RBI leader with 108 in 1965
- Seven times hit 30 HRs
- Six times had 100 RBIs
- Six-time All-Star

a park he can't drive 'em out of with his power . . . Even if you fool him on a pitch, he can still hit the ball out of the park."

In addition to his power, many believed that Rocky had the strongest throwing arm the majors had seen since Bob Meusel of the Yankees in the 1920s. In pre-game exhibitions, Rocky would stand at home plate and toss the ball over the center field wall 424 feet away. He was so strong that he had to warm up with a catcher using a heavily padded glove.

"How fast is he," Indians manager Joe Gordon asked J. W. Porter, who he noticed was rubbing his hand after catching Colavito.

"Faster than anybody," Porter said.

"Faster than Herb Score or Ryne Duren?"

"Faster than anybody."

In one game, Gordon brought him in to pitch three innings and Colavito didn't allow a run, prompting the manager to say, "He's my right fielder—period. But I'll tell you this. As a pitcher, he'd be a 20-game winner. He has the greatest arm I ever saw."

Colavito followed his breakthrough season with a strong 1959. His average dipped to .257 but his home runs and RBI held steady at 42 (tops in the league) and 111 and he led the league in total bases with 301. He was fourth in the Most Valuable Player voting behind three future Hall of Famers from the "Go-Go" Chicago White Sox: Nellie Fox, Luis Aparicio, and Early Wynn.

The Colavito 1959 highlight was a historic feat. On June 10 in Baltimore he smashed four successive home runs, becoming only the eighth player to hit four home runs in one game and the third player to do it consecutively.

Gordon reported that after mobbing Colavito at the plate after the fourth homer, the Indians players seemed somewhat subdued in the dugout.

"They seemed too stunned to believe what they had just seen," he said.

Baseball people were predicting that Colavito would be the main gate attraction in the league once Ted Williams retired.

In addition to his ability and his charisma, "the Rock" was regarded as a great role model for children. He didn't smoke, drink, or swear and he was polite to everyone he met, signing autographs and chatting with fans for hours after the game. He owned the town.

Then in 1960, Indians General Manager Frank (Trader) Lane made the move that is generally credited with sending the Cleveland Indians into the doldrums for thirty-three years. He did the unthinkable by trading the local hero and home run king to the Detroit Tigers for batting champion Harvey Kuenn, who was three years older and didn't have Colavito's power, athletic ability, or gate appeal.

To say that the trade was unpopular doesn't come close to describing the reaction of loyal Indians followers. It was a dark day in Indians history, and ensured Lane's place in Cleveland infamy similar to the place Walter O'Malley holds in Brooklyn after moving the beloved Dodgers to Los Angeles in 1958. Many fans believe that the team's failure to compete for a pennant again for more than three decades can be traced to Lane's misjudgment.

Terry Pluto even suggests with some humor, that when the Indians traded Colavito they were cursed as the Red Sox were cursed when they sold Babe Ruth.

Indians teammate pitcher Jim "Mudcat" Grant described the reaction to the trade to Pluto: "All hell broke loose in the minds of the players when Rocky was traded," he said. "We knew what he meant to the lineup. Pitchers were scared to death of him."

Close friend Herb Score describing what Colavito meant to the team and the fans said: "Rocky had a tremendous charisma. Fans gravitated to him, not just because he hit home runs, but also because Rocky never gave a short step on the field. He always gave 100 percent. He was a courageous clutch player. With the winning run on second base and two outs in the ninth inning, Rocky wanted to be at the plate."

Colavito had some good seasons in Detroit, but he was never the icon he had been in Cleveland. He was traded back to the Indians in 1965 and led the league in RBIs and bases on balls and set a major league record by playing all 162 games without an error.

He retired in 1968, with 374 home runs and 1,159 RBIs to his credit. Colavito also appeared in nine All-Star Games (there were two a year in 1959, 1961, and 1962). He led the league in total bases twice. In his career he had more walks than strikeouts, an impressive achievement for a slugger.

But who knows what those numbers would have been if Colavito had remained in Cleveland where, in 1976, fans voted him the most memorable player in Indians history?

Sal (The Barber) Maglie

P, 1945, 1950–1958, Giants, Indians,
Dodgers, Yankees, Cardinals

When pitcher Sal Maglie came strolling into the Brooklyn Dodgers clubhouse to meet his new teammates in 1956, it was as if John Dillinger had suddenly joined the FBI.

The hated "Sal the Barber" of the enemy New York Giants, along with his combative former manager, Leo Durocher, came to symbolize the Manhattan side of the greatest rivalry—no, feud—in the history of baseball.

The scowling, menacing Maglie, who never hesitated to throw "the purpose pitch" at the heads of Dodgers batters since he returned to the majors from exile in 1950, was now one of them. The heavily bearded Maglie, whose "high hard one" touched off more than one brawl and many "incidents" in the ongoing battle for National League supremacy and New York City baseball pride, at thirty-nine years old, was now one of the "Boys of Summer."

Everyone was especially conscious of how Maglie's arrival would affect outfielder Carl Furillo, who viewed all the Giants as his enemies. Furillo had been the target of several of Maglie's sailing fastballs. Furillo detested the Giants, especially Durocher and Maglie.

Author Roger Kahn, who chronicled the exciting post–World War II baseball scene in New York, describes the event: "The Brooklyn clubhouse was electric as Maglie entered it on the afternoon of May 16, 1956. He had knocked down Dodger hitters for six years. Carl Furillo continued to swear vengeance.

"As Maglie entered, Erskine, and Reese, and Campanella looked curiously toward Furillo.

" 'Hello, Dago,' Furillo said."

" 'Lo, Skoonj,' said Maglie." .

And that was it. The two became good friends, even roomed together for a while. Sal Maglie, "the Mephistopheles of the Mound," won 13 games that year,

Sal Maglie *at a glance*

- His .657 ranks among top winning percentages of all time
- Six seasons below 3.00 ERA
- Led NL in winning percentage .818, with an 18–4 record and five shutouts in 1950
- Led NL in victories with 23–6 record in 1951
- Pitched a no-hitter (1956)
- NL All-Star team 1951–1952

including his only no-hitter against the Phillies on September 25, and the Dodgers went on to win the pennant over the Milwaukee Braves by one game. They never would have done it without him.

"When I saw Maglie standing in our clubhouse wearing our uniform, I knew nothing in this world would ever surprise me again," said Brooklyn pitcher Carl Erskine.

The Barber also pitched two fine games against the Yankees in the World Series that year. He was the winning pitcher in Game One and he was on the losing end of Don Larson's perfect Game Five, giving up only 5 hits, one a game-winning home run to Mickey Mantle in the seventh inning.

Sal Maglie, a native and resident of Niagara Falls, New York, came up with the Giants in 1945 and posted a respectable 5–4 record, with three shutouts and an impressive 2.35 ERA. That winter, Maglie pitched in Cuba where he caught the eye of the Pasquel Brothers of the Mexican League who were raiding the majors for players.

Maglie accepted their offer to pitch south of the border. He was assigned to Puebla, where former Giants pitching coach Dolf Luque was the manager. It was there, under the astute tutelage of Luque that Maglie said he really learned how to pitch. He called playing for Luque the best thing that ever happened to him.

After two 20-win seasons in Mexico, Maglie left over a salary dispute only to learn that he and the other "Mexican Jumping Beans" had been banned for life by Baseball Commissioner Happy Chandler. He was out of baseball in 1948 and pitched for an independent team in Canada in 1949. When the ban was lifted, he returned to the Giants in 1950 at the age of thirty-three.

Maglie pitched effectively during spring training but was used in relief, except for one start in June. Then, in July, the Giants went into a nine-game tailspin and Durocher gambled on Maglie. The curveballing righthander beat the Cards 5–4 and then went on to win eleven straight games, the last four were shutouts, tying a National League record. When the year ended, "the

Barber," who received the nickname either because he gave the batter a close shave with his high inside fastball or because of his habit of shaving the corners of home plate with an effective variety of curves, finished the year at 18–4 with a .271 ERA. His .818 winning percentage led the league.

For the next few years, he was one of the top pitchers in the major leagues. Maglie was 23–6 in 1951, the year the Giants won the pennant when Bobby Thomson hit his famous "shot heard round the world" to beat the Dodgers in a National League playoff. He was 18–8 in 1952.

The key to Maglie's game was his pinpoint control and his ability to work the batter high and low, inside and out, but he always maintained that the key was to keep the batter off-balance with the high inside pitch.

"Pitch 'em high inside and low outside," Maglie said. "If you pitch high inside, the batter can't get set on you. The high inside pitch forces the batter to back away from the plate or duck to avoid being hit."

In 1952, Arthur Daley of the *New York Times* wrote: "The experts will tell you that Maglie has the best curve ball in the big leagues and now he knows what to do with it and how to control it."

Richie Ashburn had these thoughts about Maglie in *Diamond Greats* by Rich Westcott: "He had a good fastball, a great curve, and a whole assortment of other pitches. He was nasty."

Nobody knew how nasty Maglie could be better than the Dodgers, who were the frequent targets of his high inside set-up pitch.

Once Maglie, angry because of a triple that had been hit by George Shuba of the Dodgers, threw the ball behind Furillo's head, prompting the Dodgers right fielder to let go of the bat on the next pitch, sending it clear over Maglie, almost hitting shortstop Alvin Dark.

In the most famous incident of his career, Maglie threw the ball behind Jackie Robinson. In retaliation, Robinson laid a bunt down the first base line, his clear intention was to run over Maglie, who should have been covering the base. However, "the Barber" was a little slow getting over there and Robinson, the former UCLA halfback, barreled into Giants second baseman Davey Williams, who was there to cover. Williams's back was injured on the play.

Despite the longstanding blood feud between the two teams, Maglie was welcomed into the Dodgers family in 1956.

"They said I hated the Dodgers," Maglie said. "That was only because of the tough competition. I never hated anybody. When we were teammates I got along fine with Robinson, Furillo, and all the guys."

Maglie had a relatively brief major league career, but he made a major impact. During the early and mid-1950s, he was one of the best and he always performed in the center ring.

(Smokey) Joe Wood

P, OF, 1908–1915, 1917–1922,
Red Sox, Indians

T alk to any Boston Red Sox fan these days and bring up the Hall of Fame, and chances are you'll hear a pitch for Luis Tiant, whose career is chronicled elsewhere in the pages of this text. People in Boston just can't understand why Tiant isn't in.

But long before Sox fans cried for el Tiante's induction, they clamored for Smokey Joe Wood—one of their links to days when the Sox actually did win World Series.

In 1912, Smokey Joe, who hailed from the prairies of Kansas, had one of the greatest seasons ever produced by a pitcher—a year that has him labeled by some as a one-year wonder. He was never the same after that, getting hurt the following year, but that doesn't mean 1912 was all he ever did.

He beat Walter Johnson head-to-head, 1–0, that year. It's not clear at what point in that season Johnson made a comment about Wood that would turn into one of the great baseball quotes of all-time: "Can I throw harder than Joe Wood?" Johnson asked. "Listen, my friend, no man alive can throw harder than Smoky Joe Wood."

Technically, Johnson was wrong—research showed Johnson threw 99.7 miles per hour, while Wood came in at 94.5. Apparently, though, Johnson didn't know that.

Wood was 11–7 in 1909, his first full season in the major leagues, and then went 12–13 in 1910—with a 1.68 ERA. In 1911, he won 23 games for the fifth-place Red Sox, including a July no-hitter. It was soon after that gem that *Boston Post* writer Paul Shannon was given credit for tagging the right-hander with his nickname. And 1911 was just a setup for what was to come.

In 1912, the Red Sox won the World Series. Wood was 34–5, tossed 10 shutouts, and ran up a stretch of 26 wins in 28 decisions—just missing

Joe Wood *at a glance*

- Pitched a no-hitter in 23-win 1911 season
- 34–5 in 1912, and then 3–1 in the World Series
- 1915 AL ERA title
- Became an outfielder because of arm troubles
- .283 lifetime hitter
- 116–57 lifetime record
- Still number one in Red Sox history in winning percentage and ERA

winning those other two starts for a 28-game winning streak. In the World Series, he went 3–1 for 37 wins for the year. The last of those wins, in a Game Eight of the World Series [Game Two ended in a tie] saw Wood leave for a pinch hitter [he normally would have batted for himself but his pitching hand was swollen after being hit with a line drive], trailing 2–1 in the bottom of the tenth. The Red Sox rallied for the win and the title—capping Wood's dream season.

"I've seen some pretty fair pitching, but I've never seen anything like Smokey Joe Wood in 1912," said teammate Harry Hooper.

Joe Wood, who would become the long-time baseball coach at Yale after his playing days, wanted only to be a baseball player, bragged that as a youngster he always had a baseball glove on as he rode "on the front seat of that covered wagon next to my father." He not only pitched, he hit—something that came in handy when a broken right thumb, suffered in 1913, led to a shoulder injury that would end his pitching career but couldn't end his playing career.

"I never pitched again without a terrific amount of pain in my right shoulder. Never again," he said.

Pain and all, he won the ERA title in 1915 but that was it. He was done at age twenty-six. Well, not quite. There was more to come.

He sat out the 1916 season and, with the Red Sox allowing him to make his own deal, hooked up with old teammate (and roommate) Tris Speaker in Cleveland in 1917. Getting himself ready to play the outfield, Wood returned to the field in 1918—and batted .296, with five homers (remember, people didn't hit home runs yet), and 66 RBI in 119 games.

Wood got an early indication his return to the field would be a success—on May 24, 1918, in a nineteen-inning game at the Polo Grounds, he hit a home run in the seventh inning, made a game-saving catch in the ninth, threw a runner out at second base in the twelfth, and homered again to win the game in the nineteenth.

Wood played only one more year as a full-time player in 1922 and hit .297, with 8 homers and 92 RBI for the Indians. He played in the World Series in 1920 and hit .366 in a reduced role in 1921.

For his career, he was 116–57 with a 2.03 ERA as a pitcher and hit .283, with 23 homers and 325 RBI as a hitter (with 23 stolen bases).

He's been gone from the Red Sox for more than eighty-five years, but his place in Boston history will always be there. A check of the 2002 Red Sox media guide shows Wood first all-time in winning percentage (.676) and ERA (1.99), third in 10-strikeout games (18, behind only Roger Clemens and Pedro Martinez), fourth in complete games (121), fifth in wins (117), sixth in strikeouts (986), fifteenth in innings (1,416), and tied for eighteenth in games started (157, tied with Mike Torrez). As of the mid-1980s, he was the holder of fifty-one Red Sox pitching records.

If Wood hadn't slipped on wet grass in 1913, there's no telling what he could have accomplished the rest of his career. As it was, his numbers were impressive—many feeling impressive enough to get into the Hall. As things stand, though, he remains out by a step.

Bob Meusel

OF, 1920–1930, Yankees

Bob Meusel, the handsome Yankees left fielder from the 1920s, the third power bat on "Murderers Row," would probably be in the Hall of Fame now if only he had tried harder, if only he looked like he cared. His not-quite-ready-for-Cooperstown career, however, has earned him a spot on our "Out by a Step" list.

A true five-tool player, Meusel is thought by many to have had the strongest and most accurate throwing arm of any outfielder in the history of the game. He batted in more runs in the decade of the 1920s than everyone but Babe Ruth. He knocked in more than 80 runs nine times and more than 100 runs five times. He is eleventh on the all-time list of RBIs per game (.76), and everybody ahead of him is in the Hall of Fame. In 1925, he won two-thirds of the Triple Crown with 33 home runs and 138 RBIs. Meusel hit above .300 seven times in his career and .309 lifetime.

Would you like to know more? He batted in the fifth slot in what was possibly the greatest lineup of all time (batting cleanup before Lou Gehrig became established) and along with Babe Ruth and Earle Combs comprised what many believe was the greatest outfield of all time. He hit for the cycle three times and contributed generously to six Yankees championship teams.

He led or tied for the team lead in stolen bases five times.

In the 1921 World Series, Meusel stole home after warning Giants catcher Earl Smith that he was going to do it. And, because Ruth hated to play the sun field, Meusel moved to right field in several American League parks. (It is believed that Meusel's chronic headaches were caused by constantly looking into the sun.)

"Long Bob" (at 6'3", he was one of the tallest players in baseball at the time) is best remembered for his magnificent throwing arm and his "miserable" attitude.

Because he's on our Top 100 list, let's start with the positive—the howitzer right arm.

Bob Meusel *at a glance*

- Member of Murderers Row Yankees and started in six World Series
- Best outfield arm in baseball
- Seven-time .300 hitter, five-time 100 RBIs
- Hit for the cycle three times
- In 1925 led the AL in HRs (33) and RBIs (138)
- Stole home twice in World Series play

Yankees teammate Joe Dugan swore that "Meusel could hit a dime at 100 yards and flatten it against a wall."

Sportswriter Fred Lieb, who covered the Yankees, claimed he never saw a player with a stronger arm than Bob Meusel.

"Nothing pleases him more than to have a hostile base runner gamble with his 'whip' by attempting to score from second on a single or from third on an outfield fly," Lieb said.

No matter where he was in the outfield, Meusel was capable of throwing strikes, on a clean line drive to any base. He tied for the lead in outfield assists in 1921 with 28, and led the league the following year with 24. After that, people usually didn't run on him. They say that even Ty Cobb held third base on sacrifice flies to Meusel.

Yankees manager Miller Huggins was keenly aware of Meusel's value to the team. "There is one thing fans don't get about Meusel. The number of runs he prevents by just standing out in left field. Coaches will not send many in when a ball is hit to him."

Huggins marveled at Meusel's all-around skills: "I know of no hitter who can hit the ball harder than Meusel—excepting, of course, Babe Ruth. He had everything to make him great: a good eye at bat, strength, a natural, easy swing, and that wonderful steel arm."

Hug, who was continually frustrated by Meusel's apathy, also used to speculate on how good the enigmatic outfielder would have been if he had a different disposition

"His attitude is one of just plain indifference," Huggins said.

"Languid Bob" was not a crowd favorite in New York because of the easy, nonchalant way he loped after fly balls and hits. Sometimes, he didn't run out ground balls and showed no difference in emotion whether he hit a home run or took a called third strike. He hustled when he wanted to. He seemed to have no desire to please anyone and he was immune to both praise and criticism.

In 1926 Meusel told *Baseball Magazine* that "hustling is rather overrated in baseball. "It's a showy quality that looks well and counts for little."

Reporters claimed that Meusel spoke rarely, but when he did it was in a surly manner.

Meusel, whose older brother "Irish," a fine outfielder for the Giants in the early 1920s (they opposed each other in the 1921, 1922, and 1923 World Series), was as gregarious as Bob was quiet. The two shared an apartment in New York and, it is said, that when Irish came home from a road trip, Bob would pack and leave for the Yankees road trip, without saying a word.

When he became friendlier with reporters late in his career, one reporter wrote that "Meusel is learning to say hello, just when he should be saying good-bye."

Despite his reputation as a loner, Meusel was close friends with the Bambino, often running with Ruth after hours.

The two defied Commissioner Landis's warning against a 1921 postseason barnstorming tour and both were suspended for the beginning of the 1922 season.

When his Yankees career ended in 1929, Meusel spent one year with Cincinnati and then retired to his native California. Those who interviewed him as an older man found him accessible, candid and articulate.

Meusel made an appearance in the movie *The Pride of the Yankees* and he returned to Yankee Stadium in 1948 to honor the dying Babe Ruth.

When Ruth passed on two months later Meusel was quoted as saying, "Babe Ruth will never die. He did more for the game than anyone. As long as baseball is played he'll live. There is only one Babe."

Bob Meusel was a superior hitter and fielder and an important member of Murderers Row and the first Yankees dynasty, but a slight attitude adjustment probably would have made a place for him in the Hall of Fame.

Larry Bowa

SS, 1970–1985, Phillies, Cubs, Mets

Larry Bowa brings it up with honor in his voice—not bitterness from not being recognized by Hall of Fame voters.

"I've had people come up to me and say, 'your numbers are like (Phil) Rizzuto's and (Pee Wee) Reese's,'" the former Phillies and Cubs shortstop said not too long ago, "Just to hear them say that makes me very proud to do what I did.

"It's tough to get into the Hall of Fame."

Rizzuto and Reese, who made their names in New York City and were part of a storied chunk of baseball history (when there were three teams in New York), are both in the Hall. Bowa isn't even close. He got eleven votes in 1990 and was gone from the ballot. He quickly drifted into history (and this book) but shouldn't be forgotten.

And while this isn't a contention that he belongs in the Hall, consider those numbers Bowa was talking about in relation to Reese and Rizzuto. Reese was a .269 lifetime hitter; Rizzuto, .273. Bowa batted .260. Reese had 2,170 hits in 2,166 games; Rizzuto, 1,588 in 1,661. Bowa had 2,191 in 2,247. Reese had the power over both, hitting 138 homers to Rizzuto's 38 and Bowa's 15, and Reese drove in more than twice as many runs as the other two. But Bowa stole 318 bases; Rizzuto, 149 and Reese, 34. Reese hit .272 in forty-four World Series Games; Rizzuto .246 in fifty-two postseason affairs. Bowa hit .254 in thirty-two.

Toss into all this Bowa retiring with the highest fielding percentage of any shortstop ever (.980) and you can see it's not that far-fetched to consider him for the Hall of Fame. Bowa has to go down as one of the more underrated and underappreciated (except by his teammates and those who played against him) players of his time.

Larry Bowa *at a glance*

- Five-time All-Star
- Two Gold Gloves
- 2,191 career hits
- 318 career stolen bases
- .980 lifetime fielding percentage, highest by a shortstop

"Larry Bowa was a good player," says Joe Torre, who played against Bowa through their careers and then managed against Bowa the player before both became members of the managerial fraternity. "He probably was the best artificial surface player, which is not easy to play on.

"He was a terrific player. He made himself a hitter: Bowa and Ozzie Smith. He was pesky. He made contact, he could run like hell, and was very reliable at shortstop."

Elsewhere in the pages of this book, you'll find Bowa talking about fellow shortstop Davey Concepcion and saying his Cincinnati rival was "the guy that pushed me as hard as anybody. I always wanted to stay up with him."

But anyone who really knows Bowa knows this was a player who didn't have to be pushed by anyone. Seen him as a manager? Seen that intense look? That's the way Larry Bowa was as a player.

"I think Larry Bowa's a great baseball man," says former teammate Darren Daulton. "I don't think everybody can play for him but nobody knows the game better than Bowa."

Bowa, a five-time All-Star and two-time Gold Glove–winner, spent a long time learning the game—and while he was never the hitter Concepcion was when the two of them were battling on two of the best National League teams of that era, Bowa made himself into a solid man at the plate on some very good teams.

"He was a guy that broke in and couldn't hit a lick," said Daulton. "And now he's got over 2,000 hits."

And could he ever play the field. "I wanted him on defense," says Daulton. "He's got the all-time best fielding percentage."

Bowa, the son of a former minor leaguer, wasn't even drafted. But he was determined and became the Phillies shortstop in 1970. He stayed there until after the 1980 season—helping the Phillies end their World Series drought with the 1980 Championship. In the postseason that year, Bowa hit .316 in the Championship Series and .375 in the World Series win over Kansas City.

When Dallas Green took over the Cubs, he swapped his shortstop—Ivan DeJesus—for Bowa, and also got a kid named Ryne Sandberg in the deal. Bowa and Sandberg settled in as the Cubbies' double play combination and played an important part in the Cubs' return to the playoffs in 1984. Bowa was released by the Cubs during the 1985 season and actually finished his career with 14 games with the Mets.

"Here's a guy who made himself into a hell of a player—a little, skinny kid who just believed he could play and he wasn't going to have anybody tell him he couldn't," offers Buck Martinez. "He is the epitome of a self-made player. He understood he wanted to be a ballplayer and he played his ass off to become a good player."

Adds Rod Carew, who would coach with Bowa in Anaheim before Bowa returned to manage the Phillies: "He played on teams where guys made sure that you got the job done—you don't make the play, they let you know. He still is that way today. He's still intense. He's a great teacher. He knows a lot about the game. He hates losing—and that's what this is all about."

Intense? "One of the stories Eddie Bachman, who signed him with the Phillies, tells is he came to watch him play a junior college game and he got thrown out before he ever came to the plate in both games of a double-header," says Martinez. "He was intense!"

And so were the Phillies. "He was good on that team because he was sort of youngish and then grew into that role [as a leader]," says Torre. "I see them all coming together where you had Gary Matthews and him and [Mike] Schmidt and [Bob] Boonie, that was an impressive group over there at that time."

(Cannonball) Dick Redding

P, 1911–1938, Negro Leagues: New York Lincoln Giants, Brooklyn Royal Giants

Jose Mendez (The Black Diamond)
(P, 1908–1926, Negro Leagues: Cuban Stars, Kansas City Monarchs)

Ray Brown (P, 1930–1948, Negro Leagues: Homestead Grays)

"Cannonball Dick" Redding was "the Black Walter Johnson," and like "the Big Train," Redding relied entirely on his blistering fastball until he developed a curve later in his career. This overpowering right-hander with the no-windup delivery, starred for the New York Lincoln Giants and the Brooklyn Royal Giants in the 1910s and 1920s. He often pitched doubleheaders and was rarely removed for a relief pitcher. He was also an excellent hitter.

Redding, who is credited with thirty no-hitters in his career, is forever linked with his contemporary Smokey Joe Williams both as an opponent and teammate. The two engaged in some of the classic pitchers battles of the time, and when they were together, they were practically unbeatable.

In 1999 the Veteran's Committee voted Smokey Joe Willams into the Hall of Fame, and many baseball historians think Redding should also be honored.

Dick Redding *at a glance*

- Considered the hardest-throwing Negro League pitcher of all time
- 43–12 record in 1912
- Won 17-straight games as a rookie in 1911 with New York Lincoln Giants
- Won 20-straight games for Lincoln Stars in 1915
- 3–1 record and batted .385 in Lincoln Giants 1915 Black World Series Championship
- Credited with 30 no-hitters

When he broke in with the Lincoln Giants in 1911, the 6'4", 210-lb. Redding chalked up 17 straight victories with a fastball that has been called the best in black baseball history. He had pinpoint control, often using the hesitation delivery that Satchel Paige made famous many years later. Halfway through the delivery, Redding balanced on his front foot with his back to the hitter for a second before sending the pitch on its way.

In 1912, the year Williams joined the Lincoln Giants, Redding had his best year, compiling a 43–12 record that included a 17-strikeout perfect game.

When the Lincoln Giants played a game against a local team in New London, Connecticut, a reporter who covered the game wrote: "New London was helpless in Redding's hands. Redding hasn't Williams' control but he has more steam throwing a ball that goes at a terrific speed."

In 1915, as a member of the Lincoln Stars, Redding won 20 straight games, several against teams of major leaguers. He served in the army during World War I, seeing combat in France.

When he returned from the war, he served as player-manager for several clubs including the Brooklyn Royal Giants for six years. Redding, a good-natured, easy-going man, without formal education, commanded respect as a manager.

Jose Mendez and Ray Brown were given strong consideration for the Top 100 and should be remembered for their outstanding careers. They share the number sixty-six spot on our list with Dick Redding.

Jose Mendez, the great Cuban right-hander, was a dominant pitcher in his country and in the United States early in the twentieth century. He was a smart pitcher with a great curve and a fastball that was compared favorably to that thrown by Smokey Joe Williams. In 1911, Mendez and his Almendares club of Cuba defeated Williams and the New York Lincoln Giants in an extra-inning battle to decide the black baseball championship of the world. After nine innings, Williams had pitched a no-hitter and Mendez a two-hitter.

Mendez's success against major league competition made him a national hero in Cuba. In 1912, he pitched against a combined Dodgers-Giants squad managed by John McGraw. Mendez, who was 8–7 lifetime in exhibition games against major leaguers, defeated Christy Mathewson and then on one day's rest he topped Nap Rucker 2–1. McGraw compared Mendez to Walter Johnson and Grover Alexander and said that he would have welcomed him on the Giants staff.

Mendez was the ace of the racially-mixed All-Nations team that toured the United States from 1912 to 1916. He served as player-manager of the Kansas City Monarchs from 1920 to 1926, leading the Monarchs to three-straight Negro National League pennants, 1923–1925. In 1924, he had a 20–4 record and was 2–0 against Hilldale in the Negro League World Series, tossing a shutout in the final game.

Ray Brown was the ace of the Homestead Grays staff. Brown led the team to nine consecutive Negro League pennants in the 1930s and 1940s. Brown was a right-hander with a great fastball and curve who could also go to a sinker, a slider, and even a knuckleball when he needed it. He was also a fine switch-hitter who played the outfield when he wasn't pitching.

"I'd take Ray Brown over Satchel," Grays shortstop Sam Bankhead said. "Ray was a better team pitcher than Satchel. If there was one game I wanted to win—one game—I'd take Satch. But for a team I'd take Raymond Brown."

Brown had a 104–30 lifetime record and his winning percentage of .776 is the highest in Negro League history. Over one stretch covering the 1936–1937 seasons, Brown won 28 straight games.

In 1938, the height of the Grays dynasty, Brown was a perfect 10–0, inspiring Jimmy Powers of the *New York Daily News* to write: "Ray Brown is the greatest pitcher in baseball today." Powers, who was white, begged the Giants to add Brown to a team that included Hall of Famers Mel Ott and Carl Hubbell.

That same year, an article in the *Pittsburgh Courier* guaranteed the Pittsburgh Pirates a pennant if they would sign five Negro League players—Brown, along with now Hall of Fame members Cool Papa Bell, Josh Gibson, Buck Leonard, and Satchel Paige.

Brown's career highlights included a 3–2 record in four Negro League World Series. One of his victories was a one-hit shutout in 1944 against the Birmingham Black Barons. Brown also pitched in two East–West Negro Leagues All-Star Games.

A fan favorite in both Puerto Rico and Cuba, Brown led the Cuban League in wins in 1936–1937 with a 21–3 record including a no-hitter.

George Scales, a former Negro League great who also managed in Puerto Rico paid Brown the highest compliment. "You want to know the best pitcher I ever saw—The old-timers will tell you Smokey Joe Williams and Cannonball Dick Redding. But I think the greatest was Ray Brown."

Monte Irvin, a former member of the Hall of Fame Veteran's Committee, believes that one day Brown will be properly recognized with selection to the Hall of Fame.

Dwight Evans
(Dewey)

OF, 1972–1991, Red Sox, Orioles

I n talking to people about Dwight Evans for the purpose of writing this
book, the first thing that always came up was the way he played right
field, the way he handled the difficult position at Fenway Park, the way
he threw.

Quickly, though, the conversation would turn to other things.

"He's probably one of the most underrated players of his time," future Hall
of Famer Paul Molitor says. "I don't think people realize the type of career
numbers he's been able to put together, kind of getting lost in the middle of
being on some teams that had people stealing the headlines. He was just out
there being consistent and he was able to do it for a long time."

"He was the glue to that Boston team," said rival Lou Piniella. "He was out
there every day. He played hard. He played to beat you. He finally put it
together hitting wise—for a period there of six to eight years, he hit the ball as
well as anybody, and for power."

It didn't happen right away. Evans arrived in Boston in 1973, two years
before Jim Rice and Fred Lynn came along to form what some people think is
the best outfield of its era. But while offensive success came early for Rice and
Lynn, Evans was a mediocre hitter who second-guessed himself and changed
stances like most of us change underwear. He was an outstanding right fielder
(known for a great World Series catch off Joe Morgan—and that wonderful
arm), but hardly a factor at the plate.

"The older he got, the better he got," says long-time Red Sox favorite
Johnny Pesky. "When he was young, he was insecure. Darrell Johnson had him
in the minor leagues, in Louisville and Evans was going so bad he went to
Darrell and said, 'Darrell, I'm like a fish out of water.' He says, 'Send me back

Dwight Evans *at a glance*

- Eight Gold Gloves
- 385 career homers
- .373 career on base percentage
- Three-time All-Star
- 1,384 career RBIs
- Tied for AL home run lead 1981 (strike season)
- Drove in 100 runs four times

to Allentown.' Darrell says, 'I'm gonna sink or swim with you' and he wound up being MVP of the league."

"When I had Dwight, he was a struggling hitter," says former Red Sox manager Don Zimmer. "Always a great right fielder, probably the best that ever played in [Fenway Park]. He struggled to hit .260. This man's put up some big numbers and he put them all up after I got fired. Dwight became a real, real good hitter. He turned out to be a heck of a player. There's nobody who could play right field like he could, at Fenway Park, especially. He excelled in right field [at Fenway]."

Molitor talked about adjusting his running style with Evans in right. Hall of Famer Rod Carew said of the eight-time Gold Glover: "You didn't run against him. He made sure you didn't run against him. He dared you to run on him. He came up telling you, 'you go and I got you.' You better make sure rounding second you were 100 percent sure you're gonna make it because if you're not he's gonna throw you out."

But the hitting didn't turn around until batting coach Walt Hriniak got Evans going in 1980. Evans became one of the better producers in the American League. He shared the home run title in the strike-shortened 1981 season, with 22 and would hit over 30 twice. He drove in 100 runs four times, including three years in a row from 1987 to 1989. For his career, Evans wound up hitting .272, with 385 homers, 1,384 RBIs in twenty years (the last spent in Baltimore). He struck out 1,697 times, but 1,391 walks left him with a .373 career on-base percentage. His 251 homers from 1981–1990 were the most by an American League player and his 605 extra base hits led all players in the 1980s.

"Dwight Evans was a very intense player," says Buck Martinez. "He got hit in the head early in his career and for awhile became somewhat timid. But then Walt Hriniak gave him a pretty good stance where he felt confident that if he did get something up around his head he could get out of the way—and he became a hell of a hitter.

"He used to talk a lot to himself at the plate, about staying back, 'stay on this pitch and this guy's not gonna get you out,' and he was a battler."

"It was absolutely amazing what he did out there in right field," recalls Hawk Harrelson. "The reason they were in it in 1975 was nothing hit the ground out there. Everything hit was caught."

"I haven't seen this guy out in Seattle [Ichiro Suzuki] throw [in person] yet, but I watched him the other day make a throw from right field [and] he reminded me of Dwight Evans, the way he threw the ball and his style," Red Sox rival Willie Randolph said in 2001. "He was a hell of a competitor, a hell of a gamer who played hard all the time. He was a little bit overshadowed at the time by players like Fisk and Rice, but a guy who would beat you late in the game, not only offensively but defensively, catch the ball, throw the ball. You need those types of people—everyone always wants to talk about the big guy, the stat guy—but you don't win championships, you're not a good team unless you have a great supporting cast."

The Red Sox never won a championship with Evans in right field, but Evans did hit 3 homers and drive in 14 runs in fourteen World Series Games.

"He was a very, very hard-nosed player, a guy who came to play every day, great throwing arm, accurate, played hard," offers Frank White. "Toward the end of his career he was about as dangerous a hitter as they come. I like the fact he didn't duck anybody, he just wanted to play every day and to play right field in Fenway and play it the way he played it. I enjoyed watching him play. He was fun to watch. Fundamentally, he was just so good."

Bill Madlock
(Mad Dog)

3B, 2B, DH, 1B, 1973–1987, Rangers, Cubs, Giants, Pirates, Dodgers, Tigers

Ask the average baseball fan for memories of Bill Madlock and you'll probably get the following: good hitter, not much power, played with some winning teams, moody, maybe even surly.

What you probably won't get is the fact that Bill Madlock won four batting titles during his fifteen-year major league career. Four batting titles! He's the only eligible four-time winner in baseball history not in the Hall of Fame.

Is there even a hint of Madlock becoming a Hall of Famer? No.

"He's a legitimate candidate," offers Bobby Wine. "You win four batting titles, somebody's gotta vote for you."

Not if they don't remember. "He's probably the most anonymous of all batting champions," says former player and executive Tom Grieve. "He won it four times [with averages of .354, .339, .328, and .341, the first two back-to-back]. That's incredible. How many guys win four batting titles and don't get consideration for the Hall of Fame?"

None.

"I think he was overlooked because—and I don't want to touch on this as a rap—but he was basically an offensive player," says fellow "Out by a Stepper" Larry Bowa. "That sorta shocks me because the Hall of Fame looks like it goes for offensive players—and he definitely had some numbers."

Adds Joe Torre: "All the batting titles. He played third base . . . OK . . . but four batting titles is pretty incredible."

"The Mad Dog," says Paul Molitor. "You ask somebody how many batting titles Bill Madlock had and they'd say maybe one or two. I don't think anybody would say four."

Bill Madlock *at a glance*

- Four-time batting champion, including back-to-back years
- .305 lifetime batting average
- 4 homers, 10 RBIs in ten LCS games
- Hit .375 in only World Series (1979)
- Three-time All-Star
- Struck out more than 41 times in a season only twice
- Had career-high 32 stolen bases 1979

Buck Martinez takes it a step further, saying, "He was Tony Gwynn before Tony Gwynn. He could hit whatever pitch you had and you couldn't fall into a pattern with him—and you couldn't establish one particular area of the plate because he had a swing for whatever you were featuring on any particular day."

But, for whatever reason, people tend to forget a player who hit .305 lifetime, who had 4 homers and 10 RBIs in ten playoff games and hit .375 in his one World Series (a Pirates' championship in 1979)—a guy who started his career by being traded for Hall of Famer Ferguson Jenkins and then taking over for Ron Santo (number six in this book)—and ended it by being traded to contenders who needed his bat and competitive drive for stretch runs.

"I played with Doggie [in Detroit]," says Alan Trammell. "What a short stroke. I don't think I've ever seen a guy with a shorter stroke. This guy, when he played with us in '87 was basically on his way down and he was a little bit overweight but he could still hit. He believed he could hit. He'd tell you he could hit. The good hitters do that. They don't come in wishy-washy, 'well, I don't feel too good today, blah, blah, blah.' They talk themselves into they can hit, they can hit anybody—and he always felt that way."

Madlock was not a power hitter—nor a great fielder—during a career that took him from Texas to Chicago to San Francisco to Pittsburgh to Los Angeles to Detroit. He hit 163 home runs and drove in 860 runs. He didn't walk a lot and only struck out more than 41 times in a season twice. He stole as many as 32 bases in a season (1979) and swiped 174 in his career. On more than one occasion, when he appeared to be done, he moved on and helped a team win.

There's a rap on him that says he sat out against tough pitchers, but the numbers are there.

And he could compete. Some people even say he was nasty. He wasn't the greatest guy to have around a losing club, but show him a chance to win and the numbers went up. "He wasn't a real flashy kind of a guy and he was surly," says Jim Kaat. "That's probably why he wasn't real popular. If he wasn't getting into trouble with the umpires, it was with his teammates, so maybe that's why he wasn't accepted as being as good a player as he was."

Others dispute this claim, acknowledging only Madlock's desire to compete but ending it right there. Yes, there was an infamous incident with umpire Jerry Crawford that led to a fifteen-game suspension for Madlock, but people make mistakes.

"He might have pissed some people off, just because of his tone and his moods," says Trammell. "He didn't care and to his credit that's probably what helped him become the hitter he was. He had a little sarcasm to him. He was cocky—he believed in himself."

"He was tough, tougher than the situation," says Hall of Famer Rod Carew. "You knew he was going to come through in every situation." Carew thinks the batting titles tend to get overlooked and people forget other things you do (Carew added that this applies to him, too).

"People think Bill won batting titles and didn't do anything else," says Carew. "He was a hard-nosed player [Bowa said he "hated" to see him coming into second base], he played the game hard, he knew how to play the game because he was brought up in an era where you had to know how to play the game."

Was Madlock mean? "Yeah, he was," says Carew, "because he was out there to do a job. He went out there and played hard every day, every single day. He didn't have friends [on the other teams]."

Concludes Wine: "He was a legitimate hitter."

And a legitimate member of this Out by a Step fraternity.

Charles (Buddy) Myer

2B, 3B, 1925–1941, Senators, Red Sox

T he mission of the Hall of Fame Veteran's Committee is to give worthy players who've been overlooked by the baseball writers' election another shot for admission into Cooperstown. The Washington Senators second baseman, Charles "Buddy" Myer, is one deserving candidate who has been overlooked by the Veteran's Committee as well.

Myer was brought up from the minors to play shortstop at the end of the 1925 season, hit an impressive .304, and appeared in the World Series. The young Mississippian showed enough promise in the field to make the Senators think they had their shortstop of the future. It didn't quite work out that way.

The following year Myer got off to a slow start and Tris Speaker, acquired from Cleveland in the offseason, convinced Manager Bucky Harris that the Senators were only a shortstop away from being a true pennant contender. "Speaker" was also sure that Red Sox shortstop Topper Rigney was the man to lead Washington to the pennant.

Harris took Speaker's advice, went out and got Rigney and sent the twenty-three-year-old Myer to Boston in return. Rigney flopped with the Senators and was out of the league by 1928. Meyer had two fine years with the Red Sox—in 1927 he hit .281 and then moved to third base in 1928 and hit .313 and led the league in stolen bases with 30.

Owner Clark Griffith called it the "worst trade I ever made," and Walter Johnson, named Washington's manager after the 1928 season, begged Griffith to get Myer back on the club. He opened negotiations with the Red Sox and by the time the deal was made, it cost the Senators five players to reacquire Myer.

"Walter Johnson was our new manager and I wanted to do something nice for him," Griffith said later. By this time a young Joe Cronin, at the beginning of a career that would lead to the Hall of Fame, had won the shortstop job and

Buddy Myer *at a glance*

- AL Batting Champion with .349 BA in 1935
- Nine-time .300 hitter (.303 lifetime)
- Beat out 60 bunts in one season
- Twice led AL second basemen in fielding percentage
- Led AL in stolen bases with 30 in 1928

Myer was moved over to second base, where he remained a standout and a favorite of Washington fans for the next decade.

A terrific player both offensively and defensively, the left-handed hitting Myer was a peppery leader, who served as team captain. Though unspectacular, he was steady, one of those players who managers love "because he does all the little things that help the ball club."

He did some of the big things as well, including hitting and fielding—he batted .300 nine times and was an outstanding second baseman, whose great speed enabled him to cover a lot of ground. In 1938, he led American League second basemen in fielding percentage and tied for the lead in 1931. And with his strong arm, Myer worked well with Cronin on the double play.

In addition, Myer walked more than twice as often as he struck out and was considered the best bunter in the league, reportedly bunting for 60 hits in one season. Though he was not a combative player, the 5'10", 163-lb. Myer was tough and handled himself well in two notable fights with much bigger opponents who tried to rough him up at second base.

The Senators won the pennant in 1933, with Myer leading off and future Hall of Famers Heinie Manush, Goose Goslin, and Cronin and fine hitters such as Joe Kuhel and Frank Schulte hitting behind him. Though they were defeated four games to one in the World Series by a powerful Giants squad that featured Carl Hubbell (ERA of 0.00 in two victories in the Series), Bill Terry, and Mel Ott (who hit .389 in the Series), it was a team long-revered by Washington fans and the last Senators outfit to taste postseason glory.

Myer reached the peak of his career in 1935 when he edged out Joe Vosmik of Cleveland for the batting crown with a .335 average. Vosmik was ahead by 10 points with four games to play, but Myer closed the gap to 2 points on the last day of the season. The Indians protected their man by benching him in a doubleheader against the Browns. Myer went out and got 4 hits in 5 at bats. When word reached the Indians camp, they sent Vosmik in as a pinch hitter in the first game and he failed to get a hit. He went 1-for-3 in the second game and Myer was the batting champ by a fraction of a point—.3495 to Vosmik's .3489. Myer also had 215 hits, 100 RBIs, 115 runs, and 96 walks.

Early in the 1935 season, *Washington Post* columnist Shirley Povich, who always thought Myer rated a slight edge higher defensively over the Tigers' Charley Gehringer, evaluated the Senators' second baseman's performance: "This season Myer is a demon player. In the field his daily work has shamed even the play of a Gehringer," Povich said. "At bat he is not only making more hits, but he is making them with men on bases and that is when the pay-off takes place. He is harder to pitch to than is Gehringer, and consequently, he draws more walks.

"Like Gehringer, Myer is the personification of steadiness out there on the ball field. Like Gehringer's, his second basing is the poetry of motion, the pinnacle of the art but, unlike Gehringer, Myer has always been possessed of the flash and fire that the Tiger star never boasted even at the peak of his play."

Myer stayed with the Senators until the 1941 season. He retired with 2,131 hits, 850 RBIs, 1,174 runs scored, and a lifetime batting average of .303.

When his playing days were over, Myer, a Mississippi A&M alum, declined several offers to manage and became a successful mortgage banker in Baton Rouge.

Jud (Boojum) Wilson

3B, 1B, 1922–1945, Negro Leagues:
Baltimore Black Sox, Homestead Grays,
Philadelphia Stars

The stories about Jud Wilson make Ty Cobb seem as gentle as Mr. Rogers.

When they talk about the most intimidating batters in baseball history, Jud "Boojum" Wilson has to be rated number one. The left-handed line-drive hitter who starred for several great Negro League teams over a twenty-five-year career, was not only one of the most prolific hitters of all time, but he was also one of the most ferocious competitors. His disagreements and fistfights with umpires, opponents, and teammates are legendary. Although reputed to be a quiet, friendly man away from the diamond, on the field the 5'8", 185-lb. Wilson was considered "the toughest man to handle in baseball."

As a ballplayer he had the respect of his contemporaries, and, according to statistics and eyewitness accounts of his ability, should be in the Hall of Fame.

Longtime manager Cumberland Posey placed Wilson on his all-time all-American team, and Satchel Paige considered him one of the two all-time best hitters in black baseball. Early in his career, Wilson was nicknamed "Boojum" because of the sound his line drives made when they hit the outfield wall. He was considered the hardest hitter in whatever league he played in and it didn't matter who was pitching. He destroyed lefties, righties, overhanders, sidearmers, fastballers, and curveballers with equal success. Nobody scared Wilson and Wilson scared everyone. His defense as both a first baseman and third baseman was rated as adequate. He was described as a "crude but effective workman" in the field.

Jud Wilson *at a glance*

- .347 lifetime hitter
- Batting Champion of Eastern Negro League with .408 BA in 1927
- Led championship teams with Baltimore Black Sox, Homestead Grays, Pittsburgh Crawfords, and Philadelphia Stars between 1929 and 1934
- .455 BA in first three East–West Negro Leagues All-Star games

---

His maniacal competitiveness must have been infectious because wherever Wilson went, victories followed. His first taste of the Negro major leagues came in 1922 with the Baltimore Black Sox, and he hit well over .400 in his rookie year as the team won the championship of the South. Baltimore used him primarily as a first baseman. In his nine years with the team, Wilson hit under .350 only once. The Black Sox won the American Negro League pennant in 1929 with the "million-dollar infield" composed of Wilson, Frank Warfield, Dick Lundy, and Oliver Marcelle.

When he left the Sox,, he continued to perform for winners. In 1931, he joined the Homestead Grays whose lineup included catcher Josh Gibson, first baseman Oscar Charleston, second baseman George Scales, shortstop Jake Stephens, outfielders Vic Harris and Ted Page, and a killer pitching staff of Willie Foster, Ted "Double Duty" Radcliffe, and "Smokey Joe" Williams.

The following year, Wilson and many of the star players jumped to the Pittsburgh Crawfords, joining future Hall of Famers Cool Papa Bell, Judy Johnson, and Satchel Paige on a virtual All-Star team that was named the unofficial champion of black baseball.

In 1934, he was a member of the Philadelphia Stars when they won the Negro National League pennant. Manager Webster McDonald named him team captain and Wilson showed fine leadership qualities but lost control and punched an umpire during the playoffs.

He was named player-manager of the Stars in 1937 and remained with the team until 1939, a year in which he hit .373 at the age of thirty-eight. As a manager, the stormy Wilson "was a strict disciplinarian who did not tolerate loafing or grandstanding."

Wilson was the East's starting third baseman and cleanup hitter in the first three East–West Negro Leagues All-Star Games.

In Wilson's declining baseball years, he went back to the Grays and contributed to their glory years of 1940–1945 when they won the Negro National League pennant each year. Wilson was a part-time player during the dynasty that was built around mainstays first baseman Buck Leonard, pitcher Ray Brown, shortstop Sam Bankhead, and center fielder Jerry Benjamin. Wilson managed to hit over .330 in half of his seasons.

When he retired, Wilson had a lifetime batting average of .347. He also won two batting titles in the Cuban winter league and hit a phenomenal .442 against major league competition.

Despite all of his glorious achievements on the field, Wilson is perhaps most remembered for his uncontrollable temper that made him one of the "four big bad men of black baseball." The others were Oscar Charleston, Vic Harris, and Chippy Britt. It probably wasn't any fun to face them when they all played for the Homestead Grays.

Many of his altercations involved his good friend and roommate, the equally rough Jake Stephens. When they were playing for the Philadelphia Stars, Wilson, for once in the role of peacemaker, tried to break up an altercation between Stephens and an umpire. Stephens reached around Wilson and sucker punched the ump, who thought the blow was landed by Wilson. He threw old Jud out of the game and Mt. Boojum erupted. It took three blackjack-wielding cops to subdue him, stuff him in a paddy wagon, and cart him off to jail.

In one of the most told stories in Negro League lore, after the East–West Negro Leagues All-Star Game in Chicago, Stephens was reported to have returned to their room early one morning after a night of carousing and woke Wilson up. Wilson picked up the 5'7", 150-lb. shortstop and held him out of the sixteenth story window by one leg. Stephens was drunk enough to keep kicking at the hand that held him from sure death, but when he kicked the powerful Wilson just kept switching hands until he decided to let his roommate live.

Another time a teammate threatened Wilson with a bat in order to keep him from seriously hurting an umpire who had made an objectionable call.

Jud Wilson was one tough guy and one of the great competitors. It's a shame he never got to show what he could do in league play against the likes of Lefty Grove, Dizzy Dean, or Carl Hubbell. And it's a greater shame that they never had the opportunity to face Boojum in a major league game.

Mickey Lolich

P, 1963–1976, Tigers, Mets, Padres

Tim McCarver says he was warned about Mickey Lolich before the 1968 World Series. "Roger Maris had told us that Lolich was going to give us the most trouble," McCarver says, looking back on the less-than-svelte left-hander who took a backseat to teammate Denny McLain in those days, but probably shouldn't have. "I had seen Lolich during spring training, too, so he didn't surprise us at all."

McLain won 31 games that season, losing only 6 in one of the greatest seasons of the modern era. Lolich was a more-than-respectable 17–9, nothing compared to the 25 games he would win in 1971 or the 22 in 1972. But in that 1968 World Series, when the Tigers came back from a 3–1 deficit to beat the defending-champion Cardinals in seven games, Lolich was amazing in winning the Series Most Valuable Player award.

McLain was 1–2 in that Series, beaten twice by Bob Gibson and going all the way in a 13–1 win in Game Six. Lolich posted a 1.67 ERA, pitched 3 complete games, and beat the legendary Gibson with a 5-hitter that included sixth-inning pickoffs of Lou Brock and Curt Flood. The Game Seven effort came on two days' rest.

Three games, 27 innings, 21 hits, 21 strikeouts, 6 walks. He even went 3-for-12 at the plate and hit his only home run of the season, one of three Tiger homers in Game Two. He evened the Series at 1–1, kept the Tigers alive when they were down 3–1 and then won Game Seven. The performance may never be topped because people just don't pitch this much anymore.

"McLain had several good years but he doesn't belong on this list—not the way I look at it," says McCarver. "Lolich does, though. You talk to any of the hitters in the American League in those days and they'll tell 'ya Lolich was a lot tougher pitcher than McLain—a lot tougher."

"That's exactly right," says former infielder Cookie Rojas. "He was a mainstay of the Detroit Tigers—the consistency, winning 3 games in that World

Mickey Lolich *at a glance*

- Three-time All-Star
- Went 3–0 with a 1.67 ERA in the 1968 World Series, pitching three complete games
- A lifetime .110 hitter, he hit a home run in the 1968 Series
- 25-game winner 1971
- Led AL in strikeouts and wins 1971
- 217–191 lifetime

Series. I know he had a lot to do with them being in that World Series. I know McLain won 30 games but that left-hander won a lot of big games for them and showed it in the World Series."

Talk to many people about Lolich, who also pitched for the Mets and Padres (10–16 over his last three years) and finished 217–191 with a 3.44 ERA, and they call him an earlier version of David Wells—a guy who looked like he'd be more comfortable in front of the TV set or at the bar than winning big games. Both won big games, though.

"Mickey was good—he was a workhorse," says former rival Lou Piniella. "Big old guy out there, uniform shirt coming out of his pants—he's David Wells, that's exactly what Mickey was, a durable guy that took the ball every four days at that time, pitch you 250 innings. I'm gonna tell you—I enjoyed hitting off of him but he had an excellent slider, darn good fastball, he came at you. He's another one—you want to win a ballgame, and you need a left-hander on the mound, give it to Mickey Lolich."

Adds Joe Torre, another member of our club, "Lo Lo's like Spahn. McLain won 30 games but all Lolich did was win 3 in that World Series in '68. Plus the fact that he was like Warren Spahn—I'd put Warren Spahn, Lolich, and David Wells in the same category where they could get up Christmas morning and throw the ball as good as they're going to throw it.

"Those rubber arms—didn't matter what they looked like, they could still pitch. That's why, you keep challenging David Wells, he's going to keep winning. His arm is not going to wear out—the rest of his body may, but his arm is not going to wear out."

"He enjoyed life. God he enjoyed life!" Torre said of Lolich. "It was only appropriate he went into the doughnut business when he went back to Detroit. I like Mickey. We were teammates in New York."

Added former major leaguer and long-time pitching coach Bill Fischer: "He looked like he was a bartender. But he had a good fastball, he was durable, good breaking ball, threw strikes. He's a durable guy."

Lolich's career almost didn't happen after he was temporarily blinded by a line drive that hit him in the head while pitching for Denver on opening day in 1963. He quit, but returned later that season and joined the Tigers. He didn't make an All-Star team until 1969, but in 1971 went 25–14, with 308 strikeouts and 29 complete games—29!

"He had a great arm," says McCarver. "He was like Chris Short in that he never had a sore arm, never ran into things. He was a sinker/slider pitcher and you don't usually find the sinker/slider pitchers as dominating as Mickey was in the World Series. Sinker/slider pitchers are guys that give up four runs every seven innings, those type guys—keep you in the game, a lot of ground balls, stuff like that. You don't talk about sinker/slider guys in a dominating fashion but he could be dominating as he proved in '68."

Piniella might sum Lolich up best when he says, "Mickey could pitch!

"He was a good pitcher, he was a real, real good pitcher—and you said to yourself, especially on a hot, muggy day in Detroit, 'well let's just be patient with this guy and make him throw pitches and by the sixth inning we'll have a better shot at him.' Well, hell, he was throwing harder and harder in the sixth inning than when the game started."

Fred Lynn

OF, DH, 1974–1990, Red Sox, Angels,
Orioles, Tigers, Padres

Noted baseball character Don Zimmer, interviewed for this book on Dodger center fielder Pete Reiser, said the following:

"Pee Wee Reese often told me that if Pete Reiser didn't run into walls, he might have been the greatest player in the game," Zim said. "But that's something we'll never know."

He was talking about Reiser. But in a sense, he also could have tossed Fred Lynn's name into the comment. Lynn didn't always run into walls, but he always ran into something that kept him from being one of the all-time greats. Some said it was what was inside him that caused little injuries to become big ones. Others argued that—and the list of hurts was very, very real—they did keep him from immortality.

"He was pretty to watch," says former rival Lou Piniella. "Everything flowed easily. He had a very pretty batting swing, classic batting style. It's something that if you had to teach to kids, just take a look at Freddie Lynn and copy that and if you've got ability you've got some success to go along with it. No effort."

Lynn arrived in the major leagues late in the 1974 season—and immediately started posting numbers far better than the ones he ran up in the minors. In 1975, he and fellow rookie Jim Rice (a member of our club's Top 10) burst onto the scene like no two rookies . . . probably ever. Lynn was American League Rookie of the Year *and* Most Valuable Player. Rice finished third in the MVP, second in the Rookie vote.

What they did as a pair that year was remarkable—and started a ten-year run for both that had them among the game's best.

Fred Lynn *at a glance*

- 1975 AL MVP
- 1975 AL Rookie of the Year
- Nine-time All-Star
- 1982 ALCS MVP
- 1983 All-Star Game MVP
- Hit .407 in postseason play
- AL rookie record 47 doubles 1975

"Freddie Lynn to me was a [Don] Mattingly when he first came up—you didn't know how to get him out," says fellow "Out by a Stepper" Joe Torre. "He could run—Mattingly couldn't run . . . but Freddie, he was a pretty player to watch. The great swing, hit the ball all over the place, played center field at Fenway and looked so easy doing it.

"He had a nice, easy gait to him. Willie Mays contends he loved playing center field because there were no walls—well you couldn't convince Freddy Lynn of that."

There were walls. And Lynn would find them. But he posted excellent numbers in a career that would last through 1989, when he finished with the San Diego Padres. Remember, this was a career that started with Lynn becoming the first player ever to win both the MVP and Rookie of the Year awards in the same year, something that Ichiro did in 2001. Lynn set a league rookie record with 47 doubles, led the league with 103 runs, and also became the first rookie ever to lead the AL in slugging average (.566). He was second in the league (to future teammate Rod Carew) in batting (.331), third in RBIs (105), fourth in total bases (299), and mixed in 21 homers. He drove in 10 runs in one game and had a record-tying 16 total bases (3 homers, a triple, and a single) in another. He also hit .364 in the playoffs (when the Red Sox ended the three-year reign of the Oakland A's) and .280 in the World Series.

Lynn was a nine-time All-Star, four-time Gold Glove winner, the first player on the losing team ever to be named MVP of a League Championship Series (1982, with the Angels, when he was 11-for-18 with a .611 batting average and had a homer and 5 RBIs—the hit total tying a record) and the 1983 All-Star Game MVP, thanks to his grand slam at Comiskey Park.

His .517 LCS batting average is the best ever for anyone with more than 25 at-bats.

Lynn batted .283 lifetime, with 306 homers, and 1,111 RBIs. In two visits to the postseason, he hit .407, with 2 homers and 13 RBIs in fifteen games.

Some felt Lynn's career was jolted when he was traded from the Red Sox to the Angels after the 1980 season—Lynn returning home to southern California but leaving a park that was suited for him. He hit .300 four of his six years with the Red Sox, batting a career-best .333 with 39 homers and 122 RBIs (both career highs) in 1979, when he finished fourth in the MVP voting. After leaving the Red Sox, the closest he came to .300 was a .299 season with the Angels in 1982, when they won the first two games of the ALCS from Milwaukee and then lost three straight in Lynn's final visit to the postseason.

So many felt Lynn should have stayed in Boston. Said Pinella: "He had power he had power to left-center, he had power to right, played the outfield very well . . . a complete ballplayer, and when you start talking about the three outfielders in Boston—Rice, Lynn and [Dwight] Evans—just three complete players. You start talking about those three guys, and you're talking about three darn good ones—I mean *good* ones."

73

Dick Groat

SS, 1952, 1955–1967, Pirates, Cardinals, Phillies, Giants

D ick Groat won a National League batting championship and Most Valuable Player award, was a leader and key player on two World Championship teams, and was the shortstop in two of the best double-play combinations—and baseball wasn't even his best sport.

Groat, the former Duke University basketball all-American and NCAA Player of the Year in 1952, who later played for the NBA's Fort Wayne Pistons, was not exactly Roy Hobbs on the baseball diamond, but he was one of the smartest players of his time and drove himself to become an effective shortstop and one of the fine hitters in the National League.

Early in his career, scouts focused more on Groat's flaws than on his abilities. The book on him was that he was slow afoot, with no power and an average arm. Somehow this added up to one great baseball player.

"Groat was an unusual player," said David Halberstam in *October 1964*, "He was one of the smartest athletes in the game, a man who had to work exceptionally hard to maximize his abilities and overcome his physical limitations.

"Not fast with leg speed but in terms of reflexes, he was exceptionally quick. He had great hand-eye coordination and deft hands."

Groat didn't have great range but his knowledge of his pitchers and opposing hitters gave him the advantage of almost always being in the right position to scoop up grounders no matter where they were hit.

"Playing position means doing what the pitcher wants you to do, relying on his judgment rather than your own opinion about how to play a hitter," Groat said. "I rely on the pitcher's idea of how the infield should play."

As an athlete, Groat was much more "a natural" on a basketball court.

"I never had real confidence in my baseball ability. It was different in basketball. I was quick and I knew how to put the ball in the hoop. Nobody ever

Dick Groat *at a glance*

- 1960 NL MVP
- 1960 NL batting champion (.325)
- Four-time .300 hitter
- Shortstop on 1960 Pirates and 1964 Cardinals World Champions
- Five-time All-Star
- Lifetime .286 BA, with 2,138 hits

said I couldn't do this, that, or the other thing. On a basketball court, I didn't have the faults they emphasized in baseball."

As a basketball player, Groat was one of the best. Red Auerbach, who rated Bill Sharman as the best shot in the game, said "second best isn't even playing— Dick Groat."

Branch Rickey signed Groat out of Duke and had him inserted directly in the Pirates lineup at shortstop without his ever having played a minor league game. He hit .284 in 94 games for a terrible Pirates team that was still years away from benefiting from a youth movement that would form the nucleus of the 1960 World Champions.

When the season ended, Groat played most of the next year for the Fort Wayne Pistons, where, before being drafted into the Army, he averaged in double figures and showed that he would have had great career in the NBA.

However, Rickey convinced Groat to concentrate on baseball, because he couldn't continue to play two sports professionally. He came back to the Pirates in 1955, combining with second baseman and future Hall of Famer Bill Mazeroski to form the best double-play combo in the league. He remained a fixture and fan favorite in Pittsburgh until he was traded to the Cardinals in 1963.

Groat, who was the team captain, hit .300 three times for the Bucs, peaking at .325 in the 1960 Championship year. He won the batting crown on the last day of the season, returning to the lineup after missing two weeks because of a broken wrist, and was voted the National League's Most Valuable Player. The Pirates, of course, beat the Yankees in the World Series that year, when Mazeroski smacked his dramatic home run in Game Seven.

Longtime birddog and manager Mayo Smith, who admired Groat's play observed: "He doesn't look like a hitter . . . but he knows what to do with the bat. He can keep a rally alive and he's toughest up there when the big chips are down.

"For that matter, he isn't fast enough to look like much of a shortstop. But he plays position so well that he gets in front of almost everything like he's popping out of a trap door. His arm doesn't seem strong either, but he throws you out by a step because he gets the ball away so fast."

Besides being noted as one of the greatest curve-ball hitters of his time and a master of the hit-and-run, Groat was regarded as an outstanding clutch hitter with a special talent for moving the runners into scoring position.

According to former Pirates teammate Bill Virdon: "In the seven years he and I batted 1–2 in the order, I could probably count on one hand the number of times Groat failed to advance me with one out."

Groat modeled his game after Giants shortstop and Out by a Step member Alvin Dark, who he thought was the smartest player in the game. In his rookie year, Groat approached Dark after a game for some pointers and Dark, right there under the stands at Forbes Field, demonstrated how to get out of the way of a runner at second base. In later sessions, the older player gave Groat batting tips on the hit-and-run and protecting runners by throwing your bat at the ball on an outside pitch, as well as fielding tips on shifting on the hitters and moving with the count.

When the Pirates, thinking that Groat had lost a step, traded him to the Cardinals in 1963, the shortstop was motivated by pride to prove them wrong. He batted .319 and anchored one of the great infields of all time, with Julian Javier at second, Bill White at first, and Ken Boyer third, to a second place finish. All four started in the 1963 All-Star Game—marking the only time an entire infield from one team was elected to the mid-summer classic. Groat received more All-Star votes than anyone in the league.

The following year, the Cards—who also featured Hall of Famers Bob Gibson and Lou Brock, as well as perennial Gold Glove center fielder Curt Flood—overtook the Phillies on the last day of the season to win the National League pennant. They went on to beat the Yankees in the World Series.

Groat's leadership and example were key elements in the Cards' title run.

Flood said he found it easier to steal when Groat was at bat because "Dick is so good at hitting at a hole that the infielders hesitate longer than usual before covering the base. I often got to second base before they did."

The shortstop was also instrumental in Javier's maturation into the best-fielding second baseman in the league, and is, in fact, credited with bringing the entire All-Star infield together and helping to mold them into a unit.

As one opposing player observed: "They were a bunch of individuals until he came along. Defensively they were loose. Now they were the best." Groat was traded to the Phillies after the 1965 season and his career ended with the San Francisco Giants in 1967. He had a lifetime batting average of .286, more than 2,000 hits, and led or was near the lead most years in putouts, assists, and double plays for a shortstop. He went to the All-Star Game five times and earned two World Championships rings.

Pretty darn good for a basketball player who couldn't run, throw or hit for power.

Graig Nettles (Puff)

3B, OF, 1967–1988, Twins, Indians, Yankees, Padres, Braves, Expos

The story, related by a Yankee teammate years later, goes something like this: Rich Gossage on the mound, Carl Yastrzemski at the plate, tying run on, two out in the bottom of the ninth of the one-game playoff for the American League East title. Graig Nettles is playing third base and talking it up.

"C'mon, Goose, c'mon, baby, pop him up, Goose, pop him up," Nettles allegedly yelled. Yaz swung—and popped the ball up to Nettles, who started shouting, "Not to MEEEEEE," and was screaming, "NOOOOOOOO!" as the ball was coming down into his glove.

"I was playing right field so I can't say for sure," says Lou Piniella. "But I wouldn't be surprised. That's the witticism you would attribute to Nettles."

Funny man this Nettles—one of the quickest wits you'd ever find—always there with something to loosen up a teammate, always there to help the Yankees through those stormy early years of George Steinbrenner. But Nettles was also more—much more.

"There was nobody better than him at third base—nobody!" says Hawk Harrelson. "Brooks [Robinson]? Oh yeah, sure, you gotta lump those guys together. You can't say that Brooks was better than Nettles or Clete Boyer—and some National Leaguers tell you [Mike] Schmidt was better than all of them."

Robinson's in The Hall of Fame. So is Schmidt. Nettles doesn't get a sniff, but the man Alan Trammell calls "the vacuum cleaner," had a career that produced 390 home runs, 1,314 RBIs, plenty of winning, one memorable World Series (his defense in Game Three of the 1978 Series turned things in the Yankees' favor), and a real place in Yankee history.

"Nettles hit more home runs than anybody from the left side during the time that he played," says Piniella. "He had a great glove at third base, a power

---

Graig Nettles *at a glance*

- 1981 ALCS MVP
- 2,225 career hits
- Two-time Gold Glove winner
- 390 homers, an AL-record 319 as a third baseman
- Six-time All-Star

---

bat in a ballpark that you needed left-handed power. Those plays he made in the '78 World Series against the Dodgers basically, in a nutshell, tell you what Graig's all about.

"Great glove. He knew how to play the position. In the years that I played, he probably played the position only second to Brooks Robinson—and not a distant second.

"He was quick-witted. He had intensity. He played to win. Just a great ballplayer. His batting average [.248] would be the only deterrent, if any at all, but when you look at his era and the third basemen that played, the defensive prowess that he had, the ability to get big hits for you and hit home runs . . . he's another guy that people should look at [for the Hall of Fame]."

If you scan the records section of the Yankee media guide, you'll see (entering the 2002 season) Nettles, who won a pair of Gold Gloves (1977 and 1978, both Yankee championship years), sixth in home runs (250, behind only Hall of Famers Ruth, Mantle, Gehrig, DiMaggio, and Berra), twelfth in RBIs (834), thirteenth in games (1,535), fifteenth in at-bats (5,519), and twentieth in runs (750). He was knocked out of the top twenty in hits in 2001.

Overall, Nettles—who also played with the Twins (he came up with them), Indians (before the Yankees), Padres, Braves, and Expos—had 2,225 hits. He won the American League home run title in 1976 (with 32) and was the ALCS Most Valuable Player in 1981. He played in fifty-three postseason games, hitting five homers, driving in 27 runs, and providing great defense. The six-time All-Star hit 319 home runs as a third baseman in the AL, the most in that league at that position.

"Graig never had to take a back seat to anybody, the way he played defense," says Joe Torre. "They seemed to be a little bit different. I think Nettles tried to be a little more acrobatic and Brooksie was unusual—he'd come in and make that play coming in and throw *over*hand to first base."

Adds teammate Willie Randolph: "He was one of those real quiet big-game guys, you know what I mean? Nettles had a real subtle demeanor about himself, but he was like a sly fox.

"It was almost like you wouldn't notice him in big games, but he always did something to kinda hurt you. He would strike out but if you made a mistake he would hit a home run. He would not look spectacular at third base but he would make a spectacular play. One of those kinda quiet assassins who puts the nail in the coffin when you least expected it. He wasn't someone who wowed you or stood out but he was very smooth, very fundamental and he always seemed to step up in the big game."

"Tremendous instincts," says Paul Molitor. "You knew how important it was to him to know what the pitcher was throwing—slider down and in I could always see him taking that crow hop to his right." It was Nettles who told Gossage [that] George Brett's bat had too much pine tar and should be checked if he hit a home run, which he did. It was Nettles who always seemed to be in the right place at the right time—and when it mattered most."

"Graig Nettles—hands at third base . . . Brooks is going to get all the credit for being the ultimate defensive player there but I don't recall this guy missing any balls," says Frank White, who knew a thing or two about defense.

And, if you made a mistake to Nettles: "I came into the league in 1963 and in all these years he's probably the best fastball hitter I've ever seen—he and Frank Howard," offers Harrelson. "I was in the top fifteen fastball hitters I've ever seen but Nettles was number one or two. Nobody was better than Graig."

Frank White

2B, 1973–1990, Royals

In a perfect world, Frank White will follow Bill Mazeroski into the Hall of Fame—striking another blow for the great defensive players in the game. And the rule change passed during the 2001 season may be the thing that gets White the recognition many feel he deserves.

In short, the new structuring of the Veteran's Committee and the rules that go along with it reopens the door for people like White, who had been forced out by the previous rule change that said the Veteran's Committee couldn't consider a player who didn't get enough votes while on the ballot.

"In '95, when I came up for the vote, they linked me with him because our numbers were so close at that time, so I only got eighteen votes," says White, the former Royals second baseman considered the Mazeroski of his era. "Now that he's been put in the Hall, there was another rule change so I'm not even eligible for the Veteran's Committee, which is the way it goes sometimes."

But that changed. Now, White does have a chance.

White seemed philosophical about the change that previously said that a player had to garner 60 percent of the ballots in any one year to even warrant consideration from the Veteran's Committee. That didn't happen. So, White, a product of the old Royals Baseball Academy and one of those classy individuals in sports, was set to settle for basking in the glory of what he did—and in the words of others talking about him.

"Frank White to me, if you look at the best second basemen in the game of baseball, all-around second basemen, was one of the best," says Cookie Rojas, also an ex–Kansas City second baseman: "I'm not only talking about defensively—[yes] I'm talking about great range, great arm, great pivot, [but he] could run, steal bases, hit for power, and did it for say fifteen years in the major leagues and became the best second baseman in the league for many, many years.

Frank White *at a glance*

- Eight Gold Glove awards
- ALCS MVP 1980
- Five-time All-Star
- 42 postseason games
- 407 career doubles
- Graduate of the Royals Baseball Academy

"Definitely, in my opinion, Frank White should be in the Hall of Fame, without a doubt."

Mazeroski finally got in—and there was talk even he wouldn't have made it had it not been for Ted Williams's health problems (Williams had to miss the vote and was not in favor of Maz because he was a defensive guy and not known as a hitter). White is out. But if you look at their careers, the only thing Maz had that White didn't was a home run to win a World Series.

"Defensively, there's nothing [White] could be envious of from Mazeroski," says Rojas. "Mazeroski was one of the best in the game—one of the best pivots, double-play men in the game of baseball. But when you're talking about Frank White and you put all the things together—the offense and the speed, the home runs, and everything else, he's got a better record than Bill Mazeroski. If Bill is in, why shouldn't Frank White be in?"

"He was as good as there was in baseball," says Hall of Famer Rod Carew.

Says White: "I actually wanted to be the best second baseman in the American League. That was something I worked hard for and I strived for."

The Mazeroski debate? Both had eight Gold Gloves. Both turned incredible double plays. Maz hit .260 lifetime, with 138 homers, and 853 RBIs in 2,163 games. White batted .255, with 160 homers and 886 RBIs in 2,324 games (playing his home games in a spacious park). White, playing the speed game on turf (at home, anyway), out-doubled Maz, 407–294, and had 178 stolen bases to Mazeroski's 27. Both had great postseason moments—Maz a .320 hitter with two homers in the World Series he won with one swing of the bat; White the MVP of the 1980 American League Championship Series, even though he hit just .212 in forty-two career postseason games.

"Frank was a guy who just knew his pitchers, knew his ballpark, knew how deep into right field he could play against some hitters," says future Hall of Famer Paul Molitor, who, when talking about White on the double-play pivot, said, "The ball never really stopped, it just changed direction."

"He was fearless in the pivot. It didn't seem like he had to work so hard to make the special play. He was as good as Roberto Alomar, even though Robbie is more flamboyant. In terms of consistency, I'd give Frank the edge."

Recalls former rival second baseman Willie Randolph: "He was so sure-handed. We all talk about making the routine plays and how championship teams have to have a certain solid middle—I thought he was really the glue to hold that middle infield together for the most part. Freddie Patek and Amos Otis and [Darrell] Porter were in the middle but Frank was the guy that really made the plays.

"He always turned the tough double play—always did the little things. He had a little more power than I did and I was more of an on-base guy than [he was]. Our careers really paralleled each other. We kinda had a little friendly rivalry thing going because every year we played Kansas City in the playoffs. Frank was one of those glue kind of guys—that don't get a lot of play but are very important to the success of the ballclub."

Randolph says he kids White about having the Series rings while White has the Gold Gloves, but White did win the World Series known as the "I-70 Series" with the Royals in 1985. He hit a home run and drove in three of his six Series runs that year while batting cleanup for an injured Hal McRae in a Game Three win that brought the Royals back from 2–0 to the Cardinals.

White matured as a hitter. And, looking back, it was a career that almost never happened—White coming out of an academy set up by Royals owner Ewing Kauffman. "We had about 475 players in that camp and he stood out as a graceful athlete," says long-time executive Syd Thrift, who set things up for the owner. "We put him at third base because he had good hands. We put him at shortstop and he absolutely had great range and a good arm and could learn so fast. We moved him to second base because of (Fred) Patek."

We all know what happened after that. Now, we'll see what happens with the new Veteran's Committee.

Cecil Cooper

1B, DH, 1971–1987, Red Sox, Brewers

I f we had an all-underrated section of this book, Cecil Cooper might be right up there at the top of the list.

Think of this guy's career. In Boston, he was overshadowed by some huge names and never really got much of a chance to play full-time. In Milwaukee, where he spent the major part of a proud career, he was an important part of a Brewer team that almost won it all in 1982. Hall of Famers Robin Yount and Rollie Fingers were on that team, as was future Hall of Famer Paul Molitor—in a small market that didn't get the media attention.

Through it all, there was Cooper: quietly putting up some huge numbers while playing a strong first base—and posting numbers that would see him finish his career with a .298 batting average, 241 homers and 1,125 RBIs. And no one seemed to know about the five-time All-Star.

"Cecil Cooper, my God—he played in a smaller market over there in the Midwest," says Lou Piniella. "When you look at what came out of there during that era, Cecil Cooper, Ted Simmons, Robin Yount, Paul Molitor. That's unbelievable talent and to have it all together on one team for such a long time is amazing."

"I think a lot of guys get overlooked because of the team that you play on and how much media is coming out of there?" offers Hall of Famer Rod Carew. "I think where you play and the fact the writers who vote on you never see you play."

Says former manager Buck Rodgers: "People don't notice him because he's so steady. He really doesn't have many highs or lows. He just goes out day after day and does the same thing."

Adds Piniella: "Cecil could hit! He's another one that had that Charley Lau-type of approach, almost like a George Brett-type approach to hitting. He would

> ## Cecil Cooper *at a glance*
>
> - .298 career batting average
> - Five-time All-Star
> - Two-time Gold Glove
> - Hit .300 seven-straight years
> - Had at least 106 RBIs four-straight years

lean back on that back side and just shift his weight through the hitting area. My God, he became a heck of a hitter and he was a pretty good first baseman.

"Cooper had power. He could hit left-hand pitching, he'd hit for average and he used the whole field to hit. He could rifle a ball down the left field line as well as the right field line, and he could hit you a home run to left-center field as well as right-center field. A tremendous, tremendous hitter."

But how tremendous?

Cooper posted mediocre numbers with the Red Sox in the early stages of his big-league life (he never got consistent playing time at first base on a crowded depth chart)—and his career took off when he was traded to Milwaukee for George Scott and Bernie Carbo after the 1976 season. Cooper then hit .300 for seven-straight years, a period that also saw him drive in at least 106 runs in four-straight full seasons (he also had a 99-RBI season later in his career).

The lefty hit .352 with 25 homers and 122 RBIs in 1980—the batting average good enough for a batting title in most years. But that was the season George Brett threatened to hit .400, winding up at an American League–best .390.

As good as this season was, it was just a warmup for what Cooper would do in 1982 and 1983. After a strike cut down the 1981 season (Cooper hit .320 and had 60 RBIs in 106 games), Cooper went crazy the next two years, hitting .313 and .303 with 62 homers, 247 RBIs, and 408 hits.

The Brewers, who lost a divisional playoff series to the Yankees in 1981 (Cooper, 4-for-10 in the 1975 American League Championship Series with the Red Sox and just 2-for-19 in the 1975 World Series, was 4-for-18 in the 1981 postseason) and fell behind the California Angels in the 1982 ALCS after winning the American League East. Cooper went just 3-for-20 in that series, but had the hit that brought in the tying and winning runs in the fifth game—Milwaukee becoming the first team to rally from a 2–0 deficit to win what was then a five-game playoff format.

Cooper then hit his only career postseason homer in Game Three (a Milwaukee loss) of the World Series and the Brewers led that Series 3–2 going back to St. Louis for Games Six and Seven—only to lose the last two games and leave Cooper without a career World Series ring (the 1975 Red Sox had lost that marvelous seven-gamer to the Cincinnati Reds).

For his career, Cooper wound up with 2,192 hits and 415 doubles. He went out quietly in 1987—about as quietly as he had played his entire career. No fanfare, no special days—the ultimate background guy.

"Smooth," former rival Frank White says when summing up Cecil Cooper. "Great bat control, smooth around the bag. He always reminded me of Rod Carew a lot, with his hitting style, ability to put the ball in play the other way, didn't strike out much—got big clutch hits for the Brewers. The '82 team he was on really impressed me a lot."

Kirk Gibson

OF, DH, 1979–1995, Tigers, Dodgers, Royals, Pirates

The words, while they might not ring through history quite as loudly as "the Giants win the pennant," will never be forgotten by any baseball fan.

"I don't believe what I just saw! I don't believe what I just saw!" the legendary Jack Buck sang as a crippled Kirk Gibson hobbled around the bases after hitting a 3–2 pitch from Dennis Eckersley into the right field stands at Dodger Stadium to win Game One of the 1988 World Series.

Gibson, who couldn't play because of a severely pulled left hamstring and strained right knee ligaments, started that game in street clothes—and wasn't even around for the opening introductions of the players. He ended it by dragging his wounded body up to the plate and dragging himself into the history books—in his only at-bat of a Series that the Dodgers eventually won. The two-run homer, listed as number six on a *Sporting News* top baseball moments list, was basically hit with one hand and no leg drive—and made a loser of Eckersley, who wasn't exactly known for postseason failure.

Like Bobby Thomson and Bill Mazeroski before him, Gibson had become identified with one swing of his bat—and one joyful trip around the bases, his being a rather difficult one despite the elation of the moment.

Thomson was a solid player (.270 lifetime, 264 homers) who had one great moment. Mazeroski is a Hall of Famer, regarded as the best fielding second baseman of his era. How about Gibson? Where does this former wide receiver from Michigan State—who played baseball like it was really a football game—fit in, in terms of baseball history?

Many loved Gibson. Some thought he was a football player playing baseball. "I think so, definitely. That's his game," former infielder and long-time baseball man Cookie Rojas said.

Kirk Gibson *at a glance*

- 1988 NL MVP
- 1984 ALCS MVP
- 7 HRs, 21 RBIs in twenty-one postseason games
- 284 stolen bases

The stats don't make Gibson a Hall of Famer—a .268 lifetime batting average, 255 homers, 870 RBIs, actually not even equaling Thomson. Gibson played in only 1,635 games because of injuries (Thomson played in 1,779), making his career way too short for Hall of Fame consideration.

Hall of Fame? Nah. Heck, Gibson won the Most Valuable Player award in 1988 and drove in only 76 runs. There was just something about him that gets him into this book—and into the hearts of a lot of baseball people. One of those people, Wade Boggs, called Gibson "a fierce competitor."

In his book *They Call Me Sparky*, Gibson's manager in Detroit, Sparky Anderson, says, "Gibby will probably never go into the Hall of Fame. But he was a Hall of Fame performer. He hit more game-winning home runs than anyone I ever saw in my career.

"Gibby was a true winner. He's the perfect team player."

"Gibson was an athlete," says former rival Lou Piniella. "He had tremendous foot speed that probably comes back from his football days. He competed—he reminds me a little bit of Paul O'Neill, although not to that [extreme].

"I enjoyed watching him play—I had fun watching him play. You didn't know how he was going to respond at times, but he was an excellent outfielder, had tremendous power—not as fluid as a Freddy Lynn, somebody you would think would have to work on his skills to keep refining them. Power and speed. Just a solid, complete player."

Gibson hit .282 with 27 homers and 91 RBIs in helping the Tigers to the runaway 1984 American League East title. He was then MVP of the American League Championship Series, going 5-for-12 with a homer and 2 RBIs in a three-game sweep of Kansas City. He batted .333 and hit 2 homers in Game Five of the World Series as the Tigers won it for the first time since 1968.

In 1987, Gibson hit the fourth of his seven postseason homers (in a twenty-one-game postseason career) but it wasn't enough for the Tigers to beat the Twins in the league championship. He batted just .154 in the NLCS win over the Mets in 1988, but hit 2 homers—and then one more in his only at-bat in a second World Series title.

Kirk Gibson never drove in 100 runs in a season. He never hit 30 homers, either, and played the first and last parts of his career in bandbox Tiger Stadium. He never won a Gold Glove. He stole 284 bases and played the game so hard every time out there.

"I like the way he competed on the baseball field," said Piniella. "I mean, he played to beat you. He played hard and he had the tools to do it. He played the game with a little reckless abandon and he played it win."

Adds Joe Torre, "He was a big-game guy."

"We'll be seeing that home run he hit off Eckersley forever," Torre said. "It will be like the Bobby Thomson home run. He led the Dodgers to a very unlikely victory in the World Series in '88. He was a football player, Michigan State, hard-nosed type of guy, the MVP with a sub-.300 batting average which I think is an indication of what he possessed."

Cito Gaston said, "Kirk Gibson was quite a player. I don't think people really knew how hard he played and how intense he was playing. And his speed—he had great running speed, he could beat you with a home run, beat you with his speed."

Anderson said Gibson was a problem early on—because of his "meanness." Said Sparky: "He probably was the toughest project I had in my career." But Gibson matured, Anderson said, adding, "I ain't ashamed to say that I love Kirk Gibson."

Vern Stephens (Junior)

SS, 1941–1955, Braves, Red Sox,
White Sox, Orioles

Johnny Pesky still isn't sure why Red Sox manager Joe McCarthy moved him from shortstop to third base after Vern Stephens arrived in Boston from the St. Louis Browns.

To this day, Pesky doesn't care. Junior was a special player and Pesky knew it. He was happy to have him on his team.

"I knew Stephens was a shortstop and I was willing to play anywhere," Pesky says now, looking back. "I'd have played right field if that would have let Stephens play. I knew how good a player he was."

With all the bad deals the Red Sox have made through the years—yes, starting with shipping Babe Ruth to the Yankees—the one that brought Stephens from St. Louis to Boston ranks as one of the good ones. The Browns, in need of cash (sound familiar, Sox fans?), shipped Stephens and Jack Kramer to Boston for six no-names and $310,000. The transaction didn't turn out to be Ruthian, but it had its impact.

As you probably know, the Sox didn't win the World Series with Stephens. They didn't even make it to the World Series, losing a one-game playoff for the American League title to Cleveland in 1948 and blowing the pennant to the Yankees on the final weekend in 1949—as painful back-to-back seasons as the Sox have had through these many decades of not winning it all. But Stephens, who jumped to the Mexican League during a holdout in 1946 and was smuggled back into the country after playing two games there, put up some incredible numbers in Boston.

"He just loved to play the game," says Pesky. "He hit a lot of home runs and drove in a lot of runs and he could run [even though he didn't steal bases]. He

Vern Stephens *at a glance*

- 1945 AL home run leader
- 1945 AL RBI leader
- Tied for AL RBI lead in 1949
- Two-time All-Star
- 1,147 career RBIs

had great instincts for the game and loved to talk about the game. We used to talk baseball all the time on trains."

In Stephens's first three years in Boston, he hit 98 home runs and drove in 440 runs. Think about that. A shortstop! Those are the kinds of numbers that would make today's power shortstops proud. He tied teammate Ted Williams for the league RBI lead in 1949 (159) and teammate Walt Dropo for the same title in 1950 (144). All this after delivering 137 runs in 1948.

"He had an open stance and he stood on top of the plate," recalls former lefty Billy Pierce, another member of our club. "Great power. He was probably underrated because he had some good years with St. Louis during the war. People tend to discount those years, especially with the Browns. Vern was without a doubt one of the stars of that era."

So much so that a web site exists where you can compare Stephens and fellow "Out by a Stepper" Joe "Flash" Gordon to Red Sox second baseman Bobby Doerr, who is in the Hall of Fame. The comparisons are quite favorable.

Of his time in St. Louis, playing at Sportsman's Park, the site notes Stephens hit right-handed in a lefty-friendly park but that his numbers more than held up against lefty Hall of Famer Stan Musial. Stephens won the National League home run title in 1945 (Musial was in the service that year)—a year after finishing third in the MVP voting. He tailed off in 1946 and 1947 before being dealt to Boston. "Think about it," the author states, "he was averaging about the same HR and RBIs as Stan Musial! And it was a better park for Musial in which to hit."

The Red Sox hope was that Fenway Park, with its righty-friendly Green Monster awaiting, would regenerate Stephens's career. It worked—Stephens became a monster in front of the Monster.

"I can remember in those years, you talked about guys you wanted on your ballclub—Junior was one of those guys," Pesky says. "He could do a lot of things. When we had him and Ted and Dropo in the same lineup—those guys were scary together."

Stephens, who led the National League in errors in 1942 and 1948 but was still regarded as a good fielder, was angry at the Browns for not rewarding him for leading the National League in homers in 1945. Even though Happy Chandler was threatening five-year suspensions for any player who jumped, Stephens signed a big contract in Mexico but never cashed any of the checks—and was spirited out of the country and back into the United States by a group led by his father (not even taking his clothes with him).

The Browns gave him the $17,500 he wanted, instead of the $13,000 they'd been offering, and his stay in Mexico was over. His stay in St. Louis lasted two more years before the move to Boston—and the big years of 1948–1950 were followed by injuries. He lasted until 1955, but was never the same player. He died in 1968.

"He was a big handsome kid, big grin and all that," says Pesky. "He was always out at night [they were roommates] but he always got his work done. And he was as good as there was."

For his career, Stephens wound up hitting .286, with 247 home runs and 1,147 RBIs. Like so many others, his career numbers tend to get lost in the fact he played for the Browns (he did get to the World Series in 1944, going 5-for-22 with no homers). Toss in the numbers he posted during World War II, when many of the game's best players weren't around, and you can see why there's a tendency to overlook what he's accomplished.

But those numbers he put up in Boston at the end of the 1940s and into the 1950s can't possibly be overlooked.

Bob Boone

C, 1972–1990, Phillies, Angels, Royals

Wade Boggs, one of the best hitters of his day, had nothing but admiration for Bob Boone, one of the best catchers.

"He was probably the smartest catcher that I ever had to deal with behind the plate," the five-time American League batting champion says of Boone, who played nine years with the Phillies, seven with the Angels, a couple with Kansas City, and went on to become a big-league coach and manager.

"It was almost like he was in your head and he would call a game on what you would think and set you up that way."

There was more, according to Boggs, who said, "He could get more calls by either sticking his arm out or catching the breaking ball against his chest. He just had an uncanny way of getting strikes when he needed to get them.

"A guy threw a high breaking ball and he'd just let it sink and he'd catch it against his chest to give an illusion that it's a strike. Or, if they'd throw a low fastball, he'd stick out his hand before it got any lower to get the illusion that it's a strike. He would catch balls at the end of his glove, half the ball would hang out, this part of the ball's on the corner and the ball's off the plate, so he would give the illusion that he caught it on the corner but in actuality the ball's hanging out of the edge of his mitt, which is that far outside. He was so smart."

Boone batted only .254 in his long big-league career. But he caught more games than any catcher in history (2,264), won seven Gold Gloves, and batted .311 in thirty-six postseason games, winning the World Series with the Phillies in 1980 and batting .412 in that Series.

"Longevity in a position that's not known for that—I have the greatest amount of respect for Bob Boone," says Tim McCarver, whose job was taken over by Boone in 1973—before McCarver was brought back to be Steve Carlton's personal catcher. "I mean, to have done what he did and to have

Bob Boone *at a glance*

- Caught 2,225 games, the most by any catcher until past by Carlton Fisk
- Seven Gold Gloves, the last at age thirty
- Hit .311 in 30 postseason games
- Hit .412 in the 1980 World Series
- One of three generations in big leagues, all hitting at least 100 homers

made himself the type of player that could last as long as he lasted, the pride he took in one of the more important areas of the game and that was calling the game . . . constantly trying to learn and get better.

"And when he ended up doing what he did and achieving what he achieved, I was not surprised. I knew the type of person he was. If Jim Hegan was remembered for the way he handled pitchers, Bob Boone, who caught nearly a thousand more games than Jim, should be equally remembered."

The Phillies thought Boone, the middle rung of three generations of Boones in the big leagues, was all done after the 1981 season, but he became reborn in the American League with the then-California Angels.

"He was one of those guys . . . you didn't like him because it was almost like it was two against one: the pitcher and him," says former rival Willie Randolph. "He was very good at knowing what your weaknesses and strengths were. It was like having a coach on the field—he was like Carlton Fisk at double-teaming on you.

"He knew how to set you up. He was one of those guys that was always kind of annoying behind you because you always felt he was in your head. He knew how to back you off, go away. He played a lot of psychological games with the hitter."

Boone's best year at the plate was probably 1988 when, at the age of forty, he batted .295 for the Angels. He won a Gold Glove at thirty-eight, making him the oldest non-pitcher to do so. In 1987, he passed Al Lopez's mark for games caught. In 1988, he hit his 100th homer, making the Boone's the second family with a father and son hitting 100 homers. His son, Bret, made it three generations in 1999.

"His longevity is amazing," says former catcher Randy Hundley. "He fought through some pretty bad knee injuries. He was a complete catcher—the best at digging the ball out of the dirt. He also knew how to work the pitchers and he was a tremendous asset as a leader on that team."

Added Joe Torre, also a former catcher before switching to third base: "He was very proud of what he did behind the plate. He had a lot of success behind the plate. Pitchers had a lot of confidence in him and that's half the battle when you're a catcher—to get that pitching staff to believe in you. He had a lot of qualities you don't find in the record books."

Former rival Lee Mazzilli recalls Boone as "a cerebral catcher," and said Boone "fit in" as a hitter on some good teams. "Bob improved as a hitter as time went on," offers Cito Gaston, a former outfielder who has managed and worked as a hitting coach.

"I know Boone called a good game because, as a hitting instructor, watching him, I used to notice a lot of times he would go back-to-back. You'd get a home run off one pitch and a lot of times he would come back with it again—and a lot of times he got guys out with it."

Whatever it took—out-thinking the hitter, fooling the umpire, whatever. Bob Boone got it done!

Bert (Campy) Campaneris

SS, 3B, OF, 2B, 1964–1981, 1983, A's,
Rangers, Angels, Yankees

When you look back at all the big names adorning the Oakland A's roster back in the early 1970s, it's easy to forget the skinny shortstop who did so much to help those bad boys win three-straight world championships.

Think about it. There was Reggie Jackson, Catfish Hunter, Rollie Fingers, Joe Rudi, Sal Bando. The manager, Dick Williams, was high profile. So was the owner, Charles Finley. And then there was the shortstop, a quiet leader, one of those parts every winning machine has to have. The "Road Runner."

"Campy was one of the best shortstops in the game," says Hall of Famer Rod Carew. "Campy knew how to play the game."

"When I came into the league as a rookie, they were really good," says fellow shortstop Bucky Dent. "He got overlooked because of some of the guys on that team but he kinda made them go a little bit."

"He was the kind of guy that just made things happen. He'd jumpstart their offense at the top. He was a steady shortstop, made the plays—he did a lot of things well. He would put pressure on you, he could run, he handled the bat very well—he did a lot of little things that kinda made you aware of him when you played them."

Says former player and general manager Tom Grieve: "You start with Reggie, you'd say Joe Rudi, you'd go to Sal Bando, you might even get to Gene Tenace—hell, some people might say Billy North or someone like that. You do tend to forget about Campy—you do take him for granted, but there's a good chance that those A's teams wouldn't have been what they were without him."

Bert Campaneris *at a glance*

- 649 career stolen bases
- Led AL in steals six times
- Six-time All-Star
- 2,249 career hits
- 1,181 runs scored
- Once played all nine positions in a game

Adds Tommy Harper: "You have to have those kind of players in order to win. You just can't have a Reggie Jackson and a Joe Rudi and leave it at that."

In his autobiography, Jackson, discussing Charlie Finley's blueprint for a champion, ran down the Oakland lineup and said, "Campy: Good with the bat in the second spot. Move North around. Get on himself. Steal 50 bases himself."

And while Campaneris was widely known for his defense, there was much more to him. Consider what Lawrence Ritter and Donald Honig wrote in *The Image of Their Greatness*: "At shortstop, Bert Campaneris, born in Cuba in 1942, sparked the team with his speed and competitive drive. Campaneris is generally thought of as a defensive wizard and a speedster with a light bat. And a star on the basepaths. He has over 600 lifetime stolen bases (649)—the only men who have stolen more bases than Campaneris are Lou Brock, Ty Cobb, Eddie Collins, Max Carey, and Honus Wagner.

"But his bat was not all that light: one year he hit 22 home runs, and indeed in his very first major league game he hit two of them, a feat accomplished by only two others in baseball history."

Frank White was a kid in Kansas City and saw that feat, which included the first homer on the first pitch Campy saw from Jim Kaat. "Because he played for the A's, I followed him—he led the A's," White says. "He was a key to that team."

Adds former teammate Bill Fischer: "He was about two clicks less than Luis Aparicio. He was in the same category. Luis had good speed, a good arm; Campaneris had good speed, good arm. He was good—he could steal a base, get a base hit, throw you out from the hole."

While other names overshadowed Campaneris, two things in his career also tend to hide what he did. In 1965, he played every position in a game—even pitching both ways depending on the hitter in his two innings on the mound. And then there was the 1972 playoffs, when Detroit manager Billy Martin, already tired of watching Campy tear his team apart in the first two games, told Lerrin LaGrow to throw at Campaneris's legs. The pitch hit Campaneris above the ankle and he fired his bat at the mound, LaGrow ducking as the bat sailed over his head.

Martin tried to get at Campaneris, ripped him apart in the media after the game and called for a suspension. He got one—Campy was out of the rest of the series. He was reinstated for the World Series, batting just .179, but the A's won the first of their three-straight anyway.

Campaneris, who also played for Texas, California, and the Yankees in a career that spanned 1964–1983, batted .259 lifetime. He had 2,249 hits and scored 1,181 runs. He was a six-time All-Star. He led the American League in stolen bases six times and finished second once.

"Campy was one of those guys that could disrupt the other team with his speed," says Grieve. "He was a very good shortstop. He used a huge bat and didn't hit for a lot of power and I don't know how high an average he hit for. But he was a big-time base stealer; he was a very daring kind of a player.

"When he got on base at the beginning of a ballgame, he was a guy the pitcher really had to take notice of. He could disrupt the pitcher's concentration with his presence on the bases. He scored a lot of runs ahead of Reggie and Rudi and Bando by getting on base. He was also a guy who knew how to play the game—like another coach on the field, even though he didn't have tremendous command of the English language, he was still a very, very bright player and a leader at that position on that great team."

Great team. Great players. Big-name players. And Campy.

Elroy (Roy) Face

P, 1953, 1955–1969, Pirates, Tigers, Expos

No man did more to change the role and perception of the relief pitcher than Elroy (Roy) Face of the Pittsburgh Pirates. Face, along with a handful of his contemporaries, redefined the role of the short reliever and paved the way for terms such as "closer," "fireman," "short reliever" and "ace reliever" to be added to the baseball lexicon. The job description for these career relief pitchers was to come into the game in pressure situations and shut down the opposition. In the late 1950s and early 1960s, nobody did that better than Face.

According to Pirates catcher Hal Smith, "before Elroy, relief pitchers were guys who couldn't make the starting rotation. You were usually happy to knock the starter out and face the relief pitcher. The hitters were definitely not happy to see Elroy Face come into the game."

The slightly built (5'8", 155-lb.) Face, who popularized the forkball (which came to be known as the split-finger fastball), is usually remembered for his greatest season—1959, perhaps the greatest season ever by a relief pitcher. Face was 18–1 with a 2.70 ERA and 10 saves. (Saves were much harder to come by in those days.).

However, by dwelling on that one year, we tend to overlook the contribution that Face made to the Pirates and to the changing landscape of baseball over his sixteen-year career.

Teammates remember Face as a courageous pitcher who could be counted on to kill opposing teams' rallies. They point to his 193 career saves, (he led the league three times) his 96 career victories in relief, and his performance in the Pirates' 1960 World Series victory over the Yankees, during which Face pitched in four games and saved three.

"Elroy was the greatest reliever in the game when he played," said long-time teammate Dick Groat. "When he walked out on the mound, he lifted the

Elroy Face *at a glance*

- Credited with popularizing the "forkball" (now the split-finger fastball)
- 18–1 record as a relief pitcher in 1959 (17 victories in a row)
- 18 relief wins in a season is all-time record
- 96 career relief wins ranks sixth all time
- Led NL in saves three times and appearances twice
- Eleven years with 50-plus appearances, 848 lifetime

whole team up. We always knew he would get us out of a jam. And he was great in other aspects of the game. He had an excellent pickoff move, he was a great fielder, and he was a fine bunter. If you needed him to sacrifice he was usually successful. Elroy did everything you asked of him."

Face began his career in the late 1940s in the Phillies organization and was later drafted for the Dodgers by Branch Rickey. Rickey, who moved on to Pittsburgh to try to rescue the Bucs from one of baseball's worst runs of ineptitude, picked Face out of the Dodgers system in 1952.

Originally a combination starter-reliever, Face was primarily a reliever by 1956, leading the league in appearances with 68. In his career, Face pitched in more than fifty games eleven times and led the league again in appearances in 1960 with 68.

After Danny Murtaugh took over as manager of the Pirates in 1957, Face never started another game. Armed with a full assortment of pitches including an effective curve and fastball, Face's out pitch was the "forkball" which he had learned from Joe Page, who was his teammate on the Pirates in 1952. Hal Smith remembers Face holding two baseballs in his right hand to get his fingers to spread farther apart for the forkball.

Groat described the movement on Face's forkball. "When it started coming at you it looked just like a fastball and then when it got to the plate it just died. It was almost impossible to hit."

Face led the league in saves in 1958, which set the stage for his incredible 1959 career year. Manager Danny Murtaugh told the story of how important Face was to the Pirates.

"We were playing in Cincinnati and Face had pitched in eight or nine consecutive games and I thought I'd give him a rest this night," Murtaugh said. "The game went along, we got a couple runs, they got a couple. Then in the eighth inning, when we were ahead 8–6, the Reds got the bases loaded.

"I walked out to whoever was pitching and said: 'If you were me, what would you do in a spot like this?'"

"And he said: 'You'd be a damn fool if you didn't bring in the little guy.'"

Critics claim that Face's record 18 victories in 1959 was somewhat tainted because on several occasions he lost the lead only to go on and get the victory when the Pirate batters won the game in later innings. His teammates think the criticism is unfair and that the rare times that this happened did nothing to diminish Face's achievement.

"That's nonsense," Groat said. "I've never seen a relief pitcher that consistent."

Describing Face's dominance of National League batters, pitcher Vern Law said:

"As far as I'm concerned, there hasn't been anybody that has been as effective in a relief role. Bases loaded, nobody out, more than once the bases were still loaded and there were three out."

Smith, who joined the Pirates in 1960 said: "Face was a great competitor. You had to be to pitch all the time as he did. He had the most rubber arm of any pitcher I've ever seen. And he always kept the ball down. He never walked anybody."

In 1962, longtime Pirates announcer Bob Prince talked about Face to Gene Cuneo of the *Erie (Pa.) Times*. "He has pitched in 57 or more games for the past six years. Nobody has ever come close to that feat," Prince said. 'It's a wonder he's got an arm at all. There never was a relief pitcher like him."

Face, who kept his hands strong by working as a carpenter in the offseason (and after he retired), made it seven years in a row with 63 appearances that year.

Face's achievements may not look as impressive today, because his relief appearances and save numbers have been exceeded by many in an age in which managers go to the bullpen much more frequently. However, Elroy Face had a lot to do with the later trend to rely more on the relief pitching, especially the career closer. He and Hall of Famer Hoyt Wilhelm were the forerunners of later relief artists such as Rollie Fingers, Goose Gossage, and Bruce Sutter.

Reggie Smith

OF, 1B, 3B, DH, 1966–1982, Red Sox,
Cardinals, Dodgers, Giants

T om Grieve will never forget the first time he saw Reggie Smith—
Grieve a teenager in awe of a young man just three years his elder.

"When someone says Reggie Smith to me, the first thing that comes to my mind is Clapp Park, a high school field in Pittsfield, Massachusetts, where we played our high school games," the former outfielder and general manager says. "When the Pittsfield Red Sox first came into being in probably 1965, Reggie Smith and George Scott were on that first team that came to Pittsfield. And they worked out, Wikona Park probably was under water and they weren't able to practice there. So they practiced at Clapp Park and we knew they were going to practice so we went out there to watch them.

"It was the first time we'd ever seen professional players—they were bigger, stronger, they could hit, but the one thing that stood out that we couldn't believe was when he threw from right field. We had never seen anything like it—we couldn't imagine that someone could throw like that. He was in deep right field taking infield practice and he looked like Roger Clemens throwing a pitch from the mound to home plate, only it was going from right field to third base. It was incredible. I was probably sixteen.

"His arm stood out. We would go to watch them play almost every night and it was pretty obvious, even to high school kids, the physical ability he had. He could run—nobody looked better in a uniform than he did. He had a great arm, good defensive player, switch hitter."

Smith, then around twenty, was impressive. He was always impressive. He may not have compiled the numbers some thought he should have, but he always looked good doing whatever it was he was doing.

Reggie Smith *at a glance*

- Seven-time All-Star
- Led NL in total bases 1971
- Gold Glove 1968
- First player to hit 100 home runs in each league
- .287 lifetime hitter, with 314 homers and 1,092 RBIs

"The thing I liked about him is he could do everything and he looked good doing it," says Grieve. "He just had that style about him—Roger Maris was like that.

"Some guys have maximum effort, they grunt when they throw it and their head's flying when they're running, but with him everything was smooth. When he threw the ball like that it didn't even look like he was trying to throw it, he had an effortless swing, a switch hitter. He looked good. He made the game look easy."

Reggie Smith played seventeen years in the major leagues. He batted .287, hit 314 homers, drove in 1,092 runs, scored 1,123, and stole 137 bases. He was a seven-time All-Star who led the American League in total bases in 1971, the same year he led in extra-base hits and one of the two years he led in doubles. He won a Gold Glove in 1968. He was also the first player to hit at least 100 home runs in both leagues.

"I thought he was as good a player as we had in those days," says long-time Red Sox fixture Johnny Pesky. "In fact, I think Reggie Smith was as good a player as we've ever had. He could run, he could throw, he could hit."

Tim McCarver calls Smith "A guy who knew how to hit—a guy with a gifted body."

And Lou Piniella says: "More power from the left side—just a good hitter from both sides with more power from the left side. Excellent, excellent out-fielder who probably, in his era, had the best throwing arm of anybody.

"He had a cannon. He could steal a base, could drive in a run for you, whether it be with a base hit or a home run ball and then win a game for you defensively in the outfield. A great player."

Six times in his career, Smith, originally signed as a shortstop by the Twins and lost to the Red Sox for $8,000 in the minor league draft, homered from both sides of the plate in the same game. He was a triple-A batting champion in 1966 before reaching Boston, batting just .246 as a rookie. That year also marked the first of Smith's four trips to the postseason—and he homered twice in a seven-game loss to Bob Gibson and the Cardinals. He got to the World Series four times, but didn't play on a winner until the 1981 Dodgers rallied from down 2–0 to sweep the next four games from the Yankees.

Smith hit six homers in thirty-two postseason games, with 17 RBI. He won his Gold Glove in his second year in the big leagues, when he also led the American League in putouts. But his days in Boston would end after a series of controversies and his feelings of racial problems on the club and in the city.

"They don't want a black star," he once charged. He was shipped to the Cardinals with Ken Tatum in the deal that sent Rick Wise and Bernie Carbo to Boston. The Red Sox had once accused Smith of delaying his return from a knee injury and now all that was behind him. He hit over .300 in both his full years in St. Louis and was traded to the Dodgers for Joe Ferguson less than a month after hitting 3 homers in a game. He would stay with the Dodgers through 1981, finishing his career with a strong season with the Giants in 1982. He did play two years in Japan after that.

"As great a physical talent as he was, he had a fine career, I don't know that he ever reached the level that some people might have predicted for him looking at his physical tools and the ability he had," says Tom Grieve. "He ended up having an excellent career, but I think some people thought he might even have a better career than he did."

Burnis (Wild Bill) Wright

OF, 1932–1945, Negro Leagues:
Baltimore Elite Giants

Integration came a little too late for Burnis "Wild Bill" Wright, the switch-hitting Negro League star who spent the first half of his career with the Elite Giants and the second half as one of the premier outfielders in the Mexican League.

He was one of those players who was caught in the middle, still active and producing primetime numbers, but a little too old for the major leagues to hire due to the tortoise-like gradualness of integration. Wright, Hall of Famers Ray Dandridge, and Leon Day, and star players such as Piper Davis and Max Manning were still young enough to make a difference on major league rosters, but were kept in the minors, the Negro Leagues, or Latin leagues as their playing days slipped away. Other outstanding Negro Leaguers such as Willard Brown, Quincy Trouppe, Bus Clarkson, and Artie Wilson were brought up for a "cup of coffee," and players such as Luke Easter and Sam Jethroe produced in the majors but were gone as soon as they showed any sign of diminished skills.

Wright was a large man (6'4", 225 lbs.) who hit for power and average and was fast enough to be regarded as one of the top defensive center fielders and base stealers of his time. He was also adept at laying down a nifty bunt and legged out many infield hits throughout his career.

"Bill could run like a deer," said Hall of Famer Monte Irvin. "He was a great drag bunter and he could steal 40–50 bases. As a hitter, he had both power and dexterity, usually batting about .350. Anyone who saw him will attest to the fact that he should be in the Hall of Fame."

Irvin became friends with Wright when the two were teammates in the Puerto Rican Winter League in 1941, but he was aware of Wright's ability before that.

Bill Wright *at a glance*

- Hit .318 in seven East–West Negro Leagues All-Star games
- .336 lifetime BA
- .488 BA to lead Baltimore Elite Giants to NNL championships
- Often among league leaders in BA, HRs, and SBs
- Won the Triple Crown in the Mexican League in 1943
- Elected to Mexican Baseball Hall of Fame

"In the late '30s I was a third baseman for the Newark Eagles and we were playing against Bill and the Elite Giants," Irvin said. "I knew he could bunt so I came in a couple of steps. He was hitting left-handed and swung away. He hit a shot that would have decapitated me if I hadn't gotten my glove up just in time. I never played in on him again. If he wanted to bunt, I'd let him."

Wright, a native of Milan, Tennessee, started out as a pitcher with control problems, thus the nickname Wild Bill. He joined Tom Wilson's Nashville Elite Giants of the Negro Southern League in 1932 and in one of the most stable careers in the Negro Leagues stayed with the organization when it moved to Columbus, Washington, and then Baltimore.

In the late 1930s, Wright, a perennial All-Star, was the bellwether of a strong Baltimore Elite Giants squad that fought the Homestead Grays and the Newark Eagles for Negro National League supremacy. His teammates included pitchers Bill Byrd and Jonas Gaines, first baseman Jim West, outfielder Bill Hoskins, and catchers Biz Mackey and a young Roy Campanella. Wright was Campy's first roommate.

In 1939, Wright was the Negro National League batting champion, hitting .404, the second time in his career he exceeded the .400 mark.

That year, the title was decided by a four-team playoff series in which the Elite Giants topped the Grays 4–1 in the finals for the unofficial league championship. Wright was outstanding on both offense and defense in the series. He drove in two key runs in the first game, doubled in the fifth game of the series, and scored the run that gave the Giants a 1–0 victory in the championship game, a pitching duel between Gaines and the Grays' Roy Partlow.

In that game, which was played at Yankee Stadium, Wright, an extraordinary outfielder, especially for his size, sprinted to the 467-foot mark to haul in a shot by the legendary Josh Gibson to keep the score deadlocked at 0–0.

The following year, Wright was one of many who jumped to the Mexican League. The league featured Negro League stars such as Hall of Fame members

Gibson, Cool Papa Bell, Willie Wells, Martin Dihigo, Dandridge, and Day. Wright was considered in that class as a ballplayer.

He stayed in Mexico for the 1941 season and won his first of two batting crowns, hitting .390 and beating out Gibson and Dandridge.

In 1942, it was back to the Elite Giants, and then a return to the Mexican League for a most spectacular 1943 season. Wright won the Triple Crown and missed the stolen-base title by only one steal. He hit .366 to nip Dandridge and the two tied for the league-lead in RBIs with 70. His 13 homers topped Campanella's 12.

After a productive 1945 with Baltimore, Wright returned to Mexico for good, becoming one of the country's most popular players. He eventually settled there and opened a restaurant in Aquascalientes named "Bill Wright's Dugout." He was later inducted into the Mexican Baseball Hall of Fame.

In 1958, the TV show "This Is Your Life" honored Campanella, the great Brooklyn Dodgers star who was paralyzed in a car accident. Wright, a former teammate and friend, made an appearance on the show as a surprise guest. His only other public appearance was at a reunion of Negro Leaguers in 1990.

There were two other true marks of Wright's greatness. He made seven appearances in the East–West Negro Leagues All-Star Game, compiling a .318 average against the crème de la crème of black baseball hurlers. He also pounded out an impressive .371 average while facing a number of major league pitchers such as Bob Feller, Dizzy Dean, and Ewell Blackwell.

"Bill was a great guy to have on a team and he was adored in Mexico," Irvin said. "Some day the Veterans Committee should recognize him and elect him into the Hall of Fame."

Carl Furillo

OF, 1946–1960, Dodgers

The most underappreciated member of the great Brooklyn Dodgers teams that would come to be known as the "Boys of Summer" was right fielder Carl Furillo. "Skoonj" (short for Scungili, the Italian word for snail) was a consistent clutch hitter and an excellent right fielder with the strongest and most accurate throwing arm in the major leagues.

That tremendous right arm, which put fear into the hearts of base runners, is what people most remember about Furillo. It was responsible for his other nickname the "Reading Rifle." He nailed many opposing runners who tried to take an extra base. It got to the point where runners held their bases out of respect for Furillo's rifle. In the ninth inning of a 1951 game against the Pirates, Furillo threw Bucs pitcher Mel Queen out at first base on what appeared to be a sure single.

"I got more of a thrill out of throwing out a runner than I did getting a base hit," Furillo told Rich Westcott in *Diamond Greats*. "I used to love it. I really gloated on it."

His virtuosity as a fielder was especially impressive because he spent his Brooklyn career playing the unusual caroms off the oddly angled right field wall in Ebbets Field. However, sometimes the credit he received for his defense annoyed Furillo because "nobody ever talked about *my* hitting."

He probably had a right to be annoyed because over his fifteen-year Dodgers career, "Skoonj" was one of the really fine hitters in the National League.

He drove in more than 1,000 runs in his career, with more than 90 RBIs six times, and hit for a career .299 average with five seasons over .300.

Furillo played in seven World Series, often with outstanding success hitting and fielding. He hit .314 in 1955 in the Brooklyn Dodgers first and only world championship season, capping off the season by hitting .333 in the World Series as the Dodgers beat the Yankees in seven games.

Carl Furillo *at a glance*

- 1953 NL Batting Champion (.344)
- Starting outfielder for Dodgers in seven World Series
- .299 Lifetime BA, with 192 HRs, and 1,058 RBIs
- Five-time .300 hitter
- Two-time NL All-Star
- Led NL in outfield assists (24) in 1951

His best year was 1953 when he won the National League Comeback Player of the Year award after slumping because of an eye injury the year before. Furillo also won the National League batting title with a .344 average that year.

Furillo, who grew up in Stony Creek Mills, Pennsylvania, was one of six children of Italian-immigrant parents. He quit school in the eighth grade and worked a variety of jobs to help the family through the Depression. He started for his hometown Reading's minor league team and the Dodgers bought the Reading franchise for $5,000 and a bus in order to secure Furillo's services. He was brought up in 1946 to replace Pete Reiser in center field and was moved to right field to stay in 1947.

Furillo, teammate Jackie Robinson and the New York Giants manager Leo Durocher and pitcher Sal Maglie symbolized the blood feud that existed between the two New York City teams of the National League in the 1950s. Furillo was involved in a number of skirmishes with the Giants over the years and claimed to hate the Giants uniform, when it was really Durocher he hated.

In 1953, Furillo missed some time with a broken finger he sustained while attacking Durocher in the dugout, suspecting that the Giants manager had ordered pitcher Ruben Gomez to throw at Furillo's head. That incident was just another chapter in the Furillo-Durocher feud that had its roots in the late 1940s when Durocher managed the Dodgers. Furillo disliked Durocher because the skipper predicted that Skoonj would never be a full-time player because he couldn't hit righties. It was after Burt Shotten took over the team that Furillo hit his stride and became one of the game's great right fielders.

In 1949, Giants pitcher Sheldon Jones hit Furillo in the head, causing a concussion. Jones insisted that he had beaned the Dodgers right fielder on Durocher's orders. The following year, after Maglie had come really close with two-straight brush back pitches, the hot-tempered Furillo tossed his bat at the pitcher.

"I have heard Durocher threaten to fine pitchers who didn't throw at hitters," Furillo said. "That happened when I played under him."

Despite the well-publicized flare-ups, Furillo was a quiet, serious man and a great team player who went about his job with professionalism and proficiency. While watching Furillo take batting practice, Dodgers manager Walter Alston observed, "There's a fellow who doesn't give anybody a bit of trouble. He plays hard, never gripes and does a helluva job . . . He's a real competitor."

Though the on-field melees were uncharacteristic of Furillo, he was not one of the more popular "Boys of Summer" in the clubhouse. In a 1950 profile in *Sport Magazine,* sportswriter Milton Gross observed: "Few of the Dodgers know him well. He is close to none, maybe because it's the way he wants it to be, or perhaps because he knew of no way to change it."

Furillo looked at baseball as a job and a living.

"You go out and do the best you can every day you play. Either you do or you don't. That's all there is to it," he told Gross.

It's sad, given his ability, work ethic, and all the great years he gave the Dodgers organization, that his career ended in controversy and bitterness.

In 1960, the Los Angeles Dodgers gave Furillo his release early in the season. Claiming that he had a baseball-related injury when he was let go, Furillo sued the team for his full year's salary. He won the court case, but left baseball a bitter man, claiming for years that the sport had blacklisted him because of the lawsuit.

In his later years, Furillo made peace with the game and became a regular staff member at Dodgers fantasy camp in Vero Beach, Florida, where he joined other Dodger greats in reminiscing with the fans.

In a 1968 interview, Furillo said he had "No regrets, none at all. Look at that career I had."

Former Dodgers general manager E. J. "Buzzie" Bavasi thinks that Furillo should be a Hall of Famer and probably would be if he could have kept his lifetime average at or above .300.

"One or two more hits or one or two fewer outs in his career, and I think Carl would be in. He was such a great all-around player," Bavasi said. "There are outfielders in the Hall of Fame, contemporaries of Furillo, who I wouldn't take over him."

Stan Hack

3B, 1932–1947, Cubs

I t's possible that "Smiling" Stan Hack's greatest personal attribute—his winning smile—has overshadowed his outstanding major league record and has contributed to his being overlooked by the Hall of Fame. Most newspaper and magazine stories about the Chicago Cubs third baseman emphasized his wonderful character and winning smile before his skills as a ballplayer were even mentioned.

Wendell Smith wrote in the *Chicago American*, on the occasion of Hack's being named manager of the Cubs: "He was the smiling, gentle hero to everyone from the front office to the bleacherites."

Or this newspaper account by Chicago writer Jack Ryan during a thirty-eight-game Hack errorless streak: "Hack's grin, the trademark he has worn ever since the Cubs brought him in from Sacramento in 1932, isn't the least impaired as he piles up chance after chance in a flawless succession that now totals 158."

In 1933, a young Bill Veeck ran a promotion "Smile with Stan Hack" in which he gave mirrors with Hack's photo on the back to the Wrigley Field bleacher bums. Of course when the fans reflected their mirrors into the faces of the Pittsburgh batters that day, the game had to be stopped until all the giveaways could be confiscated.

The gleam from that grin may have obscured the record that shows Hack to have been a superb hitter and an excellent fielder comparable in his all-around game to Hall of Fame third basemen George Kell, Jimmy Collins, Freddie Lindstrom, and even Pie Traynor. One of his former teammates likened Hack's game to that of Wade Boggs, who will surely be in the Hall of Fame one day.

Hack, who spent his entire sixteen-year career with the Chicago Cubs, was considered the top leadoff hitter of his day. He hit .300 six times, finishing with

Stan Hack *at a glance*

- Seven-time .300 hitter
- Four-time All-Star
- .301 lifetime BA, with 2,193 hits, 1,239 runs, and 1,092 BBs
- .348 BA in four World Series
- Led NL twice in hits and twice in SBs

a lifetime average of .301, socked 2,193 hits, scored 1,239 runs (seven seasons with more than 100 runs scored), and walked 1,092 times, while striking out just 466 times. He also led the league's third basemen in most fielding categories (fielding average, assists, putouts, and double plays) more than once.

True, he didn't have the power numbers—his top figures for home runs and RBIs were 11 and 79, and that hurts you when your career is being evaluated decades after your retirement.

However, his teammates and opponents knew how valuable he was. Charlie Grimm, a Cubs teammate and manager, compared Hack favorably with Traynor, who was for a long time regarded as the third baseman against whom all others were measured.

"He doesn't bat in as many runs . . . but you must remember that Traynor hit in the cleanup spot with men on the bases in front of him," Grimm said. "Stan may never have batted in 100 runs in a season, but what leadoff man ever did?

"In fielding, throwing, place-hitting, and every other department of that third base business, he's the payoff, the greatest of modern times for my money."

Hack, who hit sharp line drives to all fields, was at his best in clutch situations, winning many games with late-inning heroics. He hit .348 in four World Series and an even .400 in four All-Star games.

"He was especially good when the chips were down," said longtime Cub Phil Cavaretta. "The kind of guy you liked to have at the plate when the big hit was needed."

Hack was also respected for his durability. He was hurt many times but usually played through his injuries without complaining. His wrist was broken by a Roy Parmalee pitch and was in a cast for most of the winter, but he came back the following season and took his position in the lineup while the wrist healed. He took several fastballs to the ribs and always returned ahead of the recovery schedule. In one game, Hack was knocked cold at third base by a line drive off the bat of Hank Leiber and was back in the lineup a few days later.

Hack was the consummate professional: consistent, even-tempered, respected by the press, and beloved by the fans. He often signed autographs for adoring followers long after the game ended.

Once a St. Louis Cardinals player, observing Hack signing autographs and chatting with a crowd of his fans, said: "That man has more friends than Leo Durocher has enemies."

In his book *Mitts*, John Curran best summed up Hack's personality and abilities when he wrote: "I guess the Cubs' genial Stan Hack came closest to an earthly manifestation of the ideal third baseman of the day. Tall, slender, handsome, and confident, Hack was the idol of every sandlot urchin playing third in a pair of torn knickers. I never saw Stan swagger, but it would have been forgivable in his case. He was fast, aggressive, graceful. A lifetime .300 hitter, he sported a glove of 24-karat gold."

When they held a tribute day for him at the end of his career, he was handed a full-length portrait of himself by an admirer. On the back was inscribed "May life be as kind to you as you have been to other people."

That's the way everyone felt about Stan Hack

When Hack died in 1979, Dave Condon eulogized him in the *Chicago Tribune*: "Hack's smile was a singular attribute. There has been none other quite like it in sport. Not even, perhaps in the movies."

Condon remembered that Hack had once told him: "I enjoy playing baseball and this grin is just my way of showing it."

Bobby Grich

SS, 2B, 1B, 3B, DH, 1970–1986, Orioles, Angels

I f you fed Bobby Grich's vital statistics into a computer, chances are he
would not come out a second baseman. But that's exactly what he
was—and there weren't many better during his time.

"When you look at him, you would categorize him as a major league offensive second baseman," Lou Piniella says of Grich. "But if you look further, you
see a pretty darn good complete player."

At 6'2", 190-lbs., the gritty Grich, who had an outstanding seventeen-year
career that included six trips to the All-Star Game—all in the American
League—was, in the words of Wade Boggs, "a third baseman playing second—
that kind of build."

And that type of power. But Grich wasn't a third baseman trying to play
second. He was a second baseman with a big body who won four-straight Gold
Gloves—from 1973 to 1976. In a sense, he may have helped pave the way for
the lanky Cal Ripken Jr. to have a chance to make it so big as a shortstop.

"[Grich] was a big guy, a strong guy, but a mean guy," says Frank White,
generally regarded as the best-fielding second baseman of his era and also a
member of the class in this book. "He played the game hard. He didn't give an
inch on the field. He blocked guys off the base, fought when he had to fight,
battled guys at the plate, got big hits. He was a winner."

Grich, who hurt his back lifting an air conditioner later in his career and
saw his fielding suffer from the injury, was a legitimate threat at the plate.
After being named the *Sporting News* Minor League Player of the Year in 1971
(he hit .336 with 32 home runs), he hit 224 career homers playing for
Baltimore and California (he grew up an Angels fan in southern California and
always wanted to play for them).

He drove in 864 runs and stole 104 bases in 2,008 big league games. His
best year at the plate was 1979 with the Angels, when he hit .294, with 30
homers, and 101 runs batted in and helped the Angels to their first postseason.

Bobby Grich *at a glance*

- Six-time All-Star
- Four-straight Gold Gloves at second base
- *Sporting News* Minor League Player of the Year in 1971
- Tied for AL home run title in 1981 (strike season)
- Hit 224 career homers, 864 career RBIs

In what should have been his best offensive year, Grich hit .304 and shared the American League lead with 22 homers in the strike-shortened 1981 season.

He played on winners, but never made it to the World Series—despite five trips to the American League Championship Series—and wasn't a great post-season hitter (.182, 3 homers, 9 RBIs in twenty-four playoff games). He was a member of the 1982 California team that won the first two games of the ALCS against Milwaukee before dropping three straight. The Angels suffered a similar disaster in 1986 and have never been to the World Series.

Postseason woes aside, Grich could play, and could, as they say, compete. "He reminded me a little bit of Davey Johnson, before him—a second baseman that had size, was durable, that stayed in there and turned the double play very, very well," says Piniella, a rival throughout Grich's career. "For a big guy, he had much better than adequate range, good hands—and he swung the bat like a third baseman or a left fielder.

"He could hit the ball for power, he could hit the ball for average, he had the ability to drive it to left-center, right-center, out of the ballpark. Just a really, really solid major-league second baseman."

White says he was happy Grich shifted to shortstop in 1977 (the year he hurt his back lifting the air conditioner in February), opening the door for White to be the new Gold Glover (a title players tend to keep once they latch onto it). White kept that honor even after Grich, who made only five errors and set a major-league record with a .995 fielding percentage in 1973 (a mark topped by Jose Oquendo, who played his home games and many of his road games on artificial turf, with truer bounces), returned to second base for the 1978 season after hurting his back the year before. That was a year after Grich left Baltimore via free agency, signing a five-year, $1.69-million contract with the Angels.

"Bobby was an ultimate professional," White says. "He was a no-nonsense kinda guy. He played the game hard, played it right.

"He was one of the better clutch hitters in the league, very consistent, didn't have a lot of range but knew how to play the game—one of those hard-nosed professional guys who came every day to play the game.

"I actually wanted to be the best second baseman in the American League," added White. "That was something I worked hard for and I strived for and he was the perennial Gold Glove winner at that time at second base. Then when he went to California as a free agent as a shortstop, I said, 'OK, this is my chance to do what I need to do,' and that's when I got my first Gold Glove and five in a row after that. I think if he had stayed at Baltimore and stayed at second base, I don't think I would have had a chance to win a Gold Glove."

Added Boggs: "He revolutionized big guys playing a small-man's position. He'd do whatever it took to win—drop a knee on you at second to block the bag . . . whatever it took he would do it."

Former second baseman and long-time coach and scout Cookie Rojas had a slightly different view of Grich. "He wasn't a good fielder," Rojas says. "He was positioned right all the time.

"He knew how to play the game, he turned the double play very well. But he did not have, in my opinion, all of the tools, when you look at it." But Rojas said, "He was a tremendous ballplayer, a winning ballplayer."

Alvin Dark

SS, 3B, 1946, 1948–1960, Braves, Giants,
Cardinals, Cubs, Phillies

In the song "Talkin' Baseball" Terry Cashman sings of "Willie, Mickey, and the Duke," the three great center fielders on the three New York teams in the 1950s. There were also three great shortstops, but you never hear anyone sing about "Pee Wee, Scooter, and Al Dark."

While the Giants shortstop wasn't the equal of Hall of Famers Reese and Rizzuto in the field, he did get the job done and was a team leader for three pennant winners, and he was a better hitter. His .289 lifetime average is 16 points higher than Scooter's and 20 points above Pee Wee's. He also had a little pop in his bat, hitting 14 homers or more five times.

A great running back at Lousiana State University and Southwestern Louisiana University, Dark could have played professional football. If he listened to his early critics, he probably doubted that he had chosen the right sport.

Sportswriters made fun of Dark's awkwardness in the field and his ungraceful swing at the plate. He went after balls outside the strike zone with a choppy swing that resembled a man cutting down trees or swatting a fly. One writer pegged him "the worst looking good hitter to come up in years."

Giants manager Leo Durocher called Dark "my upside-down shortstop. He will make the toughest play in America for you when you need it. Then he will have an easy chance with nobody on base, when it doesn't mean as much, and he will play it as if he never saw a baseball."

But Dark was determined to put in the sweat and commitment to make himself a major league shortstop. And despite his unusual style, he was a fine hitter, who became the best hit-and-run man in baseball.

When Dark came up with the Boston Braves in 1948 his keystone partner, mentor, and roommate was the feisty veteran Eddie Stanky.

Alvin Dark *at a glance*

- 1948 NL Rookie of the Year
- Three-time All-Star
- Four-time .300 hitter
- Led NL shortstops three times in double plays and three times in putouts
- .323 BA in three World Series

"They were an odd couple," Hall of Fame announcer Ernie Harwell said. "Dark was an intellectual, deeply-religious college grad, and Stanky brought his competitive spirit and the edge of the street. They worked hard together and became a mighty good double play combination, first with the Braves and then with the Giants. Durocher had a fondness for both of them because they reflected his attitude."

During that first spring training with Boston, Dark had difficulty relaxing at bat or in the field because of all the advice he received from well-meaning teammates.

One day, Braves ace pitcher Johnny Sain, known for his strong will and independence, gave Dark the advice he needed and would follow for the rest of his career. He said, "Accept what you want and reject what you don't want, but always do it your way. You didn't get here by striking out."

With "Spahn and Sain, Then Pray for Rain" and the new double-play combination of Stanky and Dark, the Braves won their first National League pennant since the Miracle Braves of 1914. Dark hit a career-high .322, and was named the National League's Rookie of the Year.

After the 1949 season, Dark and Stanky were traded to New York for four players. Dark was named team captain and inserted into the number two spot in the batting order where his abilities to hit in the clutch, hit-and-run, and protect runners served the Giants well for more than six seasons. Joe DiMaggio called Dark the "perfect number two hitter" because he could bunt, hit behind the runner, or push the ball to the opposite field.

"Dark did anything to keep the rally alive and give the fat part of the batting order a chance to come up with men on base," DiMaggio said.

In 1951, Dark played a key role in the "Miracle of Coogan's Bluff" when the Giants' furious pennant drive caught the league-leading Dodgers on the last day of the season, forcing a playoff.

With the Dodgers winning 4–1 in the bottom of the ninth in game three of the playoff, Dark singled to start the winning rally that ended with Bobby Thomson's pennant-winning homer, "The Shot Heard 'Round the World."

Dark went on to hit .417 in a losing cause in the 1951 World Series against the Yankees, and three years later he hit .412 in the Giants' four-game Series sweep of the Indians.

The Giants captain was a central figure in the brutal Giants-Dodgers rivalry in the 1950s. Especially memorable is the game in which Giants pitcher Sal Maglie brushed back Jackie Robinson, as he often did to Brooklyn's batters. Robinson retaliated by laying a bunt toward first base, expecting Maglie to cover the bag. Instead, little second baseman Davey Williams covered, and former football star Robinson, running with his head down, ploughed into Williams and knocked him out of the game with a back injury from which he never fully recovered.

In Dark's next at bat he got his opportunity to send a message to Robinson. Running from first to third on a single, Dark, ever the football running back himself, charged right past the base and crashed into third baseman Robinson, sending him toppling into foul territory.

Durocher admired Dark's toughness, but he also respected the ability of his "upside-down" shortstop.

"He's a great shortstop—fast, smart, alert, with a fine pair of hands," said Durocher. "He's an intelligent, scientific natural .300 hitter. He's my shortstop and I wouldn't trade him for any other in the league today."

Dark had a .289 lifetime average, more than 2,000 hits and more than 1,000 runs scored. He later managed five major league teams, winning the National League pennant with the Giants in 1962 and the World Series with the Oakland A's in 1974.

In 1964, when he was managing the Giants, Dark received a great deal of notoriety when he made a series of racist remarks in an interview with Stan Isaacs of *Newsday*. He said the Giants were playing poorly because they had so many "Negro and Spanish players" on the team. "They are just not able to perform up to the white player when it comes to mental alertness," Dark said.

Dark always claimed he was misquoted. And even though Jackie Robinson and Willie Mays sprang to his defense, the story damaged Dark's reputation, especially since he was known as a deeply religious man.

Former teammate Monte Irvin remembers Dark as a team leader on the Giants who helped facilitate the smooth integration of the team when Irvin, Hank Thompson, and Mays broke in.

"Dark and I are friends and I'll never speak an unkind word about him," Irvin said recently. "He was a team leader and a great guy to all of us when we came up. He misspoke that time and that was unfortunate. But I never thought he was a racist."

Vida Blue

P, 1969–1983, 1985–1986, A's, Giants, Royals

"**I**t's easy, man. I just take the ball and throw. Hard! It's a God-given talent! No one can teach it to you. They either hit it or they don't," says Vida Blue.

It's so easy to look at the career of Vida Blue and dream about what might have been—what Blue would have turned out to be without the off-field trouble, without the contract bitterness early in his career—if he had somehow managed to keep doing what he did when he exploded into the major leagues.

"I remember when he was a young guy just blowing people away," says fellow "Out by a Stepper" Willie Randolph. "He came into Yankee Stadium one day and struck out like nineteen guys. He was just the most overpowering, dominating pitcher I've ever seen.

"You just knew what was coming and he'd just challenge you. He was a great athlete, too. Tough competitor, too."

Randolph's Yankee teammate, Lou Piniella agrees: "When I first faced Vida in his first major-league start in 1970, it was the hardest I had ever seen anybody throw a baseball," Piniella says.

"Now, Nolan Ryan subsequently threw harder . . . but [Blue] threw pitches on the knees. I remember reading when I was younger about Sandy Koufax throwing the ball down and it hopping . . . well, Vida Blue was throwing the ball down, it was hopping. Overpowering, just overpowering.

"When he was with Oakland those first four or five years he was just simply, simply overpowering.

And after a ho-hum introduction to the major leagues in 1969, Blue, then twenty-one, was summoned to Oakland late in the 1970 season. He pitched a one-hitter in his first start and a no-hitter in his second—missing a perfect game only by a walk to Harmon Killebrew. There were 6 starts, a 2–0 record, and a 2.09 ERA—just a hint of what he would do the following season.

Vida Blue *at a glance*

- 1971 AL MVP
- 1971 AL Cy Young award
- Six-time All-Star
- Won 209 games
- Three-time 20-game winner
- Pitched consecutive one-hitter and no-hitter upon 1970 recall from minors

The 1971 baseball season was magical for Vida Blue, who went 24–8 with a 1.82 ERA (the league average was 3.33)—301 strikeouts and 88 walks in 312 innings. He allowed 209 hits and pitched eight shutouts—and was named American League Most Valuable Player and Cy Young award winner.

Blue would never have another year like that one on a long—and often bumpy—road that would end after the 1986 season, a road that would include going to jail on drug charges and would finally end when he couldn't pass a urine test. But few pitchers have had the kind of year he had in 1971. Still, there would be 209 total wins, five more All-Star selections, 161 losses, a less-than-mediocre 1–5 mark with 2 saves in seventeen postseason games—and the wonder of what might have been.

"He came at you with his best gun and that was it," former infielder Cookie Rojas said of Blue's heat. "With Koufax and him, when they threw the ball high on you, it would rise—that was the velocity they had on the pitch."

"The man could flat out throw the ball," says Tommy Harper, a Milwaukee Brewer when Blue came up before moving on to Boston. "In the years Vida was on, I mean, he electrified people. He was a drawing card, like Koufax; he was just something. He dominated for that 3–5 year period."

Adds Joe Torre, also an MVP in that 1971 season: "He was a bells and whistles guy . . . Vida was one of those guys who you give him the ball and give him a run and that was going to be enough. He was an overpowering pitcher, he was a great athlete."

Blue's troubles started with his first contract battle with A's owner Charles O. Finley after the big year. The holdout that ensued helped produce a 6–10 year in 1972—and reporting overweight may have led to arm trouble that cut his strikeout total down the rest of his career. Later he would admit his drug problems started in 1972. But he came back to win 20 the next year and 22 in 1975, pitching for Oakland teams that won three-straight titles.

If you've forgotten, these were the times Finley started trying to sell off his players. Blue was shipped to the Yankees for $1.5 million and Commissioner Bowie Kuhn vetoed it because of an arbitrary limit on a cash sale of a player. He was sent to the Reds for the same figure and Kuhn killed that, too. Finally, on March 15, 1978, Vida Blue was traded to the nearby Giants—for seven players and $390,000. He won 18 games for the Giants in 1978, stayed there for four years and was shipped to Kansas City for four players. He was a central figure in the Kansas City drug investigation and wound up serving three months in prison, missing the 1984 season. He went back to the Giants and was 18–18 over the next two years and was set to re-sign with Oakland when he failed the urine test. His career was over.

"I faced Vida in spring training—he was in the other league," says Cito Gaston. "When he went to San Francisco, I used to consider myself a low-ball hitter and guys who threw the ball up probably gave me more trouble inside. But he's probably one of the only left-handers I've seen where the ball down was quicker than it was up. I was surprised. I was like, 'whoa, what's this?' And that was kinda at the end when he was with San Francisco. I can imagine what he was like when he was with Oakland with that ball down."

And we can only imagine what might have been.

Bob Elliott

3B, OF, 1939–1953, Pirates, Braves,
Giants, White Sox

Bob Elliott could be the poster boy for this book. He was one of the great players of the 1940s, the National League Most Valuable Player in 1947. He drove in more runs than anyone in the decade, and he was the top producer for the 1948 Braves pennant winners—yet nobody but old time baseball people, aging fans, and baseball historians ever heard of him.

How does a man whose outstanding hitting, fielding, hustle, and leadership earned him the nickname "Mr. Team" fade so completely from public memory? There may be two reasons, other than the mere passage of time and the fact that he is not a member of the Hall of Fame.

First, his achievements have probably been downgraded because several of his best years were during World War II when many top players were in the military. He also had the misfortune of dying young (at the age of forty-nine in 1966), a fate he shares with other unjustly forgotten Out by a Step heroes such as Sherry Magee, Urban Shocker, and Joe Gordon. Many players of lesser ability who went on to long careers as executives, announcers, and managers made a more lasting public impression.

Lest you think that we pulled his name out of a hat, check out Bill James' *Baseball Historical Abstract* and Lloyd Johnson's *Baseball's Dream Teams— The Greatest Players—Decade by Decade*. Both writers named Elliott the best third baseman of the 1940s.

In making his selection, James said. "Elliott isn't remembered very much, and he probably wouldn't win a poll over Keltner, Kell, and Hack. But Elliott drove in more runs than any other player during the decade, was the only third baseman to win an MVP award in the '40s, was a good defensive player,

Bob Elliott *at a glance*

- 1947 NL MVP
- Seven-time All-Star
- Six times 100 RBIs
- Lifetime .289 BA, with 170 HRs, 1,064 runs, and 1,195 RBIs
- Led NL in BBs (131) in 1948

and would have far better statistics if he played in any park but Forbes . . . I feel sure I've got the right man there."

Johnson supports the argument for Elliott: "Bob Elliott was a powerful right-handed slugger who knocked in more than 900 runs and 109 homers during the decade. He participated in the 1941, 1942, 1944 and 1948 All-Star Games. An outstanding clutch hitter who once popped three home runs in a single game, he drove in over 100 runs from 1943 through 1945. He moved from the outfield to third base to help his team, and developed into a wide-ranging fielder. From 1942 through 1944, he led NL third basemen in assists and errors."

An outfielder in his first three years with Pittsburgh, Elliott was convinced by manager Frankie Frisch to switch to third base for the good of the team. Frisch told him that the switch would add five years to his career. In one of Elliott's first practices a hard grounder bounced off a pebble and hit him right between the eyes, knocking him out. When he came to, there was Frisch standing over him asking how he was doing. Elliott answered weakly, "Frank, I think I just lost three of those five extra years you promised."

Frisch had high praise for the slugging Californian: "He could play third base or the outfield as good as anybody. Any manager would want him on his ballclub. He played mad all the time. Baseball could use a few more Bob Elliotts."

Elliott was traded to the Braves in the 1947 season for a washed-up Billy Herman and three fringe players, in what has been called "one of the most one-sided deals in the history of the National League." He immediately became the team's inspirational leader and top performer. His 22 homers, 113 RBIs, and .317 batting average earned him the MVP award.

Boston Manager Billy Southworth, who suggested the trade, was always a big Elliott fan. "The ball games he won for me or the home runs and extra-base hits he got to put us in the game are too numerous to mention," said Southworth. "He was one of the elite, a bell cow. He was a fellow that carried a lot of the club. The other players looked up to him. He was the core of the ball club."

In 1948, the Braves won the pennant, featuring Elliott and Top 100 members Johnny Sain and Alvin Dark, as well as Hall of Fame pitcher Warren Spahn. Elliot had 23 homers, 100 RBIs (the fifth of his six 100-RBI seasons), and hit .283. He also led the league in walks with 131. In every one of his fifteen years in the league, Elliott had more walks than strikeouts.

The Braves lost the World Series to the Indians 4–2 in one of the best-pitched fall classics in years. It included two shutouts (by Sain in Game One and by the Indians' Gene Bearden in Game Three) and in the only slugfest, an 11–5 Braves victory in Game Five, "Mr. Team" smashed 2 home runs, the first off Bob Feller.

Elliott's production dropped the following year, but in 1950 he came back with a typical Elliott year with a career-high 24 homers, 107 RBIs, and a .305 average.

In 1952, the Giants put in an emergency call to the Braves when Monte Irvin suffered a devastating ankle injury, and though Elliott tried to give the New Yorkers some right-handed power, he was nearing the end of the line and wound up on the bench. He went to the American League in 1953, splitting the season between the Browns and the White Sox.

Elliott's career numbers include a .289 batting average, 2,061 hits, 1,064 runs scored, 1,195 RBIs, 967 walks, and a .393 on-base percentage. He played in five All-Star Games and was chosen for seven. These may not be Hall of Fame statistics, but they certainly establish Elliott as one of the great players of his time and a man worthy of more historical recognition than he's received.

Hal Trosky

1B, 1933–1949, 1944, 1946, Indians, White Sox

With any kind of luck, Hal Trosky wouldn't be on this list. He'd be in the Hall of Fame. While many of our Top 100 players saw their chances for Cooperstown disappear because of bad luck—injuries, illness, death, illness, late arrival or early exit, ill-conceived trades, or employment by bad teams, Hal Trosky was victimized by a double dose of misfortune.

The tall, blond-haired Indians first baseman was a premier power hitter from his first season in 1934, but arrived on the American League scene when three of the great first basemen of all time were in their prime. Though hailed as a coming star, Trosky was usually overshadowed by Lou Gehrig, Jimmie Foxx, and Hank Greenberg—all of whom are on everybody's list of the all-time best first basemen.

Trosky's other misfortune was a chronic case of migraine headaches that plagued him throughout his days in the majors and eventually ended his career many years before his time.

When Trosky came up with the Indians at the tender age of twenty-one, Manager Steve O'Neil declared: "Trosky is ready. The infielders have to play back on the grass for him because of his tremendous power. He may not be a great fielding first baseman but he sure can hit."

Trosky went on to have one of the greatest rookie years in the history of baseball. He hit .330 on 206 hits, smashed 35 home runs and 45 doubles, and was second in the league in RBIs (145) and total bases (374). Trosky also worked hard to improve his fielding and led the league's first basemen in putouts, assists, and double plays. While these numbers caused quite a stir in Cleveland, Trosky's competitors also had great years. Gehrig won the Triple Crown and Foxx and Greenberg both had a slightly higher batting average, while Foxx hit more home runs. And Greenberg, with future Hall of Fame mates Cochrane, Gehringer, and Goslin, won the pennant.

Hal Trosky *at a glance*

- Led AL in RBIs (162) in 1936
- Had .330 BA, 35 HRs, 45 doubles, and 142 RBIs as a rookie in 1934
- Six-straight seasons of 100 RBIs
- Four-time .300 hitter (lifetime .302)
- Twice hit 3 HRs in a game

Trosky's impressive start, however, did have people talking about him as the most likely new player to break Babe Ruth's single season home run record, and the press did recognize him as the next phenom in this incredible line of power-hitting first baseman.

In 1935, Trosky was the victim, to some degree, of the sophomore jinx as his batting average dropped to .271 but his 113 RBIs were good for fourth in the league behind (you guessed it) Greenberg (170), Gehrig, and Foxx. And his 26 home runs ranked fifth behind the three first basemen and the A's "Indian Bob" Johnson, another member of our Top 100.

In 1936, Greenberg was hurt, and Trosky had his career year, tying his all-time high with 45 home runs, and his highest batting average of .343. He won the RBI championship with a very impressive 162. Foxx, now a member of the Red Sox, finished slightly behind in all three categories. But Gehrig batted higher, powered a league-leading 49 home runs and his Yankees, with rookie Joe DiMaggio in the outfield and Hall of Famers Red Ruffing, Lefty Gomez, Tony Lazzeri, and Bill Dickey ran away with the pennant by nineteen games.

At this time, Trosky was only twenty-four years old and seemed headed for a long career as a superstar. But there would be only four more productive seasons ahead for the 6'2", 195-lb. slugger from Norway, Iowa.

As time went on, the public found out more about a problem that had been plaguing Trosky since his early days in the majors—migraine headaches that were so bad that he eventually had to retire from baseball in 1941. He had gone to doctors for years and they never found a cure for the headaches, which he suspected were caused by stress during the baseball season. He was assured that he would eventually outgrow them, and he did, but long after his career with the Indians ended.

The headaches got worse as the years went on and in 1940 the tension was exacerbated by the team's conflict with manager Oscar Vitt, a terrible communicator, who often criticized his players in public and to their teammates. The players also didn't think much of Vitt's skills as a manager. In 1940, Trosky led a revolt by Indians players who signed a petition calling for the ouster of the despised manager. The owner rejected the petition and Vitt was allowed to finish the season. The players were branded the "Cleveland Crybabies" and were criticized by the press and ridiculed by opposing players and fans. It left a mark on Trosky's otherwise fine reputation in Cleveland.

By this time, Trosky's headaches became so bad that he started to talk about retirement if they did not subside. In 1941, it was obvious that his ability to perform on the field was being affected by the migraines. "One day Dizzy Trout was throwing hard ones and I asked to be taken out," Trosky once said. "Then Mel Harder threw to first on a pickoff and hit me in the belly. I didn't even see the ball, I knew it was time to get out."

He left baseball after the 1941 season at the age of twenty-nine.

In 1944, with many players in the service, Trosky tried a comeback with the White Sox. His headaches were somewhat diminished at this time thanks to self-administered B-1 shots. But the old batting stroke was not the same. He took another year off and played for part of the 1946 season before retiring to his farm and a successful real estate business.

Trosky retired with 1,561 hits, 228 home runs, and 1,012 RBIs, which included six-straight seasons with more than 100 RBIs. He had a lifetime batting average of .302. But he never played in a World Series and he would never reach the great career heights of Foxx, Gehrig, and Greenberg.

Willie Randolph

2B, DH, 1975–1992, Pirates, Yankees,
Dodgers, A's, Brewers, Mets

Yankees bullpen coach Tony Cloninger, a former National League pitcher, was talking about different members of our prestigious list not long ago when his eye caught another one of the Yankee coaches seated nearby.

"My man Willie on there? You have to put my guy Willie on that list, right?" Cloninger said, nodding toward Willie Randolph. "He's gotta be on there."

He is.

Through all the tumult that was the Yankees of the 1970s and 1980s, there was a calm within the storm—a second baseman who didn't get a lot of publicity but just went about his business, didn't make waves and got the job done for a lot of good teams: Willie Randolph.

"Randolph was a very steady influence on those Yankee clubs," says former rival Jerry Remy—the opposing second baseman in the Yankees–Red Sox rivalry of that time. "With all the big names they had, day in and day out he was a very solid player."

A six-time All-Star, Randolph was hardly ever mentioned in all the books written about the Yankees—"the Bronx Zoo"—of that era. All this Brooklyn kid did after coming back home in a trade from Pittsburgh was play ball. He wasn't flashy, he didn't hit a lot of home runs or steal a lot of bases. He just played the game—and helped keep those teams together when things easily could have exploded (and sometimes did anyway).

"He was a heck of a ballplayer," says former teammate Lou Piniella. "He could run, he could field, he could steal bases, could hit for average, could get some big hits for you. He was just a little injury prone. Outside of that, Willie would man the second spot in your lineup, would swing a .300 bat for you, play a heck of a defensive second base for you."

Willie Randolph *at a glance*

- Six-time All-Star
- Played on three World Series winners
- 2,210 career hits
- Six postseason trips
- Second all-time Yankees stolen bases (251)

"With the changes that we had in the shortstop position, he and [Graig] Nettles were the glue of our infield. He was just a tremendous player and a tremendous competitor and another good person. We had a lot of good people over there on that ballclub."

Randolph, a .276 lifetime hitter who collected 2,210 hits and played in the postseason six times (he missed 1978 with an injury), was never a great post-season hitter, batting .222 in eleven series. But it didn't matter.

Randolph often talked about not letting the Steinbrenner craziness get to him—and it showed.

"He wasn't at all affected by it—he stayed out of it," says Piniella. "He was quiet, he stayed to himself more than anything else—he went out and played and played hard and played to win. No, he wasn't affected by the atmosphere we had there at times.

"He played in an era where second basemen really shone.

"Willie, in an era where there might not have been as many great second basemen, his career would be highlighted a heck of a lot more. And Willie being quiet the way he was, with Reggie there and Catfish and Guidry and Thurman and the rest of these guys, you tend to overlook him a little bit."

Frank White was one of those second basemen. He's generally regarded as the top one of that era, but Remy says he'd take Randolph.

White laughs when you mention Randolph. "My biggest thrill back in those days was competing against the guy that did play second base because they all were good—so when I went into a series with the Yankees, my competition was Willie and I wanted to outplay him that series," says White, who played for the Royals—the Yankee competition in the playoffs of 1976, 1977, 1978, and 1980. "We both played two different types of games—my game was more run production and his game was more get on base, steal bases, and that type of thing."

"He was their captain. I mean, he was solid, made all the routine plays, got on base, he ignited big innings for them. He was a guy that weathered the storm that was there in New York at the time."

Check out Randolf's place in Yankee history. Prior to 2002, he was second in stolen bases (251), seventh in runs (1,027), eighth in at-bats (6,303), ninth in games (1,694), eleventh in hits (1,731), sixteenth in doubles (259), nineteenth in triples (28).

"He was the only true constant from '76 when he came in from Pittsburgh as a rookie and he never buckled under the pressure of playing in New York—and I think a lot of that comes from him being from New York," says White. "He was a leader."

The trade that brought Randolph home was one of the greatest the Yankees ever made—and came in an era when Steinbrenner and his "baseball people" didn't always make the right moves. But on December 11, 1975, Randolph, who had played all of twenty games as a Pirate as a twenty-one-year-old, was dealt along with Doc Ellis and Ken Brett to New York for Doc Medich. The Yankees' Gabe Paul had brought a local kid home and he hit .267 as their second baseman the following year.

Two of Randolph's best years actually came after he left New York. He was hampered by injuries in 1988, leading the Yanks to sign Dodgers second baseman Steve Sax. So, Randolph signed with the Dodgers and hit .282 while making the All-Star team in 1989. He then moved to Oakland and won his third World Series in 1990 and batted .327 in 124 games with Milwaukee in 1991 before finishing his career with the Mets in 1992.

But he was always a Yankee—which is why it made sense for him to wind up as their third base coach during the wonder years (probably on his way to being a big-league manager).

Tommy Davis

OF, DH, 3B, 1959–1976, Dodgers, Mets, White Sox, Pilots, Astros, A's, Cubs, Orioles, Angels, Royals

One moment of indecision on the bases may have cost Tommy Davis a place in Cooperstown.

He was twenty-six years old and had already won two batting crowns, an RBI title, and starred in the 1963 World Series sweep of the Yankees.

Then on May 1, 1965, in a game against the Giants, Davis was about to slide into second to break up a double play when he hesitated for a split second. His spike caught in the dirt and he slid through his right leg, breaking it and tearing a ligament.

Though he was back in the lineup by September, Davis would never regain the speed that had made him one of the best all-around players in the game, and he had to adjust his batting style, because he could no longer get the power he needed from pushing off on his right (back) foot. "That injury changed Tommy's career and changed his whole life," said former teammate Maury Wills. "I have no doubt that with two good legs he would have had 3,000 hits and hit 350–400 home runs."

As it was, Davis salvaged a pretty good career, but he came nowhere near reaching his early promise when he was compared to Jackie Robinson and Rogers Hornsby.

A Brooklyn boy who starred in both baseball and basketball at Boys High, Davis grew up a Dodgers fan, but was pursued more eagerly by the Yankees. "I had a locker at Yankee Stadium and often went there to work out," Davis said. "And they gave me free tickets to their games. I was all ready to sign with them when I graduated but then the Dodgers really came on strong."

Tommy Davis *at a glance*

- 1962 NL Batting Champion (.346)
- 1963 NL Batting Champion (.326)
- 1962 NL RBI leader (153) and hits leader (230)
- Six-time .300 hitter
- Top career pinch-hitting average in history (.320)
- Batted .400 in 1963 World Series

Their sales pitch included a call from Robinson, Davis's childhood hero. "Jackie told me how important it was for a Brooklyn boy to sign with the Dodgers and how well I'd be treated in Brooklyn," Davis said.

Scout Al Campanis closed the deal at the Davis home, and the seventeen-year old went off to play in the minors, envisioning the day he would return to the old neighborhood as a Brooklyn Dodger.

In 1957 at Kokomo, Davis won the Midwest League batting crown (.357) under manager Pete Reiser. Pistol Pete loved Tommy as a person and believed in his talent, but as his mentor, Reiser's scouting report noted: "Davis needs a little more of Robby's daring in him" and "he needs to be pushed occasionally. Tommy has a habit of becoming a little too nonchalant sometimes."

Reiser wanted Davis to go up to the plate mad at the pitcher, but Davis insisted that fiery anger was just not his nature.

"When I got mad I wasn't relaxed. It tightened me up every time," Davis said years later about the nonchalance that tag followed him to the majors. "I hustled in my own way."

Davis was on-track to get to Brooklyn except for one small problem. In 1958, the Dodgers took off for California and Tommy Davis became the Brooklyn Dodger who never was.

"That was really a blow at first," Davis said. "But the Dodgers' move turned out to be a blessing. I escaped the distraction of my childhood friends. I was able to concentrate on baseball when I got to the majors. It also gave me a chance to explore new horizons and grow up a little bit," But he added: "I'm always going to be a Brooklyn boy."

With Spokane in 1959, Davis won the Pacific Coast League batting crown and the following year it was up to the big club.

By 1962 Davis had become a star, leading the league with a .346 average and 152 RBIs in just his third season. He had also developed the reputation as one of the game's best clutch hitters. That season Davis supplied the key hit in many victories, including two straight come-from-behind wins in June. The first was a three-run sixth inning shot against Houston, and the following day he broke up a scoreless Bob Gibson–Sandy Koufax duel with a ninth-inning homer into the left field bullpen.

"I'm apt to be more awake in a tight situation, a clutch situation. It gets me up. I like to see men on base," he said.

He made it back-to-back batting titles hitting .326 in 1963 and then .400 in the Series.

After an off year in 1964, Davis was optimistic that he would get right back on track in 1965.

Then came the devastating injury in May. Though he did return by season's end, Davis would never be the same. After hitting .313 part-time in 1966, he was traded to the Mets, where Wes Westrum gave him the chance to play regularly, and Davis responded by batting .302.

"I'll always be thankful to Wes. I still say 1967 was my best year in baseball because I proved to myself and my critics that I could be a full-time player again and be productive," Davis said recently.

But after the season he was sent to the White Sox for center fielder Tommie Agee, who went on to star for the 1969 "Miracle" Mets.

"It worked out great for Tommie," Davis said. "And I became a journeyman."

Actually, he became *the* journeyman. By the end of his career in 1976, Davis had worn eleven uniforms, at the time the most by anyone in major league history.

In 1971 with the A's, Davis hit .324 with 42 RBIs in 219 at bats and drove in 12 runs with 13 pinch hits. During spring training the following year, he was released. He always thought it was because he had introduced 24-game winner Vida Blue to Tommy's lawyer Bob Gerst, suggesting that Gerst handle Blue's public appearances and endorsements. The following spring, Blue turned his contract negotiations with Finley over to Gerst, and while the deal was being made, Davis was released.

"A club doesn't just release a .324 hitter even if he's been put in jail for life over the winter," Davis joked. "You get him out of the penitentiary."

Davis's name remains in the record books, thanks to his .320 batting average as a pinch-hitter, still the best in major league history.

When Wills teaches sliding at camps and clinics, he tells the Tommy Davis story.

"I tell students never to be indecisive. Always be looking to slide," Wills said. "Never change your mind at the last minute. Tommy was one of the best hitters I've ever seen, especially in the clutch. And he had speed. In the minors Tommy, Earl Robinson, Willie Davis, and I could run about the same. And Tommy was bigger than the rest of us. Were it not for that injury he'd be remembered with all the greats."

93

Dan Quisenberry (Quiz)

P, 1979–1990, Royals, Cardinals, Giants

Bill Fischer remembers a time Dan Quisenberry might have given it all up—long before he was ever the "Quiz" we came to know and appreciate.

"He was never considered a prospect," says Fischer, the former major league pitcher who would go on to a long career as a pitching coach—and who was the Kansas City Royals minor league coach when a young Quisenberry started out.

"You know how he got to the big leagues?" Fischer asked. "In 1979, I left the organization and went to Cincinnati as a major-league coach. He was at Omaha. He had pitched two or three years at Jacksonville and he came to me one day and he says, 'Bill, I'm not getting nowhere.' He said, 'I'm gonna quit and I'm gonna go home and teach school.' I said, 'don't ever quit—make them bastards make you quit by releasing you.'

"So he stuck out that year and the next spring I'm gone, he goes to Omaha and they got this guy from Atlanta—Gene Garber—he was the Royals closer and he hurt his arm. They took the best guy pitching at Omaha at that time. It was like May, they took him up to Kansas City and he stayed—he got every son of a bitch out."

They took him up to Kansas City at age twenty-six—a college pitcher who took a while to get to the show. The rest, as they say, is history—and a proud spot in Royals history. Quisenberry, the witty right-hander who threw from down under, died from a brain tumor in 1998 and left behind a proud record, mostly built with the Royals at their proudest time. Fischer may have been the man responsible.

"I told him not to quit but that's not being responsible," Fischer said. "Guys say they're gonna quit ten times and they never do. He threw sidearm, under-

Dan Quisenberry *at a glance*

- 244 career saves, 89 total in 1983 and 1984
- Only 162 walks in 1,042 career innings
- Pitched 139 innings in relief 1983
- Won Game Five of 1985 World Series
- Was 3–4 with three saves in eighteen postseason games

hand, and they figured left-handers would kill him. They never did kill him—they hit him a little better but they didn't kill him."

Wade Boggs was one of those lefty hitters—one of the best of his time. "I hit him hard but always made outs," Boggs says. "I'd line out to the left fielder, line out to the center fielder. He had such movement on his ball, he was difficult to center and he would eat up righties."

Adds former teammate Cookie Rojas: "No question, Dan was one of the best relievers in the American League. He saved a lot of ballgames for that club. If you look at the numbers in comparison to the ones that have been in [the Hall], he's got as good a record as anybody. You talk about the East Coast and you're talking about the West Coast, when you're in the Midwest, you don't get as much publicity as the other guys."

Quisenberry, who came out of college throwing underhand, led the American League in saves from 1982 to 1985. For his career, which spanned at least parts of twelve seasons, he was 56–46, with 244 saves (89 in 1983 and 1984 combined), a 2.77 ERA, and only 162 walks in 1,041 innings (with a high of 139 in 1983). He didn't have a great postseason record, going 3–4 with only 3 saves in 18 games. He was 1–2 in the 1980 World Series and was the winner in Game Six against the Cardinals in 1985—the Royals winning Game Seven for the only championship in club history.

Quiz also pitched for the Cardinals and Giants, retiring in 1990.

"He was just one of those guys that was tough to pick up," said Yankee rival Willie Randolph. "When you have guys throwing from that level, you're not used to that. It was always an adjustment. He was a guy you felt like you could get to but he would always have enough sink on the ball where it was just very frustrating because you would always hit it on the ground. He wasn't a power guy but the results were there."

Power guy? When compared to hard thrower Goose Gossage once, Quiz said: "I don't feel comfortable being compared to a guy who throws harder than God."

The man was funny. "Very funny. Very funny," says former teammate Hal McRae. "He was quick-witted—he made a habit of saying something witty each day."

And, McRae said: "He would get the hitter to swing at balls out of the strike zone. He fielded his position, had great control and was a good competitor. He was probably the inventor of the three-inning save.

"He pitched quite often because he was the best we had and he threw underhanded so they felt that his arm wouldn't turn like the conventional throwers and he pitched a ton of innings before people started keeping track of innings pitched or appearances. He was an iron man—there was no pitch count for him."

Adds Boggs: "Being a pioneer of relief pitching and taking it to another level, he gets lost in the shuffle."

Not bad for a guy who wasn't supposed to make it.

"When he reported to us in the minor league camp, he was signed as a fill-in player for the Rookie League," recalls Fischer. "A scout from California sent him in—he went to Laverne College and he wasn't considered a prospect. He joined us in the Rookie League and he was too good for the Rookie League so they sent him to Waterloo in the Midwest League.

"He threw strikes—he was a college pitcher! He was twenty-two years old. They needed somebody at Waterloo in the Midwest League so he was the guy who threw the most strikes so they sent him right there. A college pitcher, if he has to stay in the Rookie League, he's not too good of a college pitcher. So they sent him to Waterloo and he stayed there and he stayed a couple years in Double-A."

Obviously, he moved on from there.

Terry Moore

OF, 1935–1942, 1946–1948, Cardinals

The cliché in St. Louis in 1942 was that the Cardinals were built on speed, hustle, and Terry Moore.

The star center fielder whose great instinct to sense the direction and speed of the ball with the crack of the bat, was called the best friend the Cardinals pitchers had. Those who saw him play say he was among the best center fielders to ever play the game, comparing him favorably to Tris Speaker and Joe DiMaggio, the hallmarks of outfield defensive play.

The Cardinals brought Moore to the big leagues in 1935 after only one year in the minors. These were the days of the famous "Gas House Gang," and Moore became an immediate crowd favorite as he won the center field job. He batted a respectable .287 in a season highlighted by some notable games, including one in which he hit 2 inside-the-park home runs and another in which he collected 6 hits. He also had a great day against the Pirates, smashing 2 home runs and 2 triples.

Moore quickly became the Cardinals' leader and for many years served as the team captain. He held the center field job until he went into the service after the 1942 championship season. The speedy flychaser had a .280 lifetime batting average and played in every All-Star Game between 1939 and 1942 when he really came of age as a hitter, compiling a .295 batting average for those years.

But it was his fielding that drew the raves.

Leo Durocher once said, "I don't see how they can rank anybody better than Moore. What the heck, I've got no axe to grind for the guy. He's a swell fellow. But he's on the other team and he's beaten us out of two dozen ball games . . . if a ball is hit in the air, he'll get it. Nobody can do any better than that."

Giants slugger Mel Ott believed that a catch Moore made against him was the greatest catch he'd ever seen.

Terry Moore *at a glance*

- Regarded as best fielding center fielder of his time
- Four-time All-Star (1939–1942)
- Captain of 1942 and 1946 Cardinals World Championship teams
- Nine consecutive hits (1947)
- 6-for-6 in a game as a rookie in 1935

"I thought I had the slot in right center plugged with a line drive, one day at the Polo Grounds," Ott said. "I'd hit too many like it. They all went through for doubles and triples. But I rounded first base and saw Terry sliding on his shoulder with the ball in the glove. So help me, I didn't think it could be done."

Poor Ott didn't even mention the game in St. Louis in 1936 when Moore robbed him of a triple with a grab that witnesses say was one of the best in history. Moore raced from right-center to deep left-center to make a flying, bare-handed grab, and then bounced along the ground on his stomach with his hand aloft to show that he had the ball. He jumped to his feet and fired to third to double off Burgess Whitehead.

Moore's career was threatened twice by serious injury. In 1938, he missed a portion of the season after he crashed into a wall going at full speed. In 1941, Moore was hit in the head by a pitch and was out for a month with a severe concussion. Many thought the Cardinals lost the pennant to the Dodgers that year by two-and-a-half games because Moore was not in the lineup

By 1942, Moore at thirty was the old pro on the Cardinals team and had a fine year, hitting .288. In September, he hit a home run against the Phillies that put the Cardinals in first place to stay. Throughout the season, Moore helped the St. Louis pennant drive with great catches and timely hits.

His heroics continued when they met the heavily favored Yankees in the World Series. In the sixth inning of Game Three with the Cardinals leading 1–0, Joe DiMaggio hit a shot to left-center that was headed for the bleachers. Moore raced to the wall, and made a one-handed leaping catch that was called by one writer, "one of the finest exhibitions of defensive play in the history of postseason games." He made several other spectacular catches and hit .294 as the Cards beat the Yankees in five games in one of the biggest upsets in World Series history.

When he returned from the service in 1946, Terry once again took his place in center field. A severe knee injury limited his playing time, but he helped the Cardinals beat the Dodgers in a two-game playoff for the National League pennant and played an outstanding center field as they beat the Red Sox 4–3 in the World Series. In Game Seven, he made acrobatic catches on Ted Williams and Pinky Higgins that broke Boston's spirit.

After the game, a despondent Joe Cronin, the Sox manager, said, "What an outfielder! They told us Moore had bad knees. I hate to think of what he does to you when he's running on a good pair of knees."

Redbirds manager Eddie Dyer told veteran baseball writer Fred Lieb how much he appreciated Moore's all-around contributions: "I don't like to think of the day when Terry Moore won't be able to take his place in our outfield. Terry just does something for our team, and we aren't the same ball club without him. And what a loyal lieutenant he is to be working with you. I recall tough periods early in 1946 as well as this season when it was a comforting thought to know that Terry was in my corner. There never was a better team man in baseball.

"Last season . . . when we needed every game in September, Moore was in there every day, despite his damaged knee, and I would rather have had him in center field than any center fielder I know. What a ball player he is when the chips are down. Will you ever forget his five hits in those two playoff games with Brooklyn or his fielding in the World Series?"

While Moore was a good hitter, he doesn't have the offensive numbers for the Hall of Fame. If they ever begin recognizing players whose achievement was primarily on defense, Moore will definitely take his place at the head of the outfield class.

Don Baylor

OF, 1B, DH, 1970–1988, Orioles, A's,
Angels, Yankees, Red Sox, Twins

Those watching the success Don Baylor has had as a manager aren't
shocked. They saw it coming.

"I played with Donnie in New York. You can see why he became a manager—
his presence, his competitiveness, his will to win," fellow manager Lou Piniella
said during the 2001 season.

"I think he's showing that leadership this year with the Cubs," Tim
McCarver said during the 2001 season.

If Don Baylor, who started his managerial career by leading the expansion
Colorado Rockies to the playoffs in their third year of existence, were to come
up to the major leagues today they would call him a throwback. Definition? He
was intense; he would do anything to win. He was mean; he played hard all the
time—and he was a great leader, a man who got involved in the Players
Association and was in the middle of the major labor disputes that turned the
game in favor of the players.

And he could play.

"About the only thing he really couldn't do on a baseball field was throw,"
says Piniella. "He could steal a base, he could hit for average, he could hit for
power, he brought leadership to a club."

Baylor has been called "the classic designated hitter," more than filling the
role that seemed to be created with him in mind. A football injury to his right
shoulder left him with a weak arm and the DH spot basically arrived when he
did. He did play more than 800 games in left field, but DH was his spot.

In an eighteen-year career that included stops in Baltimore, Oakland,
California, New York (for the Yankees), Boston, Minnesota, back to Boston, and

Don Baylor *at a glance*

- 1979 AL MVP
- Hit by a pitch 267 times
- Hit .273 in 38 postseason games
- 1979 All-Star
- Hit 338 career homers
- .285 lifetime hitter

back to Oakland, Baylor hit a career .260 with 338 homers, 1,276 RBIs, 285 stolen bases, and was hit by a pitch 267 times.

Baylor, nicknamed "Groove," was in the postseason seven times, the World Series, three (he finally won it with the Twins in 1987). He hit .273 in thirty-eight postseason games, 4 homers, 21 RBIs—10 of those coming in the Angels' five-game loss to the Milwaukee Brewers in the 1982 American League Championship Series (4 on a grand slam). Baylor homered in the dramatic fifth game of the 1986 ALCS against the Angels, then scored the winning run and was instrumental in the Sox wins in games six and seven.

He had a game-winning pinch hit for the Twins in the playoff opener in 1987 and was a factor in the World Series, where he went 5-for-13, including a two-run homer off John Tudor in Game Six.

He was the American League's Most Valuable Player with the Angels in 1979, when he hit .296, with 36 homers, 139 RBIs, and 22 stolen bases.

"A true professional, no-nonsense kind of guy," offers Frank White, who added, "I don't think they came any tougher than that guy."

Adds Cito Gaston: "Great player—he's one of those guys who . . . you wish you could teach guys to hit like that because he gets a long look at the ball. He barely moved at all—he and Paul Molitor probably saw the ball longer than anybody before they swung that bat. And you know he was never afraid to get hit.

"Great character and a great leader."

Says Piniella: "He stood right on home plate. I always watched him and tried to figure out how he could stand so close to home plate and be so quick with the bat—he had a tremendously quick bat. And he had that ability to get the pitcher's breaking ball because he stood so close to the plate, and just hit it over the left field wall.

"He had tremendous strength—he had to be intimidating for a pitcher to face, just a big mountain of a guy up there with a short, quick power, compact swing that could beat you with one swing of the bat."

And Baylor was a terror for middle infielders. "His willingness to come out and do what it takes to win is something I won't forget," says second baseman White. "He broke up double plays—he's one of those guys I feared most coming down to second base and breaking up a double play."

Adds McCarver: "He was one of the most feared base runners of his day. Tough base runner. The only thing Don couldn't do was throw—he couldn't throw a lick. But all the other facets of the games were areas in which he excelled."

White says: "He was just a real hard guy, didn't like to lose, played the game the right way. He mellowed a little bit as he got older. I remember in '76 [when Baylor was with] Oakland, we hit him with a pitch and he charged the mound and we had the big brawl—that was our first year competing for the division and finally overcoming the A's. Then, later in his career, he had fallen into the record of 'how many times can I get hit?' and he didn't have the same temperament to go out and charge the mound as he did as a younger player."

The stats back White up on what he says. Baylor was hit by a pitch 20 times in 1976, the only time until 1984 he'd been nailed more than 18 times in a season. But he was hit 23 times with the Yankees in 1984, 24 times with New York again in 1985, a league-record 35 times with the Red Sox in 1986, and 28 times with the Sox and Twins in 1987—sometimes drawing criticism for taking one on the arm with a runner or runners in scoring position.

But none of it could take away from a fine career that left Baylor regarded as one of the great competitors of his era.

Del Ennis

OF, 1946–1959, Phillies, Cardinals,
Reds, White Sox

W hen the St. Louis fans booed Ken Boyer during an uncharacteristic batting slump in 1964, he called himself the "Del Ennis
of St. Louis."

Ennis, who was the cornerstone of the Phillies offense for a decade, is a
veritable legend for being mistreated by his hometown fans. Of course, these
were the same folks who would later give it to Dick Allen and Mike Schmidt
and, as the cliché goes, would even boo Santa Claus.

As with Allen and Schmidt, the reaction to Ennis was unjustified, ungra-
cious, and certainly ungrateful for the accomplishments of the cleanup hitter
who drove in 1,284 runs in his career. Ennis had seven 100-plus-RBI seasons,
358 home runs, and retired with more than 2,000 hits and a lifetime batting
average of .284. Only Stan Musial drove in more runs between 1946 and 1959.

Ennis, a solidly built 6'0", 195-lb. slugger was chosen for three All-Star
Games, led the Phillies' famous "Whiz Kids" to the National League pennant
in 1950 with 31 homers, a league-leading 126 RBIs, and a .311 batting average,
finishing fourth in the MVP voting. Through most of his career he was the only
power bat on a team that was noted for slap hitters and the hit-and-run.

He was also known as an excellent clutch hitter. "I was a better hitter with
men on base. I studied the pitchers and I always knew I would get the pitcher's
best pitch when he was in a jam," Ennis said.

Phillies General Manager (Hall of Famer) Herb Pennock noticed that
Ennis was a better hitter than most when he had two strikes on him.

"He's just as dangerous then as when he stepped to the plate. And he hits
to all fields. They can't throw up a special defense against him," Pennock said.

When Ennis knocked in his 1,000th career RBI in 1955, veteran catcher
Walker Cooper said: "Man, those people don't realize what they've got going

Del Ennis *at a glance*

- Named by *The Sporting News* as Rookie of the Year in 1946
- 1950 NL RBI leader with 126
- Seven times 100 RBIs, 1,284 lifetime
- Hit 3 HRs in one game (1955)
- Three-time All-Star

for them. I've been in the league a long time and I'm supposed to be a long ball hitter. And I'm not even close to 1,000."

Then why did the Philly fans boo a hometown guy who graduated from nearby Olney High School? First, you've got to realize that the Philadelphia fans were considered to be the most critical in baseball. They were officially named the worst in a 1955 *Sport Magazine* survey of major league players. But, how could they rag on Ennis, who had been such a consistent player and so cooperative and friendly to the press and to fans?

Some thought that it was because he *was* the Phillies only power hitter. When he failed to hit in a crucial situation, there was no one to pick up the slack. The crowd would leave the ballpark muttering that he cost them the ball game.

Other critics mentioned his nonchalant style going after a ball in the outfield. They said he looked lackadaisical, but management and teammates always considered him a hustling ballplayer. Actually Ennis was also one of the most consistent outfielders in the league, with good speed, quick and sure hands, and a talent for stopping hard shots in the gap and holding the runner to a single.

Did the negative treatment bother Del Ennis?

"They've stung me a few times with personal insults, but I never really let them bother me," Ennis said. "I figured they're paying their way into the park and have the right to boo."

The fans often threw objects on the field.

"Sometimes they threw food. If I spotted a good orange, I would pick it up, peel it and eat it," he told *Sport Magazine*. "One night a paper bag landed at my feet. I looked inside and found a peanut butter and jelly sandwich all wrapped up in wax paper. I unwrapped it and then started to eat it. You should have heard them howl."

Ennis, whose childhood hero was Phillies Hall of Famer Chuck Klein, was discovered in a high school game in 1942. Phillies scout Jocko Collins was there to watch a pitching prospect but came away thinking of Ennis, who hit three home runs and a double. Jocko lost interest in the pitcher and, after that, followed Ennis, eventually offering him a contract to play for the Phillies.

"Those line drives that Del hit when he was young were like lightning. He'd hit the ball and then it's in the stands, just like this," Jocko said clapping his hands.

After a stint in the navy during World War II (he saw action at Iwo Jima clearing land mines as a member of the landing party demolition crew), Ennis came up with the Phillies and was named National League Rookie of the Year in 1946, hitting .313 with 17 homers and 73 RBIs.

Former Cardinals manager Gabby Street saw Ennis as a rookie and said: "He's got the best-looking wrist action of any player I ever saw."

Ennis explained that his fine wrist action and good footwork were owed to gymnastics, the result of long hours spent on the parallel bars and other apparatus during a physical education course at Temple University.

He also thought his hitting got a little boost from his ritual soaking his bats in a drum of cylinder oil over the winter, supposedly to fill in the grain and make the bats as "hard as iron." This was at the suggestion of Phillies coach Benny Bengough, who told Ennis that all the great hitters of the past including Ruth, Gehrig, Cobb, and Shoeless Joe Jackson had used the oil-soaking method to get an extra little edge over the pitchers.

Through the years, the "wolves" gradually came to realize how valuable a player Ennis was both at bat and in the field. The booing actually turned to cheers. The team held "Del Ennis Night" at Connie Mack Stadium on August 25, 1955. The stadium was packed, thousands were turned away, and the crowd had the opportunity to thank the former object of their derision for his many years of outstanding performance. They showered Ennis with hundreds of gifts including a two-tone Cadillac sedan.

After all those years, the local boy finally made good.

Glenn (Buckshot) Wright

SS, 1924–1935, Pirates, Dodgers, White Sox

The Pittsburgh Pirates had a series of great shortstops through the first two-thirds of the twentieth century—three are in the Hall of Fame, and even more impressively, three are on this list. Everybody knows about Cooperstown residents Honus Wagner, Rabbit Maranville, and Arky Vaughan. There are also many fans who remember Dick Groat as the leader of the 1960 World Champion team and Maury Wills, who spent his greatest days in Los Angeles, but had two pretty fair seasons with the Pirates.

However, the forgotten man in Pittsburgh's illustrious shortstop history is Glenn "Buckshot" Wright, who owned the position between 1924 and 1928. At the time, he was regarded as the greatest shortstop in the game, but a series of career-shortening injuries kept him from achieving the numbers that would have assured his enshrinement in the Hall of Fame.

Wright, though not fast afoot, covered the infield like a tarp, had the strongest throwing arm of any infielder in the league and could hit .300 with power, majoring in clutch hits that drove in runs. He was an early version of Cal Ripken Jr. and Ernie Banks, with a similar game to Hall of Fame member Joe Cronin, who played in the American League in the 1930s.

Early in his career, Wright received high praise from Hall of Famer Fred Clarke, who had played and managed Pittsburgh from 1900 to 1915, and was a teammate of Honus Wagner.

"Wright is perhaps as great a fielder as Wagner was in his prime and a mighty good hitter, who is improving. The Dutchman is gone and Wright is the best. He's in a class by himself."

If you look at Wright's first two years in the majors you can understand Clarke's enthusiasm. In his rookie year of 1924, Wright hit .287 with 7 home runs and 111 RBIs, all while displaying great range in the field and that powerful, but at this point, somewhat erratic arm. That season he set the major

Glenn Wright *at a glance*

- Set record for assists by a shortstop (601) in his rookie year (1924)
- Four-time .300 hitter (lifetime .294)
- Led NL shortstops in double plays and assists his first two seasons (1924–1925)
- Four times 100 RBIs
- Made an unassisted triple play in 1925

league record for assists by a shortstop with 601, which stood until Ozzie Smith of the San Diego Padres broke it in 1980.

In his second year, he batted cleanup, leading the Pirates to the World Series. He hit .308 with 18 home runs and 121 RBIs and improved in every facet of the game. He became more disciplined and knowledgeable in the field, more accurate with his throws. The defensive highlights of his season included an unassisted triple play off the bat of the Cardinals Sunny Jim Bottomley in May, and he participated in a record five double plays in a game in September.

Wright and third baseman Pie Traynor combined to give the Pirates one of the greatest left sides of the infield any team has ever had. Some even say that Wright's solid play at short enhanced Traynor's reputation as a third baseman.

Many who saw him play, including Casey Stengel, said the sure-handed Wright was without doubt one of the top shortstops of all time.

Pirates outfielder Carson Bigbee said this about his teammate early in Wright's career: "Two years from now, when talking about shortstops, people will name Glenn Wright first and then put all the rest together in the field. That's how good he is."

In 1927, Pittsburgh again won the pennant and Wright, though his average fell to .281, knocked in 105 runs. The Pirates went on to get wiped out in four-straight in the World Series by the famed 1927 Yankees.

Wright was traded to the Dodgers after the 1928 season and before he had a chance to show what he could do for "the Daffiness Boys" he badly injured his shoulder playing in a handball game and missed most of the 1929 season.

Over the winter, a surgeon removed a bone from Wright's left thigh and grafted it to his right shoulder, and after a relatively short rehabilitation period the "miracle surgery" had the twenty-nine-year-old shortstop back in uniform.

"I may as well admit once and for all that my arm is not what it used to be," Wright said before the next season. "I can throw with most of them and better than some. But there was a time when I used to say that if I could get the ball in my hands before the runner reached first base, I cold throw him out. That's no longer true."

Though his arm would never gain its old elasticity Wright, who was named the Dodgers' captain, had one of the greatest comeback years in history. He achieved career highs, hitting .321 with 22 homers and 126 RBIs, as the Dodgers finished in fourth place, just six games from the pennant and one behind John McGraw's Giants.

Although he played three more years for Brooklyn, that one brilliant year, 1930, was the last great season for Glenn Wright. The bad shoulder and an assortment of other injuries to his back and his ankle took their toll and he never regained the form that prompted John J. Ward to write in *Baseball Magazine*: "Ask the players in the National league who is the greatest short-stop and they will say Glenn Wright."

Wright retired with a .294 lifetime average and 100-plus RBIs in the only four seasons that injuries would allow him to make more than 500 plate appearances.

Hall of Fame Manager Al Lopez, who was a Dodgers teammate, has been a big supporter for Wright's election to Cooperstown. Though Wright's career numbers would never support his selection to the Hall, there are many who agreed with Lopez's evaluation of the shortstop's all-around ability.

"The best shortstop I ever saw is not in the Hall of Fame," Lopez said. "I'm speaking of Glenn Wright. "He had a .294 average and there are many short-stops in the Hall who couldn't carry Wright's bat or his glove. And how many shortstops are powerful enough to hit fourth?"

After his playing days ended, Wright remained in baseball for many years as a minor league manager and scout.

Sparky Lyle

P, 1967–1982, Red Sox, Yankees, Rangers,
Phillies, White Sox.

Talk to any Red Sox fan about the worst deal the franchise has ever made and they'll point to the sale of Babe Ruth and others to the New York Yankees, who would only go on to do you know what over the next eighty-plus years. But ask those same Sox fans to come up with other traumatic trades the franchise has made and chances are Sparky Lyle's name would come up.

The date was March 22, 1972. The Sox acquired first baseman Danny Cater from the hated Yankees for reliever Sparky Lyle. Albert Walter Lyle had gone 6–4 with 16 saves for the Sox in 1971. Cater had batted .276 in 121 games for the then-sorry Yankees, and made Boston the sixth of seven big-league teams on his resume.

Cater would become a blip on the Boston radar screen—hitting 14 homers and driving in 83 runs in three years in Boston before ending his career with a season in St. Louis. Lyle, who called Red Sox manager Eddie Kasko, "the only big-league manager who I ever played for that I didn't like," would become a star, win a Cy Young award, right in the middle of the craziness of the Bronx that led to his own book—*The Bronx Zoo*—and a treasured place in Yankee history.

OK, so it wasn't Babe Ruth. But the Babe never sat on top of cakes naked, either—not that we know of, anyway. Lyle would become a major part of the Yankees' rebirth.

"He was a team guy and all he wanted to do was win," recalls former teammate Willie Randolph. "He wasn't on an ego trip—he just wanted to win . . . and party, keep everybody loose and just have a good time. When I first met him . . . he's the same as he is to this day."

Sparky Lyle *at a glance*

- 1977 AL Cy Young
- Led league with 72 appearances in 1977
- 238 career saves
- 3–0 with one save in thirteen postseason appearances
- Three-time All-Star

It was that type of personality that allowed Lyle to compete as a top reliever—and to help Rich Gossage when the Goose was brought to New York to take Lyle's job. It's something Gossage never forgot. It made Goose's life easier. But that was Lyle.

"Sparky was a great teammate," says Randolph.

And the lefty could pitch.

"He's one of those gut, old-time, old-school relievers," Randolph says. "The slider's coming, you know it's coming—he didn't hold runners on, he didn't care who was out there, he said, 'I'm gonna come at you with my best stuff,' and he'd hump at you every day. He had the nerve of a safecracker—it's just who he was.

"He was back from when relievers were relievers—the Rollie Fingers guys, Bruce Sutter guys who just got the ball every day no matter if they pitched 2 ⅔ or whatever, they'd come out there and just go at ya. I never faced Sparky but I know he had to be hellacious. You knew the slider was coming, but you still could hardly hit it. He had ice water in his veins, he didn't care, he left it on the field and had a good time doing it."

That slider was devastating. "Occasionally, he'd throw a fastball, but almost every pitch was a slider—and they all broke differently," says former outfielder Tom Grieve. "Some broke down, some broke across. I don't know that he tried to make them do anything different—it looked to me that he was just out there trying to throw it as hard as he could, trying to keep it down and in for a right-handed hitter.

"For a guy that really didn't have an exceptional fastball, he saved a lot of games with guts, determination, and a hard slider that he could throw to right-handed hitters."

Lyle says the pitch was developed throwing against a wall in spring training with the Red Sox. "I once asked Ted Williams [who was then a Boston hitting coach] what was the toughest pitch for a hitter there was," Lyle said. "He said it was the slider and suggested I learn it. So I started throwing it against a clubhouse wall before I was brave enough to ask a catcher to help me with it in a game."

Adds Don Zimmer, who managed the Red Sox against Lyle and the Yankees in 1978: "It's easy to say Sparky Lyle would be in trouble if you didn't swing at his slider in the dirt—especially the right-handed hitters. The ball's breakin' in on their feet. It just looks good and he had a knack of being able to throw it where he wanted to throw it all the time. Sometimes a guy can't hit a ball from a left-hander low and in but sometimes the left-hander can't get it there that many times. Sparky had a knack of throwing it there. He was a very tough pitcher."

In 1977, Lyle led the American League with 72 appearances. He was 13–5, with 26 saves and a 2.17 ERA. Thirteen of the twenty-eight Cy Young voters left Lyle off their ballots, but he won the Cy Young, anyway. Then, George Steinbrenner signed Gossage to a six-year contract and Lyle, fighting with the Boss—and not Gossage—through the 1978 season, was gone after that year in a ten-player trade that brought the Yankees Dave Righetti from Texas. His career ended in 1982.

Final numbers: 99–76, 2.89 ERA, 238 saves. He was also 3–0 with a save in thirteen postseason games, winning the World Series with the Yankees in 1977.

One other thing—Sparky Lyle, who once asked "Why pitch nine innings when you can get real famous for pitching two?" never started a game in the major leagues, making 899 relief appearances.

Wally Schang

C, OF, 1913–1931, A's, Red Sox, Yankees,
Browns, Tigers

Wally Schang considered himself a lucky man to have spent nineteen years in the American League and to have played for seven pennant-winning teams. However, as Mae West said, "Luck had very little to do with it."

Schang was an outstanding baseball player who was a key to the success of the A's, Red Sox, and Yankees during the second and third decades of the twentieth century. He was the rare breed, especially during the dead-ball era, a fine defensive catcher who could run the bases and hit for average—and he was a switch-hitter. He was the first player to hit a home run from each side of the plate in the same game.

In his career, he caught for Hall of Famers pitchers Eddie Plank, Chief Bender, Babe Ruth, Herb Pennock, Waite Hoyt, and Lefy Grove. He was regarded as a great handler of pitchers and had a rifle for an arm: in one game he threw out six base runners trying to steal. Connie Mack would often use Schang at third or in the outfield to keep his bat in the lineup.

Schang, came up with the A's in 1913, after a great year at Buffalo. When starting receiver Jack Lapp was injured, it was Bender who suggested that Mack "give the kid a chance."

So in Schang's first game behind the plate, Bender shut out the Browns 2–0, and the rookie catcher went 2-for-3. When Lapp returned to the lineup, the two shared the "tools of ignorance" for the remainder of the year, though Schang usually caught for Bender.

The A's won the pennant with Plank and Bender on the mound and the "$100,000 infield" of Stuffy McInnis at first base, Eddie Collins at second, Jack Barry at shortstop, and Frank "Home Run" Baker at third. They faced John McGraw's New York Giants in the World Series.

Wally Schang *at a glance*

- Catcher for Hall of Famers Eddie Plank, Chief Bender, Babe Ruth, Herb Pennock, Waite Hoyt, and Lefty Grove
- Hit .287 as starting catcher in six World Series (two for A's, one for Red Sox, and three for Yankees)
- Hit .357 in 1913 World Series and .444 in 1918 World Series
- Six-time .300 hitter
- Only catcher on three different World Champion teams
- Threw out 6 base runners attempting to steal in one game (1915) for AL record
- Recorded 8 assists in a game (1920), an AL record for a catcher

In his World Series preview, sportswriter Hugh Fullerton compared Schang with the Giants veteran catcher Chief Meyers. "Defensively, Schang has proved one of the wonders of the year," Fullerton wrote. He noted that Schang had the more accurate arm of the opposing catchers."

". . . Wally had cut down 50 percent of runners attempting to steal. Thanks to Mack's coaching, Schang is steadier and works with more judgment than he did during the early part of the year, studies batters better, and works better with the pitchers."

The A's won the Series in five games and Schang, who hit .357, was the catcher in all four victories. They were the first team to win the World Series three times.

The following year, Schang was behind the plate for 100 games as the A's once again grabbed the pennant, but this time they were swept in the World Series by the "Miracle" Braves. In both 1913 and 1914, Schang's sturdy play behind the plate and at the bat was recognized as he received significant support for the Chalmers Award, the MVP trophy of that time.

After that season, with competition from the Federal League causing salaries to escalate, Mack unloaded most of his high-priced talent, but kept the young catcher. However, Schang split the catching duties, as the Mackmen spent the next few years in last place. After the 1917 season, Schang was traded to the Red Sox, and once again he proved to be the good luck charm (or catalyst) as the Red Sox won the pennant the year he joined them. The Red Sox pitching staff was led that year by 21-game winner and member of our Top 100 Carl Mays and Babe Ruth, who won thirteen games. That was the year that manager Ed Barrow decided that Ruth's bat was too valuable to be in the lineup only once every fourth day and the Babe played fifty-nine games in the outfield and thirteen at first base, clouting 11 homers and hitting 300. Schang went 4-for-9 in the World Series as the Red Sox defeated the Cubs 4–2.

The following two seasons began Schang's prime years as a batter—he hit .306 and .305, and then in 1920 he became one of the items in Harry Frazee's ongoing fire sale to the Yankees. For the next few years, the Red Sox owner, who was losing money on his Broadway show investments, sent not only Schang and Babe Ruth, but a trainload of great players from the fine Red Sox team—players who would become the core of the early Yankee dynasty. They included pitchers Mays, "Bullet Joe" Bush, Hoyt, Pennock, and "Sad Sam" Jones, shortstop Everett Scott, third baseman Joe Dugan and outfielder Duffy Lewis.

In New York, Schang took up permanent residence behind the plate, as the Yankees, who had finished in third place in 1920, won the first of three pennants in a row. After losing twice to the Giants in the World Series, the Yankees finally won their first championship in 1923—that was the year that Yankee Stadium opened, and Schang was the Yankees catcher on opening day.

He remained with the Yankees until 1925 and then spent four productive seasons with the Browns. Schang returned to the A's in 1930 and once again performed for a championship team, though at age forty, he was only a backup to Mickey Cochrane and did not appear in the World Series.

Schang's nineteen-year major league career as one of the winningest players of all time ended in 1931. He had a lifetime average of .284, batted over .300, six times, and was probably the best hitter among American League backstops until Cochrane came along. Schang was considered one the great team players and was loved by his teammates and by the fans.

The Hall of Fame Veteran's Committee considered him for induction many times but he never received the needed votes, even though former players such as Waite Hoyt and Bob Feller gave him their endorsements. Baseball historian Bill James ranked Schang tied for tenth place with Roger Bresnahan among catchers in career value. Everyone ahead of him, except Ted Simmons, is in the Hall of Fame.

For his contribution to the success of so many winning teams, writer Jim Hamilton of the *Oneonta Star*, called Schang the original "straw that stirred the drink."

Tommy Henrich
(and Ten Yankee Greats)

Tommy Henrich (Old Reliable)

OF, 1B, 1937–1942, 1946–1950, Yankees

Hank Bauer (OF, 1948–1961, Yankees, A's)
Clete Boyer (3B,SS, 1955–1957, 1958–1971, A's, Yankees, Braves)
Charlie (King Kong) Keller (OF, 1939–1943, 1945–1952, Yankees, Tigers)
Gil McDougald (2B, 3B, SS, 1951–1960, Yankees)
Johnny Murphy (Grandma) (P, 1932–1943, 1946–1947, Yankees, Red Sox)
Bobby Richardson (2B, 1955–1966, Yankees)
Red Rolfe (3B, 1931, 1934–1942, Yankees)
Bob Shawkey (P, 1913–1927, A's, Yankees)
Bill (Moose) Skowron (1B, 1954–1967, Yankees, Dodgers, Senators, White Sox, Angels)
Gene Woodling (OF, 1943, 1946–1947, 1949–1962, Indians, Pirates, Yankees, Orioles, Senators, Mets)

Tommy Henrich *at a glance*

- Called "Old Reliable" for clutch hitting and fielding
- Five-time All-Star
- Starting Yankees right-fielder on six pennant-winning teams and in four World Series
- Twice led AL in triples and once in runs scored

This is where we give the New York Yankees their due. After all, they did dominate baseball from 1921 to 1964, winning twenty-nine American League pennants and twenty world championships. True, our Top 100 has been sprinkled with Yankee greats, but we felt compelled to recognize the Bronx Bombers' incredible domination of baseball over that forty-four-season span.

So, we reserve number one hundred for the outstanding Yankees who may not have been superstars like Ruth, Gehrig, DiMaggio, Mantle, Berra, and Ford, but who played a major part on multiple pennant winners. Our theory is that while they may not have the career numbers to qualify as Hall of Famers, they spent practically their entire careers playing important games for the big prize— which the Yankees usually won, often due to the contributions by our guys.

When the Yankees needed the clutch hit or big fielding play in a tight pennant race or World Series Game, it often was provided by a member of our Top 100 group. Though they were supporting players on the great Yankee teams, they probably would have been stars with less successful clubs.

Tommy Henrich is our official number one hundred (as Allie Reynolds is number twenty-three), but we take this opportunity to include (as Out by a Step honorees) eleven great Yankees.

First, **Tommy Henrich.** Outside of maybe Churchill and Eisenhower, nobody is responsible for more high-profile heroics in the 1940s than "Old Reliable" Tommy Henrich, the outfielder who expressed his love for the game and the Yankee uniform with more passion than any player in history.

Although only a .282 lifetime hitter, Henrich was one of the great clutch hitters of all time and a fine fielder, who with Joe DiMaggio and Charlie Keller, formed one of the greatest, if not *the* greatest, outfield of all time.

"Tommy was an extremely smart player," said teammate and former American League President Bobby Brown. "He was always thinking about how to do the right thing at the right time. He knew the nuances of every outfield wall in the league and worked on figuring out caroms and positioning himself to get a quick release."

All business on the field, Henrich's serious approach to the game is best exemplified by his famous quote "catching a fly ball is a pleasure, but knowing what to do with it after you catch it is a business."

He was at his best when big games were on the line, getting the game-winning hits in three of the four victories in the 1947 World Series. He also carried the team with his clutch hitting during the 1949 Yankees–Red Sox pennant race while DiMaggio was hobbled with a bad heel. Henrich's home run in the eighth inning of the final game of the season against Boston helped the Yankees win the pennant by one game. Henrich finished sixth in the Most Valuable Player voting that year.

The high point of Henrich's season came in Game One of the World Series of that year when he hit a 3–0 Don Newcombe pitch into the right field stands to win the game.

That was not the first World Series victory over the Dodgers in which Henrich was a key player. In Game Four of the 1941 Series, with the Yankees ahead two games to one, the Dodgers were up 4–3 in the bottom of the ninth with two out. Pitcher Hugh Casey worked Henrich to a full count. The next pitch was a curve that broke into the dirt and would have been ball four, except Henrich swung and missed. As the ball skipped by catcher Mickey Owen the alert Henrich hustled to first, starting a four-run rally that put the Yankees up 3–1 and the World Series out of reach for the Dodgers.

Henrich, a native of Massillon, Ohio, was originally in the Indians farm system. He petitioned Judge Landis to make him a free agent because he felt the Indians were hiding him in their organization. His request granted, the steady outfielder signed with the Yankees for a $25,000 bonus and went on to play on eight pennant winners and four World Champions. He was chosen for the All-Star Game five times.

Bob Feller, a Henrich admirer once said: "That guy can hit me in the middle of the night, blindfolded and with two broken feet, to boot."

Oh, **Hank Bauer** was tough ladies and gentlemen. Boy was he tough.

He was so tough they said he had a "face like a clenched fist."

He was so tough that he would tell non-hustling teammates "don't mess with my money."

Bauer, a World War II marine hero, joined the Yankees in 1948 and was a key ingredient in one of the greatest runs by a major league team. From 1949 to 1958, the Yankees played in nine World Series and won seven championships.

A team leader and one of Casey Stengel's favorites, Bauer played regularly in right field but was often platooned. He still managed to start three All-Star Games, and came up particularly big during the Yankees' annual march to the American League pennant and in the World Series.

"Bauer was another one of those players who was at his best in big games," Brown said. "He was a player who could do everything. He had good speed, a great arm, he was smart, and he stayed healthy. He murdered left-handed pitching."

His three-run triple and sliding catch were key plays in the Yankees' 4–3 win in the sixth and final game of the 1951 World Series. In the 1958 seven-game Series victory over the Braves, Bauer clouted four homers and knocked in all the runs in a 4–0 Game Three victory.

Bauer set a World Series record from 1956 to 1958, hitting in seventeen-straight World Series Games. He had 7 World Series home runs and 24 RBIs. When he retired, Bauer was in the top ten in a number of World Series career categories.

Clete Boyer was one of the finest fielding third basemen of all time, whose brothers Cloyd and Ken were also major leaguers, and played for the Yankees' five consecutive pennant winners from 1960 to 1964. The weakest bat in the Yankees lineup, Boyer's defensive contributions were key to that stretch of dynasty. Although he continually lost the Gold Glove award to Brooks Robinson, many Yankees believed that Boyer was Robby's equal in the field and that the voters were swayed by Robinson's batting stats. Teammate Bob Turley spoke for many Yankee pitchers when he talked about Boyer's fielding. "He was such a great third baseman. He was always making diving stops or charging topped balls and throwing out speedy runners. I just loved to watch that guy."

Brooks Robinson himself said: "In terms of catching the ball and throwing, Clete Boyer was the best defensive third baseman I played against."

However, Boyer's career did have some offensive highlights, too. He had some pop in his bat and hit double figures in home runs seven times, with a high of 26 late in his career with the Atlanta Braves.

He was also one of the hitting stars of the 1962 World Series, batting .318 and hitting a seventh inning home that proved to be the game-winner in Game One. In the Game Seven of the 1964 World Series, Clete and his brother Ken (then playing for the Cardinals) became the only brothers to hit a homer in the same World Series Game.

Traded to the Braves in 1967, Boyer finally had his big year with the bat, 26 homers and 94 RBIs that year. He finally won a Gold Glove Award in 1969.

Charlie Keller hated to be called "King Kong" but this muscular left-handed hitter did enough damage to opposing pitches to earn the nickname. The left fielder in the outfield with DiMaggio and Henrich was on his way to a Hall of Fame career but was detoured by chronic back problems and seasons lost to the service during World War II.

"Charlie had tremendous power and speed," Bobby Brown said. "He was a devastating hitter and he was probably the fastest runner on the Yankees. When he came up he hit to all fields, but then he learned to pull the ball to take advantage of the short right field in Yankee Stadium.

Keller hit .334 in 1939, his rookie year, and went on to star in the World Series sweep of the Reds, where he hit .438 with a 1.188 slugging average, knocking in 3 homers with 6 RBIs and scoring 8 runs. In Game One, he tripled to lead off the ninth and later scored the winning run. In Game Three, he homered twice with a man on, and hit another four-bagger in Game Four.

Over the next four years, Keller would average 100 RBIs and 100 runs scored. He also earned more than 100 walks five times in his career and led the league in free passes twice. He averaged more than 27 home runs a year between 1940 and 1943.

Keller had one more productive season after the war and then injuries took their toll and relegated him to part-time duty. He was sent to the Tigers before the 1950 season and the following year he led the league in pinch-hitting.

Gil McDougald was the most versatile starting infielder in the Yankees' dynasty. He excelled as a starting second baseman, shortstop, and third baseman, depending on where the Yankees needed him.

The reliable McDougald played on five Yankees champions, and started in the World Series in eight of his ten years in the majors. Like Bauer, at his retirement McDougald ranked in the top ten on many World Series career lists, including games played (53), at bats (190), hits (45), home runs (7), RBIs (20), and runs scored (23).

McDougald came to the majors in 1951 with more-acclaimed fellow-rookie Mickey Mantle, but proved more mature than "the Mick" and won the American League Rookie of the Year award alternating between second and third base. He hit .306 with 14 homers and 63 RBIs. In that rookie year, he tied a record by knocking in six runs in one inning. In Game Five against the Giants in the 1951 World Series, he became the first rookie to hit a grand slam in the Series.

McDougald went on to hit 2 home runs in the 1953 Series and homered in Games Five and Six in the 1958 World Series victory over Milwaukee.

The man with the odd batting stance appeared in five All-Star Games and had a career-high .311 batting average in 1956. He had a career-high 83 RBIs in 1953. He averaged a little over 11 home runs a year.

McDougald, who may be most famous for hitting the line drive that hit pitcher Herb Score in the face, retired after the 1960 season at the age of thirty-two, rather than go to an expansion team.

Johnny Murphy was the top relief pitcher of his time. In the late 1930s and early 1940s, "Grandma" Murphy made his living coming in to relieve the likes of Red Ruffing and Lefty Gomez on the Yankees teams of Gehrig-Dickey-Dickey—regarded by many as the greatest teams of all time.

A native New Yorker and Fordham grad, Murphy came up to the Yankees as a starter in 1934, going a respectable 14–10. After that, it was mostly the bullpen for Murphy, who developed into baseball's best reliever decades before the "career closer" came into fashion in the early 1960s.

He led the league in relief victories six times and in saves four times, retiring with a career 73–42 record out of the bullpen. He set a record of 12 wins in relief in both 1937 and 1945. He also earned 107 saves in an era in which saves were hard to come by.

In 1941, his best year, the big right-hander who relied on a wicked curveball, was 8–3 with a league-leading 15 saves and an ERA of 1.98. His highest save total was 19 in 1939.

He pitched for six world championship clubs and had a record of 2–0 with four saves in Series competition.

Later, Murphy served in the front office of the Red Sox and Mets, and put together the "Miracle" Mets of 1969.

And then there is **Bobby Richardson.** While the great power hitters grabbed the headlines and the dominating pitchers like Ford, Gomez, and Reynolds got their share of the glory, many baseball people realized that one key to the Yankees' dynasty was the procession of outstanding infielders who graced the Bronx diamond between the 1920s and the 1960s. Starting with Everett Scott and Joe Dugan back in the 1920s, the Yankees always had capable glove men who could get the clutch hit or move up the runner. Tony Lazzeri and Phil Rizzuto made it to the Hall of Fame, but the others are remembered merely as supporting players to the Yankee monuments.

The last of the great dynasty second-basemen, following Lazzeri, Joe Gordon, Jerry Coleman, Billy Martin, and McDougald, was Bobby Richardson, who covered the ground between first and second as a regular from 1957 to 1966. Known as a God-fearing man and solid citizen, Richardson played—and played excellently—in seven World Series, won the Gold Glove every year between 1961 and 1965 and appeared in seven All-Star Games.

For quickness and instincts, many compared Richardson to Gordon. Richardson led the American League in double plays four times and in putouts twice. His total of 136 double plays in 1961 is still among the highest ever recorded by a major league second baseman.

While it was his fielding that made him an All-Star, Richardson had a number of hitting achievements as well. A lifetime .266 hitter who rarely walked, Richardson topped the .300 mark in both 1959 and 1962, a year in which he led the league in hits with 209, and finished second to Mantle in the MVP voting.

However, he saved his best for the World Series, and if he were a more flamboyant personality may have justifiably laid claim to the sobriquet "Mr. October."

Richardson hit .305 in seven World Series, with his best postseason performance coming in the 1960 World Series against Pittsburgh. Even though the Yankees lost to the Pirates, Richardson was named MVP, batting .367 with 11 hits, including a grand slam and 8 runs scored, and set Series records with 12 RBIs, 6 coming in Game Three. The following year he tied the five-game Series record for hits (9) and at bats (23) for a .391 average.

In 1962, it was Richardson's memorable catch of a Willie McCovey line drive with two out and two on in the ninth that ended the Series in a 1-0 victory for the Yankees.

All this from the man about whom Casey Stengel said: "He doesn't smoke. He doesn't drink. He doesn't chew and he doesn't stay out late. And he still can't hit .250."

In 1969, the steady **Red Rolfe** was named the Yankees all-time third baseman. He's recognized here as one of the great underrated players during the team's dominance in the late 1930s and 1940s. "Red was one of my favorite players when I was a kid," Dr. Bobby Brown said. "He was a great fielder, could run like the devil, and could hit for a high average. He hit to all fields. And he played his entire career with ulcerative colitis, and there was no treatment for it in those days."

Rolfe was a true table-setter. Usually leading off or batting second in the lineup, he was often on base when DiMaggio, Gehrig, Henrich, Keller, and Dickey came to the plate.

Rolfe had a .289 batting average, topping .300 four times. He scored more than 100 runs seven times, led the American League in fielding twice, and was the All-Star third baseman four times. His best year was 1939 when he hit .329, led the league in hits (213), runs scored (139), and doubles (46) on a team that won the pennant by seventeen games and swept Cincinnati in the World Series. While he didn't hit well in that Series (.124), he did have a lifetime Series batting average of .284 in six Series, hitting above .300, four times with a high of .400 in 1937.

Bob Shawkey was a Yankee pitching mainstay from the late 1910s through 1927. Shawkey is the one representative in this section from the dynasty's first era. A four-time 20-game winner, Shawkey's 18–12 mark helped the Yankees to their first pennant in 1921.

In his first year with the Yankees, 1916, Shawkey went 24–8 overall, leading the league in relief victories with a 7–4 record and 8 saves. He struck out 15 A's in a game in 1919, a long-time Yankee record. In 1920, Shawkey was the American League ERA leader (2.45). He pitched in five World Series, including one for Connie Mack's A's in 1914. He was 196–150 in his career.

Shawkey, who became the Yankees manager when Miller Huggins died, led the team to a third-place finish in 1930 before giving way to Joe McCarthy.

An important figure in Yankees history, Shawkey was the starting pitcher in the first game played at Yankee Stadium (1923), beating the Red Sox 3–1. Babe Ruth hit the first homer at the new ballpark, but Shawkey helped his own cause when he hit the second. In 1976, the Yankees honored the eighty-five-year-old Shawkey by having him throw out the ceremonial first pitch at the refurbished Yankee Stadium.

If the slugging Yankee teams of the late 1950s and early 1960s were called "Murderers' Row II," **Bill Skowron** would have been Bob Meusel. Moose was to Mantle and Maris as Meusel was to Ruth and Gehrig, the third weapon in an extremely powerful arsenal.

One of the strongest men in baseball, the enduring memory of the right-handed hitting Skowron is of him reaching out over the plate and punching a home run to right field.

For a decade-and-a-half the Yankees had trouble finding a starting first baseman after Gehrig retired. Well, Skowron ended that talk when he became the regular first baseman in 1955. Moose was a good fielder and a free-swinger who hit for both power and average (career totals of 211 HRs, 888 RBIs, and a .282 BA).

One of the most underrated players in baseball, Skowron played in seven World Series. And he wasn't just a supporting player. Moose was another of the Yankees bats who came up big in the World Series. Against Milwaukee in 1958, he knocked in the winning run in Game Six and socked a 3-run homer in Game Seven. He also hit .375 in the 1960 classic and .353 in 1961. He compiled a .293 batting average in World Series play. He also swatted eight home runs and drove in 29 runs, both ranking in the top ten of all time. His career World Series record includes his .385 average, a home run, and 3 RBIs while helping the Dodgers to a four-game sweep over his former team in 1963.

Skowron's lifetime stats take a hit from Stengel's platoon system and from the distant left field fence that made it difficult for a right-handed hitter to pull the ball into the stands.

Nevertheless, the amiable former Purdue football player, smashed more than 20 homers four times and drove in more than 80 runs five times—the high water mark coming in 1960 when he had 91 RBIs.

Three of the major leaguers we interviewed for this book suggested **Gene Woodling**'s name as a candidate for our Top 100, and while we couldn't give him a designation of his own, we feel that he deserves to be on this list of Yankees greats. Woodling shares that one magical trait with everyone else on this list—he was a winner.

Woodling mostly batted first or second on the five consecutive Yankees' championship clubs between 1949 and 1954, and often came up with the clutch hit that started or continued a rally.

"They had nicknamed Tommy Henrich 'Old Reliable,' and since I came from near him in Ohio, Yankee broadcaster Mel Allen nicknamed me 'Old Faithful.'"

"I liked to think that nickname applied to my playing, too. I had the good fortune to be able to win ball games with late-inning hits. That was where I excelled and how I made my money"

Johnny Sain and Ted Williams thought the left-handed hitting Woodling, who folded into a deep crouch when he hit, was one of the toughest outs in the American League.

Often platooned in the outfield, Woodling was a fine all-around player who was regarded as one of the best left fielders of his time.

Woodling, a four-time minor league batting champion, hit .284 in a seventeen-year major league career. He hit better than .300 in five of his full seasons and walked almost twice as many times as he struck out.

Always a great performer during the pennant run or in the World Series, Woodling had a .318 lifetime World Series, averaging .400 in 1949 and .429 in 1950.

Bonus Coverage: Honorable Mentions (the Second 100 Players)

H ere is our list of the second 100 or honorable mentions. Many of the players listed here appeared in our Top 100 during the selection process and most were mentioned by those who were interviewed for this book.

101 Louis Santop (C, 1909–1926, Negro Leagues: New York Lincoln Giants, Brooklyn Royal Giants, Hilldale Daisies)

102 Bill Freehan (C, 1B, 1961–1976, Tigers)

103 Willie Wilson (OF, 1976–1994, Royals, As, Cubs)

104 Johnny Pesky (SS, 3B, 2B, 1942–1954, Red Sox, Tigers, Senators)

105 Charles (Deacon) Phillippe (P, 1899–1911, Louisville, Pirates)

106 Denny McLain (P, 1963–1972, Tigers, Senators, A's, Braves)

107 Elwood (Bingo) DeMoss (2B, 1910–1930, Negro Leagues: Indianapolis ABCs, Chicago American Giants)

108 Willie Davis (OF, 1960–1976, Dodgers, Expos, Cardinals, Rangers, Padres, Angels)

109 Bill Buckner (1B, OF, DH, 1969–1990, Dodgers, Cubs, Red Sox, Angels, Royals)

110 Mickey Vernon (1B, 1939–1943, 1946–1960, Senators, Indians, Red Sox, Braves, Pirates)

111 Lou Whitaker (Sweet Lou) (2B, 1977–1995, Tigers)

112 Bobby Veach (OF, 1912–1925, Tigers, Red Sox, Yankees, Senators)

113 Cliff (Gavy) Cravath (OF, 1908–1909, 1912–1920, Red Sox, White Sox, Senators, Phillies)

114 Jackie Jensen (OF, 1950–1961, Yankees, Senators, Red Sox.)

115 Heinie Groh (3B, 1912–1927, Giants, Reds, Pirates)

116 Ed Reulbach (P, 1905–1917, Cubs, Dodgers, [Federal League] Newark, Braves)

117 Jimmy Wynn (The Toy Cannon) (OF, 1963–1977, Astros, Dodgers, Braves, Yankees, Brewers)

118 Oliver (Ghost) Marcelle (3B, 1918–1934, Negro Leagues: Atlantic City Bacharach Giants, New York Lincoln Giants

119 Garry Maddox (OF, 1972–1986, Giants, Phillies)

120 Sal Bando (3B, 1968–1981, A's, Brewers)

121 Bill White (1B, 1956, 1958–1969, Giants, Cardinals, Phillies)

122 Lon Warneke (the Arkansas Humming Bird) (P, 1930–1943, 1945, Cubs, Cardinals)

123 Buddy Bell (3B, 1972–1989, Indians, Rangers, Reds, Astros)

124 George Foster (OF, 1969–1986, Giants, Reds, Mets, White Sox.)

125 J. Preston (Pete) Hill (OF, 1899–1926, Negro Leagues: Philadelphia Giants, Chicago American Giants)

126 Kent Tekulve (P, 1974–1989, Pirates, Phillies, Reds)

127 Norm Cash (1B, OF, 1958–1974, White Sox, Tigers)

128 Dave McNally (P, 1962–1975, Orioles, Expos)

129 Walker Cooper (C, 1940–1957, Cardinals, Giants, Reds, Braves, Pirates, Cubs) and Mort Cooper (P, 1938–1949, Cardinals, Braves, Giants, Cubs)

130 Willard Brown (OF, 1935–1950, Negro Leagues: Kansas City Monarchs, Major Leagues: St. Louis Browns)

131 Dave Kingman (Kong) (1B, 3B, OF, DH, 1971–1986, Giants, Mets, Padres, Angels, Yankees, Cubs, A's)

132 Jose Cruz (OF, DH, 1970–1988, Cardinals, Astros, Yankees)

133 Ken Williams (OF, 1915–1929, Reds, Browns, Red Sox)

134 Lance Parrish (C, 1977–1989, Tigers, Phillies, Angels)

135 Larry Doyle (Laughing Larry) (2B, 1907–1920, Giants, Cubs)

136 Fred (Firpo) Marberry (P, 1923–1936, Senators, Tigers)

137 Mark Belanger (SS, 1965–1982, Orioles, Dodgers)

138 Mel Harder (P, 1928–1947, Indians)

139 Jim Maloney (P, 1960–1971, Reds, Angels)

140 Spottswood (Spot) Poles (CF, 1909–1923, Negro Leagues: New York Lincoln Giants)

141 Tommy Bridges (P, 1930–1943, 1945–1946, Tigers)

142 Jack Clark (OF, 1B, DH, 1975–1992, Giants, Cardinals Yankees, Padres, Red Sox)

143 Paul Blair (OF, 1964–1980, Orioles, Yankees, Reds)

144 John (Stuffy) McInnis (1B, 1909–1927, A's, Red Sox, Indians, Pirates, Phillies)

145 Jeff Reardon (P, 1979–1994, Mets, Expos, Twins, Red Sox, Braces, Reds, Yankees)

146 Jim Sundberg (C, 1974–1989, Rangers, Brewers, Royals, Cubs)

147 Sam Leever (P, 1898–1910, Pirates)

148 Wilbur Cooper (P, 1912–1926, Pirates, Cubs, Tigers)

149 Fred (Cy) Williams (OF, 1912–1930, Cubs, Phillies)

150 Newt Allen (2B, 1922–1944, Negro Leagues: Kansas City Monarchs)

151 Wally Berger (OF, 1930–1940, Braves, Giants, Reds, Phillies)

152 Floyd (Babe) Herman (OF, 1B, 1926–1937, Dodgers, Reds, Cubs, Tigers)

153 Ken Singleton (OF, DH, 1970–1984, Mets, Expos, Orioles)

154 Harvey Kuenn (OF, SS, 3B, 1952–1966, Tigers, Indians, Giants, Cubs, Phillies)

155 Rico Petrocelli (SS, 3B, 1963, 1965–1976, Red Sox.)

156 Del Pratt (2B, 1912–1924, Browns, Yankees, Red Sox, Tigers)

157 Jake Daubert (1B, 1910–1924, Dodgers, Reds)

158 Clarence (Ginger) Beaumont (OF, 1899–1910, Pirates, Braves, Cubs)

159 Darrell Evans (3B, 1B, DH, 1969–1989, Braves, Giants, Tigers)

160 Dick Bartell (Rowdy Richard) (SS, 3B, 2B, 1927–1943, 1945–1946, Pirates, Phillies, Giants, Cubs, Tigers)

161 Clint Thomas (OF, 1920–1938, Negro Leagues: Hilldale Daisies, New York Black Yankees)

162 Bob Watson (Bull) (1B, OF, DH, 1966–1984, Astros, Red Sox, Yankees, Braves)

163 Davey Lopes (2B, OF, 1972–1987, Dodgers, A's, Cubs, Astros)

164 Amos Otis (OF, 1967, 1969–1984, Mets, Royals, Pirates)

165 Lindy McDaniel (P, 1955–1975, Cardinals, Cubs, Giants, Yankees, Royals)

166 Dave Cash (2B, 1969–1980, Pirates, Phillies, Expos, Pirates)

167 Jerry Koosman (P, 1967–1985, Mets, Twins, White Sox, Phillies)

168 Mel Parnell (P, 1947–1956, Red Sox.)

169 Ben Taylor (1B, 1910–1930, Negro Leagues: Indianapolis ABCs)

170 Dolph Camilli (1B, 1933–1943, 1945, Cubs, Phillies, Dodgers, Red Sox)

171 Del Crandall (C, 1949–1950, 1953–1956, Braves, Giants, Pirates, Indians)

172 Bobby Thomson (OF, 3B, 1946–1960, Giants, Braves, Cubs, Red Sox, Orioles)

173 Fred (Dixie) Walker (the People's Cherce) (OF, 1931, 1933–1949, Yankees, White Sox, Tigers, Dodgers, Pirates)

174 Roy McMillan (SS, 1951–1966, Reds, Braves, Mets)

175 William (Bucky) Walters (P, 1934–1950, Phillies, Reds, Braves)

176 Wilbur Wood (P, 1961–1965, 1967–1978, Red Sox, Pirates, White Sox.)

177 Mike Garcia (P, 1948–1961, Indians, White Sox, Senators)

178 Jim (Junior) Gilliam (2B, 3B, OF, 1953–1966, Dodgers)

179 Sherman Lollar (C, 1946–1963, Indians, Yankees, Browns, White Sox)

180 Jim (Hippo) Vaughn (P, 1908, 1910–1921, Yankees, Senators, Cubs)

181 Joe Adcock (1B, OF, 1950–1966, Reds, Braves, Indians, Angels)

182 Frank Howard (Hondo) (OF, 1B, 1958–1973, Dodgers, Senators, Rangers, Tigers)

183 Ron Cey (Penguin) (3B, 1971–1987, Dodgers, Cubs, A's)

184 Tim McCarver (C, 1B, 1959–1980, Cardinals, Phillies, Expos, Red Sox.)

185 Mike Cuellar (P, 1964–1977, Reds Cardinals, Astros, Orioles, Angels)

186 Sammy T. Hughes (2B, 1931–1946, Negro Leagues: Baltimore Elite Giants)

187 Camilo Pascual (P, 1954–1971, Senators, Twins, Reds, Dodgers, Indians)

188 Eddie Yost (The Walking Man) (3B, 1944, 1946–1962, Senators, Tigers, Angels)

189 Elwin (Preacher) Roe (P, 1938, 1944–1954, Cardinals, Pirates, Dodgers)

190 Mel Stottlemyre (P, 1964–1974, Yankees)

191 Rick Sutcliffe (P, 1976, 1978–1994, Dodgers, Indians, Cubs, Orioles, Cardinals)

192 John (Pepper) Martin (The Wild Hoss of the Osage) (OF, 3B, 1928–1940, 1944, Cardinals)

193 Jim Perry (P, 1959–1975, Indians, Twins, Tigers, A's)

194 John (Boog) Powell (1B, OF, 1961–1977, Orioles, Indians, Dodgers)

195 Jim Piersall (OF, 1950, 1952–1967, Red Sox, Indians, Senators, Mets, Angels)

196 Mike Marshall (P, 1967, 1969–1981, Tigers, Pilots, Astros, Expos, Dodgers, Braves, Rangers, Twins, Mets)

197 Willie Horton (OF, DH, 1963–1980, Tigers, Rangers, Indians, A's, Blue Jays, Mariners)

198 Larry Jackson (P, 1955–1968, Cardinals, Cubs, Phillies)

199 Earl Battey (C, 1955–1967, White Sox, Senators, Twins)

200 Ken Keltner (3B, 1937–1950, Indians, Red Sox)

The Not Prime-Time Players Long Enough All-Star Team

These players did not play in the major leagues or in the major Negro Leagues long enough to be eligible for our Out by a Step Top 100. But in their time, they were outstanding players.

1B   Luke Easter (Cleveland Indians), Ferris Fain (Philadelphia A's), Jim Gentile (Baltimore Orioles)

2B   Jerry Coleman (New York Yankees), Johnny Hodapp (Cleveland Indians), Kenny Hubbs (Chicago Cubs)

SS   Ray Chapman (Cleveland Indians), Charlie Hollocher (Chicago Cubs), Tony Kubek (New York Yankees), Dobie Moore (Negro Leagues)

3B   Bob Dillinger (St. Louis Browns), Whitey Kurowski (St. Louis Cardinals)

OF   Lyman Bostock (California Angels), Tony Conigliaro (Boston Red Sox), Sam Jethroe (Boston Braves), Austin McHenry (St. Louis Cardinals), Chino Smith (Negro Leagues), Taft (Taffy) Wright (Washington Senators)

C   Bill DeLancey (St. Louis Cardinals), Chief Meyers (New York Giants), Pythias Russ (Negro Leagues)

P   Johnny Beazley (St. Louis Cardinals), Dave Brown (Negro Leagues), Steve Busby (Kansas City Royals), Harry Coveleskie (Detroit Tigers), George Earnshaw (Philadelphia A's), Mark Fidrych (Detroit Tigers), Vean Gregg (Cleveland Indians), Frank (Noodles) Hahn (Cincinnati Reds), Larry Jansen (New York Giants), Stuart (Slim) Jones (Negro Leagues), Orval Overall (Chicago Cubs), Joe Page (New York Yankees), Dick Radatz (Boston Red Sox), Herb Score (Cleveland Indians), Jeff Tesreau (New York Giants), Don Wilson (Houston Astros)

Bibliography

Amoruso, Marino. *Gil Hodges: The Quiet Man*. Middlebury, Vt.: P. S. Erickson, 1991.

Anderson, Sparky, with Dan Ewald. *Sparky*. New York: Prentice Hall, 1990.

———. *They Call Me Sparky*. Chelsea, Mich.: Sleeping Bear Press, 1998.

The Baseball Encyclopedia. New York: Macmillan Publishing Company, 1969. (All chapters)

Benson, John, and Tony Blengino. *Baseball's Top 100: The Best Individual Seasons of All Time*. Wilton, Ohio: Diamond Library, 1995. (Dick Allen, Maury Wills)

Brashler, William. *The Story of Negro League Baseball*. New York, Ticknor & Fields, 1994. (All Negro League chapters)

Cairns, Bob. *Pen Men*. New York: St. Martin's Press, 1992

Canton, Ray. "Babe Will Never Die, Says Former Yankee Bob Meusel," 1948.

Carlson, Chuck. *True Brew*. Dallas, Tex.: Taylor Publishing, 1993.

Condon, Dave. *Chicago Tribune,* "Memories of Smiling Stan Hack will never die," 1979.

Creamer, Robert W. *Stengel, His Life and Times*. New York: Simon & Schuster, 1984. (General)

Curran, William. *Mitts, The Celebration of the Art of Fielding*. New York: William Morrow & Company, 1985. (Stan Hack and general)

Dawson, Andre, with Tom Bird. *Hawk*. Grand Rapids, Mich.: Zondervan Publishing, 1994.

Fimrite, Ron. *Sports Illustrated,* "Getting It All Together," April 8, 1974. (Bobby Bonds)

Fitzgerald, Ed. *Sport Magazine,* "Ted Kluszewski—The Cincinnati Strongman," July 1955.

Frommer, Harvey. *The New York Yankees Encyclopedia—The Complete Record of Yankee Baseball*. New York & Indianapolis: Hungry Minds, 1997. (All Yankees chapters)

Gardner, Robert, and Dennis Shortelle. *The Forgotten Players: The Story of Black Baseball in America*. New York: Walker and Company, 1993. (All Negro League chapters)

Golenbeck, Peter. *Bums—An Oral History of the Brooklyn Dodgers*. New York: G. P. Putnam's Sons, 1984. (Carl Furillo, Gil Hodges, Sal Maglie, Don Newcombe)

———. *Dynasty: The New York Yankees 1949–1964*. Englewood Cliffs, N.J.: Prentice Hall, 1977. (Hank Bauer, Clete Boyer, Tommy Henrich, Ed Lopat, Roger Maris, Gil McDougald, Vic Raschi, Allie Reynolds, Bobby Richardson, Bill Skowron)

———. *Wrigleyville, A Magical History Tour of the Chicago Cubs*. New York: St. Martin's Press, 1996. (Stan Hack, Johnny Kling)

Graham, Frank Jr. *Sport Magazine*, "How Del Ennis Won His War with the Wolves," May 1956.

Gross, Milton. *Sport Magazine,* "Brooklyn's Good Right Arm." June 1950. (Carl Furillo)

Hageman, William, and Warren Hilbert. *New York Yankees, Season of Glory*. Middle Village, N.Y.: Jonathan David Publishing, 1999. (Joe Gordon)

Halberstam, David. *October, 1964*. New York: Villard Books, 1994. (Ken Boyer, Curt Flood, Dick Groat)

Hamilton, Jim. *Oneonta Star*. (Columns on Sherwood Magee, Urban Shocker, and Wally Schang)

Honig, Donald. *The Greatest Catchers of All Time*. Dubuque, Iowa: William C. Brown Publishers, 1991. (Johnny Kling, Wally Schang)

———. *The Greatest First Basemen of All Time*. New York: Crown Publishers, 1988. (Gil Hodges, Ted Kluszewski)

Jackson, Reggie, with Mike Lupica. *Reggie, The Autobiography*. New York: Villard Books, 1984.

James, Bill. *Baseball Historical Abstract*. New York: Villard Books, 1986. (General)

———. *The Politics of Glory*. New York: MacMillan, 1994. (Glenn Wright and General)

Johnson, Lloyd. *Baseball's Dream Teams—The Greatest Players, Decade by Decade*. New York: Random House, 1994. (Bob Elliott and general)

Kahn, Roger. *The Era, 1947–57*. New York: Ticknor & Fields, 1993. (Carl Furillo, Gil Hodges, Sal Maglie, Don Newcombe).

Kell, George, with Dan Ewald. *Hello Everybody, I'm George Kell*. Champagne: Sports Publishing Company, 1998. (Minnie Minoso)

Kelley, Brent. *100 Greatest Pitchers of All Time*. New York: Crescent Books, 1988. (General)

Krikorian, Doug. *Long Beach Press Telegram* (Maury Wills)

Lindberg, Richard. *The White Sox Encyclopedia*. Philadelphia: Temple University Press, 1997. (Minnie Minoso, Billy Pierce)

Linkugal, Will A., and Edward J. Pappas. *They Tasted Glory*. Jefferson, N.C.: McFarland & Company, 1998. (Pete Reiser, Smoky Joe Wood)

The National Baseball Hall of Fame and Museum Archives. (All chapters)

Nettles, Graig, with Peter Golenbeck. *Balls*. New York, Pocket Sports, 1984.

Neyer, Rob, and Eddie Epstein. *Baseball Dynasties, The Greatest Teams of All Time*. New York: W. W. Norton & Company, 2000. (The Yankees Big Three and general)

Okrent, Daniel, and Harris Lewine. *The Ultimate Baseball Book*. Boston: Houghton Mifflin Co., 1991. (All chapters)

O'Neil, Buck. *I Was Right on Time*. New York, Simon & Schuster, 1996. (All Negro League chapters)

Peterson, Robert. *Only the Ball Was White: A History of Legendary Black Players and All-Black Professional Teams*. New York: Oxford University Press, 1970. (All Negro League chapters)

Peary, Danny. *We Played the Game*. New York: Hyperion, 1994. (Hank Bauer, Clete Boyer, Lew Burdette, Del Ennis, Carl Furillo, Dick Groat, Roger Maris, Gil McDougald, Minnie Minoso, Don Newcombe, Billy Pierce, Bobby Richardson, Al Rosen)

Pietrusza, David, Matthew Silverman, and Michael Gershman. *Baseball: The Biographical Encyclopedia*. Kingston, N.Y.: Total Sports Publishing, 2000. (All chapters)

Pluto, Terry. *The Curse of Rocky Colavito*. New York: Simon & Schuster, 1995.

Pollock, Ed. *Baseball Digest*, "Marty Marion—The Octopus," November 1942. Condensed from the *Philadelphia Bulletin*.

Prince, Carl E. *The Brooklyn Dodgers—The Bums, The Borough and The Best of Baseball, 1947–57*. New York: Oxford University Press, 1996. (Carl Furillo, Gil Hodges, Sal Maglie, Don Newcombe)

Redmount, Robert. *The Red Sox Encyclopedia*. Champaign, Ill.: Sports Publishing Inc., 1998

Ribowsky, Mark. *A Complete History of the Negro Leagues, 1884–1955*. Secaucus, N.J.: A Birch Lane Press Book, Carol Publishing Group, 1995. (All Negro League chapters)

Riley, James A. *The Biographical Encyclopedia of the Negro Baseball Leagues*. New York, Carroll & Graf Publishers, Inc., 1994. (Primary source for all Negro League chapters)

Ritter, Lawrence, and Donald Honig. *The Image of Their Greatness*. New York: Crown Publishers, 1979. (General)

Ryan, Nolan, with Mickey Herskowitz. *Kings of the Hill*. New York, Harper Collins, 1992.

Shatzkin, Mike, and Jim Charlton. *The Ballplayers*. New York: Arbor House, 1990. (All chapters)

Smith, David. "Maury Wills," In: John Benson and Tony Blengino, eds. *Baseball's Top 100: The Best Individual Seasons of All Time*. Wilton, Ohio: Diamond Library, 1995.

Smith, Wendell. *Chicago American*, "Hack Tireless, Resourceful Worker," April 3, 1954. (Stan Hack)

The Sporting News Archives. (All chapters)

Thorn, John, and Peter Palmer. *Total Baseball*. New York: Warner Books, 1989. (All chapters)

Trachtenberg, Leo. *Yankee Magazine*, "Quiet Bob Meusel: Mr. Indifference," June 25, 1987.

Westcott, Rich. *Diamond Greats*. Westport, Conn.: Meckler Media, 1988. (Del Ennis, Carl Furillo, Dick Groat, Ted Kluszewski, Eddie Lopat, Sal Maglie, Roger Maris, Minnie Minoso, Allie Reynolds)

www.blackbaseball.com, www.negroleaguebaseball.com, and www.majorleaguebaseball.com. (All Negro League chapters)

About the Authors

Mike Shalin is a veteran of twenty-five years in the newspaper business, much of that time spent covering baseball. He began his career working for the Associated Press and then United Press International in New York before moving on to the *New York Post* and then the *Boston Herald*, where he's been since 1983. Mike became a member of the Baseball Writers Association of America in 1979 and has been a Hall of Fame voter since 1989, a role he has always cherished. One day he looks forward to every year is the day the ballot arrives in the mail, which is usually followed by a call to his older brother and coauthor, Neil, one of the great sports mavens of our time. Their frequent baseball discussions include the players already in the Hall, those who really belong and those who are not in Cooperstown and why—that is, those who are Out by a Step.

The Shalin family lived just two miles from Shea Stadium, which became a regular summer hangout for Mike, who loved baseball and appreciated a cool spot in the upper deck on a hot night. Before covering baseball fulltime, Mike was a hockey writer and had the pleasure of covering USA's Miracle on Ice at Lake Placid in 1980. He moved to the *New York Post* later that year to cover the Yankees and in 1983 took over the Red Sox beat for the *Boston Herald*.

Since 1995, Mike has covered Boston College football and basketball, but has always kept his hand in the baseball pot. He's also worked extensively in television in both New York and Boston and authored a series of sports biographies for young readers.

He's currently coauthoring a book, also expected out this year, with former New York Rangers goaltender Gilles Villemure. Mike lives with his family, which includes three boys and a dog (aptly named Griffey), north of Boston and have two grown children.

Neil Shalin is a freelance writer in the Chicago area, who currently covers high school and college sports for *The Daily Herald*. He has been working on *Out by a Step* since he retired in 1999 as Midwest Regional Director of Public Relations, editor and speechwriter for MetLife.

A native New Yorker, who grew up in a family of Brooklyn Dodgers fans, Neil rooted for the hated New York Giants and still believes that Willie Mays, Monte Irvin, Johnny Antonelli, and Bobby Hofman are gods. Sadly, seven-year old Neil missed Bobby Thomson's swing that produced "The Shot Heard 'Round the World" because he was delivering a book of PTA raffle tickets to a neighbor. However, he returned in time to see the ball clear the left field fence. Three years later, Neil thrilled to The Catch and the four-game sweep of the Indians in the 1954 World Series. To this day part of him refuses to acknowledge that the Giants and Dodgers moved to the West Coast.

Neil began his career as a news reporter and feature writer for *The Long Island Press*, and was always part of the New York sports scene, contributing articles to newspapers and magazines. He was an announcer and publicist for Roller Derby, publicist and member of the stat crew for the New York Nets in the early days of the American Basketball Association, and he spent three years as a scout for the Philadelphia 76ers.

Neil and his wife live in a suburb of Chicago and have two grown children.